School Management in practice

General Editor: Donald Frith

Contributors

Michael Duffy, Donald Frith, George Gyte, Veronica Kerr, Florence Kirkby, Brian Knight, John Sayer, Michael Smith, Peter Snape, Pamela Stringer, John Sutton, David Williams.

Longman

Longman Group Limited
Longman House, Burnt Mill, Harlow, Essex, CM20 2JE, UK

© Longman Group Limited 1985

First published 1985

British Library Cataloguing in Publication Data
School management in practice.
1 .School management and organization—Great
Britain
1. Frith, Donald
371.2′00941   B2901

ISBN 0–900313–21–8

Printed in Great Britain by
Butler and Tanner Ltd, Frome, Somerset

Contents

List of figures

Foreword

During the last decade there has been a dramatic growth of interest in the concept of teachers as managers, and in the need for them to be appropriately trained. It has been accompanied by the growing acknowledgement that, for a variety of reasons, their tasks have become more varied and demanding, not least because they have required a change of style. Training for headship is now national policy. The publication of this book is therefore timely.

In each chapter the writers speak from their own experience and from the lessons which that experience has taught them. I know all of them as friends or through their work and can testify that their experience truly reflects the progress of their craft in our time. It is the story of how the purposes and methods of secondary education became more complex and problematic; and of how they subsequently found a unity in a heightened professionalism among teachers, and in the self-conscious, self-developing school, in which staff are both individual practitioners and members of a team with a shared philosophy and aims. Management there must be; but above all else must come the liberation and nurture of the individual within a matrix of fraternity. Headship is ultimately akin to artistry: it requires sympathetic insight into the lives of others and the ability to help others enrich that life.

This book provides both a handbook for heads and aspiring heads, and a source-book for all those who want a first-hand picture of 'what it is like' to be a secondary head. It should be of interest not only to trainers of heads, but also to all those, whether parents, politicians or administrators, who have a concern to know about the tasks which schools face.

John Tomlinson
Director of Education, Cheshire

Acknowledgements

This book is firmly based on the practical experience of members of the Secondary Heads' Association. The contributors would be the first to acknowledge the part played by many members who have regularly discussed their problems, both formally and informally, at headquarters and in the areas over many years. In a very real sense, this is an SHA book, and I commend it very warmly to all those who have leadership responsibilities in Secondary Schools.

Peter Snape
General Secretary
Secondary Heads Association

The authors and publisher wish to thank the following for permission to use copyright material: County of Avon Education Committee (fig. 9.2); Leicestershire Education Committee (Appendix: Leicestershire Education Committee revised scheme of management for a community college).

1 Introduction

Donald Frith

All the writers in this book speak from long professional experience as heads of schools. Furthermore, as is customary in this country, they moved into headship from experience as classroom teachers. Their basic commitment therefore throughout most of their working lives has been to the education of children, and, since their experience is largely limited to secondary schools, of children who in the process of their education emerge into young adulthood. The classroom encounters which have been central to their own professional development, and which in most cases have to some extent continued even since they were appointed to headship, make it likely that, amid all the day-to-day chores of 'running the school', their deepest conviction of the worth-whileness of what they do comes from their commitment to orchestrate the whole enterprise for the benefit of the pupils and of the educational experiences which they will receive.

When such people accept an invitation to write a book about education and the management of secondary schools it would not be surprising if their thoughts turned to the HMI publication *Ten good schools*. That booklet came to the not altogether surprising conclusion that the single most important factor in deciding the quality of a school was the leadership which it was given by its head. This conclusion was seized upon by heads as a public vindication of their importance. However, if the corollary was that bad schools similarly owed their badness chiefly to the indifferent quality of the head, then the judgement could be no less threatening than flattering. In the long run it is arguable that that publication has tended to increase public pressure upon headteachers. They are not only more likely now to be seen as the makers of good schools, but also as those responsible for marring schools which are judged to be bad. Already at least one head is perceived to have lost his job as a result of an

HMI report on his school. Common sense suggests that the formula 'quality of head = quality of school' can easily become over-simplified. If one set of people provide a newly appointed head with a target and the school is subsequently judged by another set of people in relation to a quite different target, the verdict may be scarcely fair on the head concerned.

Judgements about a school therefore, whoever its head and indeed its staff may be, depend not only on the quality of that head and those staff, but also upon the expectations which the judges may have, and upon the attitudes and capacities of both the pupils whom it contains and the community which it serves. Education in one sense is interference. It is a deliberate attempt to influence the minds of the young, to persuade them to learn things which adults believe to be to the advantage both of the young people themselves and of society at large. But what shall those things be? And how far will the young people themselves, their parents, their potential employers, the government and other powerful elements in society agree? Each school must live within that reality. It must surely follow that a school which is judged 'good', and whose head has received high praise for enabling it to be good, is likely also to have enjoyed, because of a complex combination of factors, a convergence of many outside influences, including the nature of its intake and the public perception of its role.

If this be granted, it is apparent how important it is, at the moment when a new head is being appointed, that those who make the appointment should make quite clear what their hopes and expectations are for the school in question: what are its perceived strengths and weaknesses; what they judge to be its limitations and which of those limitations it may or may not be reasonable to expect a new head to be able to overcome. A school's governors or an LEA may believe that if they are frank about what they see as the school's problems or handicaps, they will in some instances frighten off good candidates. Such an attitude is not only cowardly but also lamentably short-sighted. A difficult or even downright bad school will never improve unless it can benefit from an entirely honest and cooperative relationship between head on the one side and governors and LEA on the other. Such a relationship cannot develop if it begins in what will be seen by the head as dishonesty. If on the other hand a candidate finds that those who are offering a post have sought from the start to share the problems of the school, to make clear their concern and commitment to improvement and their need to seek this in partnership with the head, then a good candidate is more likely to be turned on than put off.

The newly-appointed head will also have to make sensitive

adjustments. He will bring to his new appointment all that he has learned from service in his previous schools. These are likely to have bred both positive and negative reactions. At one extreme he will have served under a head who has inspired him and he will therefore to no small extent be determined to introduce into his own school many of the techniques or systems which have seemed to operate so effectively in the previous one. At the other end of the scale he may have been getting increasingly impatient, even contemptuous, of the head under whom he has served and be eager to introduce into his own school the reforms which he could never get past the head in the previous one. It would be a poor appointee who did not have ideas and aspirations of his own, whatever their positive or negative genesis, but he too will need, like the governors and LEA, to match those ideas and aspirations against the actual situation of the school in which he finds himself. Some transplants can become very sickly in a different environment. It is true that some of the disliked factors in the new environment may be eradicable, and in real need of eradication; but others may not and may in themselves not be hostile to the educational process. This again amounts to a plea to newly-appointed heads to share with governors and LEA their own ideas and aspirations, to test them out against the views of those who are making the appointment, to acknowledge that what is to be done must be done in partnership and with mutual respect. It will be just as foolish for the head as for those who appoint him to start by deliberately concealing intentions which ultimately must come to light with all the irritation and frustration which may then ensue.

There is evidence to suggest that one of the commonest problems which faces a newly-appointed head is likely to arise from the character and practice of his predecessor – and perhaps from the disappointed deputy who was a candidate for the post. A great deal of sensitivity is needed to pick up the messages which are being transmitted. It is highly unlikely that no member of staff wants any change at all. There may be some likelihood that the older members, and those therefore perhaps in the more senior positions, may be liable to prefer the comfort of the *status quo*.

The aim must be, perhaps by the asking of Socratic questions, to discover as far as possible how the land lies, what changes seem likely to be broadly welcomed, what deals might respectably be done. The basic questions will continue to be: 'What is preventing me from doing what I believe needs to be done? How can I change that?' From time to time realistic proposals which arise when those questions have been asked do gain a sympathetic hearing. Teachers may see advantages in taking on a new role; examination boards may agree to a changed examination pattern; the LEA may somehow find an extra bit of money; the local press may agree to come and do a helpful feature on a curriculum innovation which draws in industrial support. A scheme which has been carefully worked out, combined with determined optimism can succeed. Heads can be successful enablers.

Some of what I have written so far may sound logical but mildly impractical. There are very few human situations in which we are entirely frank with each other. In any case we often find it extremely difficult to know exactly what we are aiming at, or exactly what we can reasonably expect to achieve. Many of us are for example, mildly suspicious about the present government's obsession that schools should set down clearly on paper for parents and other interested parties what the 'aims' of each school are. In that context it is interesting to read what John Dewey wrote in *Democracy and education*.

> It is well to remind ourselves that education as such has no aims. Only persons, parents and teachers etc. have aims, not an abstract idea like education. And consequently their purposes are infinitely varied, differing with different children, changing as children grow and with the growth of experience on the part of the one who teaches. Even the most valid aims which can be put into words will, as words, do more harm than good, unless one recognises that they are not aims, but rather suggestions to educators as to how to observe, how to look ahead, and how to choose in liberating and directing the energies of the concrete situations in which they find themselves.

This is not a recipe for laissez-faire, but a sensible caution against any assumption that educational aims can be cut-and-dried, a set of tablets handed down from on high. The fascination of teaching, that which prevents it from becoming a boring daily routine, is the fact that it occurs as an interaction between teachers and taught, with all the infinite variety that changing and developing personalities on both sides must bring to the process; that it is concerned not only with facts, but with imagination and sensibility and with opportunities for bringing new ideas to birth.

Nor is this interaction taking place only between teachers and taught. Any headteacher must hope for and strive to create or sustain a school in which similarly interesting and creative relationships exist between all the adults who share the responsibility for its organization and conduct. And the head has to accept that the prime responsibility for facilitating the growth of such a dynamic situation rests upon his or her shoulders. Above all this demands flexibility. The broad aim is clear, and it is one which all can be invited to share. But from day to day the approach is likely to be pragmatic. In the nature of things all must depend upon the personalities and experiences, both in and out of school, of the people who comprise the staff. Wherever possible, opportunities must be created for each individual to make the best contribution of which he or she is capable. This is likely to be a recipe for diversity rather than conformity, so that a head may be in need of persuading his governors or LEA at any particular moment to make due allowances in any suggested curriculum blueprint for the particular personalities and capacities of some members of staff who would be likely to serve their pupils less well if they were forced into some preconceived mould.

I have remarked that almost invariably heads are appointed from among classroom teachers. What most newly-appointed heads notice – unless as deputies they have already been placed in positions which widely distance them from the classroom – is that their basic sense of responsibility is felt for the pupils rather than for the staff. They may also be acutely aware that their prime source of satisfaction up to now has been from their relationship with their pupils, much of which will have been positive and appreciative. In their new post they may quite possibly feel that many of their teacher colleagues, particularly perhaps in their own subject area, do a less good job than they themselves did. Simultaneously they may feel much more isolated from the pupils – and that much more draughty round the ankles – and where they believe they see weakness or inadequacy among the teaching staff, they may find themselves emotionally on the side of the pupils against their teachers. Such a situation needs a very long, cool look. No doubt firm judgements and carefully considered plans of action need to be formulated; but the head's own emotional involvement also needs to be recognized and his understanding of his new position and the ensuing re-orientation of responsibility carefully brought into focus.

One of the best expressions of educational 'aims' which I know is the one which appears in the Warnock report: 'First to enlarge a child's knowledge, experience and imaginative understanding, and thus his awareness of moral values and capacity for enjoyment; and secondly to enable him to enter the world after formal education is over as an active participant in society and a responsible contributor to it, capable of achieving as much independence as possible.' It is anything but a strait-jacket. It provides no practical suggestions, let alone requirements, as to what shall appear in a child's timetable. But it can provide the sort of formulation which enables a headteacher and his teaching staff to agree what together in broad terms they are trying to do for pupils, of whatever background and capacity. Any pursuit of such aims cannot be a private matter, let

alone a personal indulgence, on the part of the head. It can only
become effective for the good of the pupils if it is shared, not in a
mirror image, but through the wide diversity of insights present in all
those partners with whom a head must work. Running a school can
never be more than the art of the possible. Successful headship is
likely to come not from fruitless worrying about ideals which have
not been achieved, but from skill in observing where the possibilities
lie and creating situations in which those possibilities become
actualities. First and foremost this depends upon a constructive relationship between head and staff; but it often requires also the forging
of alliances with the various groups outside the school which themselves will have legitimate ideas about what the 'aims' of the school
ought to be and will constitute a range of both resources and res-
traints in relation to which the school must operate.

There will be very few newly-appointed heads who are not already
well aware of the influences which are exerted upon schools by the
members of the local community. We tend more often to remember
the front-page headline about a misbehaving group of pupils than
the piece in an inner page about a successful concert or football
result. Similarly we remember the name of the local industrialist who
intemperately attacked the alleged inability of local school products
to spell or add up, rather than the local company which offered us a
useful piece of equipment. At a time when schools seem to be at the
receiving end of so much adverse and often ill-informed criticism, it is
salutary to start counting the occasions when we receive good
publicity so that our own perspective can be helped not to become
too distorted. In any case it is part of a head's task to find ways of
disarming critics and taking full advantage of allies. Before considering how that might best be done, it may be useful to sketch out the
likely concerns of those sections of the community who have expectations of and make demands upon schools. It must be only a
brief sketch because it will be dealt with in more detail in subsequent
chapters. The sections of society whose names need to appear in the
list are remarkably numerous: pupils, parents, further and higher
education institutions, examination boards, employers, the providers
of the schools (the spokesmen for these providers being professionals and elected politicians at both local and national level), the
police and magistrates' courts, public transport companies,
shopkeepers and residents in the vicinity of the school site, the Press.
In effect, of course, the Press seeks only to represent the view of
other sections already included in the list. But it is clear, whether
nationally or locally, that most newspapers can readily be placed at
some point on the political spectrum and that a significant part of
what they publish is a deliberate attempt to win readers over to their

political standpoint by means of whatever the current accepted dogma may be.

On the face of it most of those clients could be said to be in agreement about what schools ought to be achieving. In their view secondary schools are supposed to turn out young adults with the necessary knowledge and skills (as parents and children would put it) to get a well-paid job or (as employers would put it) be competent and reliable workers. Of course schools would be equally happy if such aims were achieved. Few people, I imagine, believe that they are deliberately obstructing such aims. So why are schools and the rest of society alleged to be so much at odds? To some extent the answer might be because schools are not processing raw materials but processing – although that now becomes an entirely in-appropriate word – human beings. The pupils in our schools may all indeed hope or expect that school will provide them with the means to earn their own living. But they have all the diversity of attitude, aptitude and aspiration that characterize also the adults who are their parents. These differences demand a flexibility in the process through which they pass which in turn places such demands upon the teachers as can never be fully met. Ultimately it is not possible to make people work, whatever their age, unless they can be persuaded that it is to their own advantage to do so. Negative persuasions, such as fear of punishment, may have their uses but can also be counter-productive. Those who are persuaded that school work is to their own advantage are the ones who find it enjoyable for its own sake – a state of affairs arising from the character of either the teacher or the pupil or most often both; and/or the ones who see it as an effective means to a personal end. If they are so persuaded they must be the sort of pupils who have sufficient trust in their parents and teachers to believe in the promise of long-term rewards in the employment market. Here home-background and the employment experiences of their parents play a crucial role. The school's task is made no easier by the absence of student allowances for the post-16's. It is to be remembered that over a very short time-span the young have had their earning prospects deferred first from age 14 to age 16, and now in effect in many cases to 17, 18 and later.

Parents are as diverse in attitude as their children. Some schools, because they are or are not selective, or because of the local com-munity which they serve, may have as their parental constituency a relatively homogeneous group. Others may have a much more diverse clientèle. One way or another they will have to cater for the wide divergencies which exist in our society and which arise from a range of factors – financial, religious, racial, educational, social. There are no other institutions in society which have to adapt themselves to the whole range of our population, with a commitment to provide them with a service tailored to their individual needs and on the basis that all must come and none may be excluded. Some of our most vocal critics would do well to meditate upon the exceptional nature of our responsibilities. The schools have to seek as much cooperation with parents as possible because they know that if school and parents are pulling in opposite directions the children in between are being forced to take sides. Even when they take the side of the school, they themselves can be placed in an invidious position.

Employers are concerned for the success of their own enterprises, for the sake of their own livelihood and that of those they employ. Whether they are bankers or manufacturers, they must keep up to date with both products and marketing if they are to prosper or even survive. Most of them are well aware that a vital ingredient of their success is a skilled and cooperative workforce. The adaptation of the workforce to the demands of new products and techniques, presents them with some of their most intractable problems. So they should appreciate how difficult it is to cope with the diverse and usually understandable concerns of a wide range of human beings. We have more in common than is generally supposed. But we have a lot to learn from them, and they from us. Many of them are just as likely to be ignorant of, or to misunderstand, what goes on in schools as we are of what goes on in places of work. If our GCEs and CSEs are less than appropriate as a preparation for adult life over the next twenty-five years, so often the entrance tests which companies set for job applicants are scarcely related at all to what those applicants will actually do if they are accepted into employment. There is a mutual need to define more clearly what the needs both of employers and of school-leavers are. Heads need therefore to seek as informed an understanding as they can of local employers and to create opportunities of bridging the gap of misunderstanding and suspicion which is never wholly the fault of one side or the other.

The influence upon the school of government, national and local, is of course unavoidable. The degree and direction of that influence varies according to the prevalent political and economic wind. The Archbishop of York in his recent book *Church and nation in a secular society* quotes some words of G. K. Chesterton: 'When everything about a people is for the time growing weak and ineffective, it begins to talk about efficiency . . . Vigorous organisms talk not about processes, but about their aims.' Few would deny that the publicized loss of faith in our maintained schools arises chiefly from our weak industrial performance and from our high level of unemployment; and that those who govern us are engaged in a search for the causes of that decline and for remedies for our perceived weaknesses. Nor must we pretend that only schools have been singled out: industry, the police, the unions and many other sectors of society have been hounded by politicians and the media. And the talk is about the need for efficiency in all these sectors. In this context the requirement that we should set out the aims of a school may seem only a device to force schools to provide measurable targets against which efficiency can be judged. This is the context within which O- and A-level examination results are seen as the only respectable measures of a school's achievement. In such a climate of opinion no head can avoid making compromises. What society demands is under-standable and up to a point justifiable, but the demands invariably over-simplify the issues and sometimes can seriously distort the nature of the school's responsibility. It is important that the staff as a whole should reach as high a degree of consensus as possible in order to cope with outside pressures. There is some encouragement in the fact that the voice of teachers seems recently to have been more heeded than in the past and that some aspects of national educational policy now seem more in line with the reality of schools' tasks. The definition of what all our children might be expected to attain during their compulsory years at school is beginning to be defined not only in terms of 'what they ought to know' but also in terms of 'what they might reasonably be expected to recognize as worth learning'. Furthermore there is a growing assent to the notion that the compulsory years of schooling provide only the foundation of the subsequent learning that they will need to undertake; for that reason alone it is essential that their school experience should lay a foundation of sober self-confidence.

What I have written cannot pretend to be more than a brief sketch of the environment in which schools have to operate. Heads have the ultimate responsibility for the performance and the reputation of their schools, taking into account the wide variations between schools of intake and social background. Their basic resource in doing so is the teaching staff with whom therefore their relationship is of paramount importance. They need also to establish a working relationship with all the outside agencies who cannot but exert important influences upon a school's aims and achievements. That relationship must seek to disarm the hostile and take the fullest possible advantage of those who are prepared to be allies. It is however important also to bear in mind that schools do not exist merely to 'turn out a product'. The value of a school to its pupils is not only related to the skills and knowledge with which they can be equipped, it is also concerned with the quality of the here and now. It provides a social milieu in the period of transition from the family to adult independence; it is a source of friendship, of shared social activities, of loyalties and a sense of belonging. This aspect of school, as of a family, provides opportunities for the young to find a sense of worth in many different contexts. It is a commonplace to remark that the boy or girl who is 'bottom of the form' may appear in a very different light on a school camp. To this extent a school is justified in looking inward as well as outward, and must seek to strike a balance between the two.

Finally, lest heads expect too much and so suffer an unnecessary sense of frustration, they would do well to remember a remark of D. H. Lawrence: 'You never know what you have done or if you have really done anything. Manual work is much more satisfying. You can see something for all your pains. You know whether you have done a job well or not, but with teaching you never know.'

2 Finance, plant and administration

Brian Knight

School finance: skills and attitudes

Skills in managing finance are essential for any headteacher. This has always been apparent in independent schools. In maintained schools it has been less so, because heads have only had direct control over, and even knowledge of, a tiny portion of their budget. But times change, and today every headteacher needs to be financially aware and competent – whether to offset inflation, resist cuts, support priorities, or exploit new opportunities.

Such skills are not easily acquired. There are virtually no training courses available, so self-tuition is necessary. The head does not need to acquire specialized accountancy techniques, (commonsense bookkeeping and straightforward arithmetic suffice) but he or she does need to acquire some key concepts, terminology and knowledge.

1 Key concepts about school finance, e.g. opportunity costs, direct and indirect costs, prime and subsidiary costs, full-cost accounting, variable and fixed costs, unit costs, cost-benefit analysis. (I have attempted to outline these concepts, and other issues discussed in this chapter, in Knight B 1983 *Managing school finance*. Heinemann Educational Books.)
2 Terminology in common use, e.g. capital and revenue, gross and net costs, continuation and development budgets, real and cash outturn prices, virement . . . the jargon isn't difficult – it just needs patience.
3 Confidence and familiarity with the budget of the school, and in maintained schools with the budget of the LEA. The school's budget must be complete; there must be no hidden pockets. So debt charges, meals and transport, and where appropriate administration

and services, should be included (see below). Incredibly, for most maintained schools such a complete budget will not be provided by the LEA, and so the head needs to build it up himself. The LEA budget is published, although the normal form doesn't make it a very functional document, as is explained below. In both cases the head does not need parrot-knowledge of the figures, but rather familiarity with and a feel for the various components.

4 Confidence in making 'What if' financial calculations. For example, the head should be able to make a realistic allowance for inflation, allowing for its compound interest effect; to work out on the back of an envelope the cost of say 4/10 of a teacher (4/10 × midpoint of scale 1 (?) + 20% for 'on costs'); to sense whether a proposed saving, or change, has marginal or substantial financial implications; to cost a new development realistically.

Skills like these cannot be learned overnight. They need to be built up over months or years, probably without initial payback except the hope that they may prove useful in future. Whether the head does acquire them, therefore, in a busy working life, will depend mainly upon his or her attitudes. And attitudes are perhaps even more important than skills. The most important attitude is a full acceptance that managing school finance is a key feature of the head's role. If the head does not believe this, he or she should skip most of this chapter. But beyond that, the head needs to accept that the financial dimension pervades, however subtly, almost all aspects of school life. Hardly any decision concerning curriculum or organization, for example, is finance-free. A simple value-judgement – is this material, course, system better than that one – implies a financial frame of reference. In our ordinary lives, as consumers and citizens, we constantly make value-judgements about goods and services which can only make sense if their cost is implicit or explicit. Would we ever choose anything for ourselves if we were ignorant of the cost? We should not suspend this practical attitude when we enter school. Our response, for example, to a question of energy conservation, or changes in school hours, or new learning technology, or outdoor activities, should always include the question 'what is the cost'? This is obviously not the only factor to be considered, but it is often an essential factor.

In maintained schools another practical attitude is needed. Here, most teachers and heads seem to believe in two currencies, 'my money' and 'their money'. 'My money' is the finance I control myself – capitation – and I look after this just like my family housekeeping. But 'their money' – the LEAs money – is different: it comes like manna from heaven; it does not need to be husbanded; its value for money is never questioned; it is spent for its original justification, even though there are higher priorities. As heads we have a responsibility – first, to look after 'their money' as if it were ours (though this is psychologically difficult) and more important, to persuade them to let us take responsibility for it and convert it into 'my money'.

Securing the supply of finance

It must be the objective of every head to preserve the supply of finance to his or her school, and to increase it if necessary. This may seem a higher priority for independent schools, because in maintained schools heads receive the bulk of their finances in kind, e.g. staffing, maintenance of buildings. In practice, such heads will strive equally to improve their staffing, the state of the fabric etc. Although it may be harder for them to influence financial battles in the council chamber, such outcomes affect them just as much as an internal decision in an independent school.

Local authority finance

The capital programme Heads will find this a difficult area to influence. Each LEA's quota for capital spending is strongly influenced by the Department of Education and Science (DES), although it may be augmented by capital receipts funds raised from sale of assets. Capital spending may be financed from borrowing from external sources or from the LEA's own capital fund, both with loan charges paid from revenue or directly from revenue (direct revenue funding).

The capital programme will include both major and minor works, and may be divided into sections such as schools, further education etc. To gain inclusion in the major works programme a head needs to present a very strong case to the local authority through his governors and to sustain a dialogue with the appropriate officers, probably over years. Projects have a nasty habit of being postponed! The minor works programme can be more easily influenced. But it will often be heavily subscribed, and so making a good case at the right time is important. A head who is finding it impossible to achieve a desired project may make a matching funds offer, i.e. finding some of the finance from other sources. Many LEAs find this attractive.

The capital programme will also include major equipment purchases, often attached to new buildings but sometimes freestanding. It may include a fund to replace equipment or furniture and fittings on a rolling programme. Bids here will often be made and paid in kind. There may be small capital budgets for health and safety programmes, for energy conservation or other special needs. Other departments within the local authority may have capital funds which are applicable to schools, e.g. architects, estates, library service. It is therefore important that the head should build up knowledge of the geography of such funds. It is often too late to begin this when a project is being launched.

Revenue estimates   Expenditure in maintained schools, other than capital, rests upon revenue estimates. If the head wishes to influence budget debates he has to make a nice judgement: to what extent should he venture into the political arena? Heads do have political influence, through their governors, parents, public opinion, and through contact with elected members. Blatant lobbying, loud publicity and exaggerated warnings of doom can be counter-productive. Quiet persuasion can be very effective. In particular, heads should be able to influence the provision of capitation by explaining that it is the life-blood of a school, the funnel through which all financial provision is poured. Most politicians will grasp the point that it is counter-productive to vote a huge salary bill and stint the means by which this is translated into classroom activity.

Most LEAs also have funds which are distributed on an ad hoc basis for curriculum development, new developments, or special projects. Such funds are often managed by LEA advisers. This is another hidden oil field which the head needs to prospect and map before it can be tapped. Although such funds are often unwise, because they absorb a great deal of time from the applicant schools and the fund holders, yet as long as they exist heads have little option but to exploit them. Similarly there will be other LEA central resources in kind – furniture stores, equipment stores, audio-visual or technology services etc. There will often be funds available under other sections of the LEA budget, e.g. further or community education, library service etc. which can occasionally be tapped.

Raising finance from government departments and agencies and from other branches of local government

A range of government departments spend funds in schools. In particular the proportion of the educational budget retained by the Secretary of State for specific grants will prove a substantial source of income. This is the new 'honeypot management', to stir the lumbering LEA bears into salivated activity. Schools will increasingly bid for such grants either individually or in groups, and so become involved in preparing a submission. Regrettably, the form and presentation of the submission may be as important as its contents. The DES is also making other specific grants, for example, for aspects of in-service training, which schools may be able to tap.

Other government departments also have funds which can be used within schools, for example the Urban Aid programme. There are also European Community (EEC) funds. There are also a whole range of quangos. Of these the most important by far is the MSC, with its massive investment in the Technical and Vocational Education Initiative (TVEI), in the Youth Training Scheme (YTS) and in community projects. Although the Manpower Services Commission (MSC) is not always well disposed to schools, it is worth developing a relationship with the local area board. There are also other bodies like the Sports Council and the regional arts organizations. In other tiers of local government substantial financial resources reside in the district councils and much smaller resources in town and parish councils. District councils are particularly likely to support 'dual use' projects.

Community education is another source of funds. Schools which have become heavily involved with their local community, such as the Leicestershire community schools, find all manner of unexpected spin-offs. The goodwill generated by the school's community activities is often reciprocated by local councils, voluntary fund raising, or industrial or other sponsorship.

Finance, other than from rates and taxes

Major fund-raising Professional fund-raisers can be valuable. They have a number of practical hints, and advise giving through covenants, which can now be limited to four years and enable schools which are registered charities to recoup the income tax of donors.

There are three principal methods of major fund-raising. First, a fund-raising consultant, or a representative of the school, may visit directly all those whose names are suggested by the school and ask for a covenant or for help with raising funds. Second, a consultant may help the school to organize its parents, well-wishers and old pupils into areas. Visits are then arranged to each area to explain the project. Those recruited in each area visit others on the list to ask for covenants. The first of these methods is normally used by either smaller schools or those seeking a smaller sum for a specific project; the second method is normally employed for a much bigger general appeal. Under the third method (only appropriate for day-schools), meetings are held at the school to promote the scheme to parents and others. This has been very successful in some maintained schools, particularly in Avon where extensive 'enrichment' schemes have raised substantial capital sums, the interest being used to 'enrich' the school in various ways. The success of such appeals appears to depend to some extent on the proportion of owner-occupiers in the catchment area, and often on an embargo on other fund-raising.

Minor fund-raising   Fêtes, raffles, sponsored walks, tuck shop etc. Some schools are very successful and heads would be well advised to tap good practice.

Trusts   A number of schools have their own foundation trusts. Others have trusts within their own area to which they can apply, or are associated loosely with charitable trusts or organizations. Schools can also make a submission to one of the hundreds of trusts listed in the *Directory of grant-making trusts*, published by the Charities Aid Foundation, 48 Pembury Road, Tonbridge. Most, however, are already heavily committed.

Direct charges   Many independent schools now allocate a proportion of their fees to a capital fund for new buildings or equipment developments. This proportion will rise as fees are increased in line with inflation though the total must be within the limits which the school's market will bear. Sometimes this addition is levied only once for each family with more than one child at the school. This is obviously not available to maintained schools, although many do make illegal charges of various sorts, e.g. 'inviting' parents to buy textbooks.

Selling off surplus assets   A number of independent schools have sold off sites with high land values to finance building and development elsewhere. Maintained schools are not so free. Some will have annexes or playing fields which could be sold off profitably, but there is no guarantee that any of the money obtained will actually be returned to the school itself, or indeed to the education department. However, careful negotiation could possibly secure this.

The need for accurate costing   When a school embarks on a major project, it is essential that neither capital nor running costs are underestimated. Although the figures may initially look uncomfortable, a project that has been thoroughly costed commands more respect and is more likely to be supported. A checklist is necessary to ensure that a full budget is drawn up for both the setting up and the maintenance of a major project. Major projects which cannot be funded from one source can often be funded by a package from several, and will have more appeal if they are of an innovative nature.

Many heads in the maintained sector will feel that this entrepreneurial approach is alien, although it will not be strange to many heads of independent schools. Heads need to decide whether they can work in an ad hoc manner, exploiting opportunities as they arise, or whether they should plan a long-term strategy. It is important for heads to realize that building up useful contacts and expertise about funds available needs to be developed over a period of years. They also need to consider whether this style of operation requires them to relinquish some more mundane tasks within their schools.

Defending supplies of finance

Finance is not always secure; it can be threatened from various sources. First there may be actual cuts. The only defence is for heads to move cautiously to the edge of the political arena, and without open politicking to make the consequences of the proposed cuts absolutely clear. But – caution is needed.

More serious are cuts that work insidiously. Sometimes these are made through devolution of items of expenditure to schools with an inadequate allowance. For example in recent years a number of local authorities devolved telephone charges with inaccurate and insufficient allowance, often concealing a cut in funds. This problem is discussed in the section on devolution below. Even more dangerous is the effect of inflation if the LEA makes insufficient allowance, particularly when inflation is high.

There are three points which heads need to understand.

1 Any shortfall in 'inflation increments' operates on a compound interest principle. For example, if an LEA allows 5% inflation for a particular financial year, say 1985–86, when inflation is actually 10%, by April 1988 the capitation index stands at 146 (April 1984 = 100) but capitation at only 121.5. If this goes on much longer it will be very difficult to make up lost ground. Even at this point it would require an increment of 32% in April 1989 to put things right.

2 The increment for inflation is calculated in many LEAs for the coming year. Some calculate it in the autumn for the previous twelve months, and provide it in the next financial year. Under this approach it takes effect eighteen months in arrears, and schools suffer when inflation is rising and gain when it's falling.

3 At times of high inflation it is important that departments spend their money as soon as they can. Obviously part of the allowance can

only be spent later in the year. But unnecessary delay devalues spending power.

Another threat to school finance is falling rolls. This will not be apparent at first, because initially financial pressures ease. Buildings and non-teaching staff serve fewer pupils; there will often be a lag in the reduction in staffing which enhances pupil-teacher ratios; there will be less pressure on textbooks and equipment. However, this gain is illusory. Central government is attempting to reduce educational expenditure as closely in proportion to falling pupil numbers as possible. The problem is that as pupil numbers fall, the proportion of fixed or semi-fixed costs rise and so the cost per pupil. It is important that heads are aware of the problem, because blind resistance to the surrender of premises or the amalgamation of schools, or clamour for curricular staffing, may well prove counter-productive in the long term.

Finally, there is the threat of structural changes in education promoted for financial reasons, such as the closure of small primary schools, the amalgamation of sixth forms, or the creation of a tertiary system. It is quite possible that changes may bring financial savings. However, heads in such a situation would be advised not to take official figures at face value. The classic illustration is the Arthur Young study *Costing educational provision for the 16–19 age group* (HMSO 1982) produced for the MacFarlane Committee. It gives very useful advice on costing alternative organizational patterns. But it painfully illustrates the hazards involved by giving an extended example showing that in a metropolitan area in a particular situation a 6th-form college would save an LEA £120,000 a year. Unfortunately this was completely demolished by Peter Newsam, Educational Officer of ILEA (*The Guardian*, 2 March 1982), when he showed that the option preferred was £120,000 more expensive than an additional option which had not even been considered.

Managing school finance

Once funds have been secured – or defended – effective management of finance depends upon various factors.

Good financial information

This is the foundation upon which good financial management rests. Information which is incomplete, inaccurate or badly presented cannot be managed properly. Of course all information is inaccurate to some degree. But it is important that there should be no gross errors or omissions, and that expenditures are not included under the wrong heading. Equally important, information needs to be complete.

In maintained schools considerable areas of expenditure are often treated as if they are of no interest to the headteacher. Apart from central administration and debt charges – the latter a very substantial element – other items likely to be omitted will be centrally provided services, often transport and school meals, and even premises and grounds. Ideally, expenditure should be accounted for at the place where the funds are actually used. In other words, even central overheads should be apportioned to the schools they service. In practice, local authorities are a very long way from this, even in such easily allocated services as the psychological service, residential centres, careers service, furniture and supplies, library service etc.

Financial information also needs to be disaggregated as much as possible. Administrators will always be tempted to amalgamate expenditures because they want to see the wood through the trees. However, for effective financial management it is much better if information is aggregated under broad headings, but disaggregated into reasonably small sub-headings. It should be presented in a format based upon the way in which education is actually provided, under appropriate, clearly understood headings. Only then can a head see the comparative costs of the range of services which the school is offering.

Freedom and flexibility

The more financial freedom and flexibility the head has, the greater the range of options he can consider. But, as always, freedom brings responsibility – and it can be illusory.

Virement Within independent schools this always exists, in the sense that the head, bursar or governors can always agree to switch expenditure between one heading and another if they so wish. In maintained schools the situation is much more varied. Three main types of virement are available. The most developed form is the 'Alternative Use of Resources' operated by the ILEA. This allocates a substantial additional resources allowance, comparable in size to the general allowance, for expenditure on additional teaching or non-teaching staff, books, equipment, minor works, etc. as the school wishes. In the second category virement is allowed across heads of already determined expenditure. Schools do not have to use virement, but can do so under certain conditions. Such virement is much smaller in scale, and does not normally involve capital or permanent staffing. Although this type of virement is limited, it does offer heads considerable flexibility, particularly with falling rolls when it is possible to close premises, kitchens and other facilities without harming the institution. Heads who do not have the good fortune to work in authorities offering this flexibility will need to persuade their LEA to adopt good practice. The third category of so-called virement is where schools are allowed to switch expenditure between one narrow budget heading such as books, and another such as school visits. This is little more than broadening heads of expenditure and doesn't really justify the use of the term.

Financial devolution ('local financial management') It is likely that heads will increasingly be asked by their LEA to take over expenditures which previously have been a central responsibility. This tends to arise for ad hoc reasons, because the authority vaguely feels that better value for money is provided or that total expenditure will be reduced. Such items have included postage, telephones, cleaning materials and have spread to examination expenses, travelling expenses, supply teaching, fuel and light. It is possible that this may spread into other areas such as duty meals for teachers, advertisement and interview expenses, in-service education.

Faced with such proposals, either piecemeal or on a broad front, how should heads react? First, they should examine the proposals critically against various criteria.

1 How sound is the data base? If the data base is inaccurate or incomplete it is unlikely that the formula for devolution will be sound, and so some schools will suffer.
2 How sound is the formula? Has it been carefully devised using existing data, or is it a 'back of an envelope' calculation?
3 What safeguards are offered during the initial period to schools where the formula can be shown to be inaccurate or where there are exceptional difficulties?
4 What provision has been made for inflation?

Purchasing freedom Freedom to purchase where one likes is important. Some authorities are very restrictive, requiring purchases through a consortium or an LEA supply department, or approval by divisional or central office. Such practices are misplaced. They restrict the freedom of schools as consumers and delay the purchasing process. Of course there is sense in the LEA getting benefit from bulk purchase discounts – but if such discounts are effective and the quality of goods is maintained, schools would not normally wish to purchase outside the consortium or department anyway.

Financial policies Each local authority and each school will have a set of policies, explicit or implicit, related to finance. They will be historical in origin, built up over years by accretion, but seldom rethought in the light of efficiency. LEA policies vary considerably and some are regrettably counter-productive. For example, some LEAs do not allow schools to carry over unspent balances at the end of the year. This is an absurd practice. It leads to a flurry of expenditure in March, and creates unnecessary bookkeeping.

Heads who can carry forward allowances should note that this tends to lead to unspent balances, either because money is being held for a purpose, or because not all invoices get paid before the year end, or because the school is nervous of over-spending and errs on the safe side. If heads find that they are carrying a balance at 1 April, they should automatically allow to overspend by that amount during the year. This cancels out the carrying forward and boosts capitation by that amount for one year only.

Some authorities do not allow schools to be credited with income from the purchase of materials. There is thus no incentive for schools to maximize such income. It would pay heads in such LEAs to volunteer an appropriate reduction of capitation so that income could be retained, as immediately this change is made income received will increase.

LEAs can sometimes be restrictive in other ways, by not providing easy means for schools to pay for items such as the running or replacement of minibuses through official LEA funds so that VAT can be reclaimed. Some LEAs have excessively laborious and slow financial procedures. Heads who are unfortunate enough to find themselves in such backward authorities should work patiently for improvement.

Allocating capitation

There are a number of questions facing every head.

1 What is the present state of provision? Which departments are well provided for, and which poorly? Such assessment is bound to be subjective, but it is still worth making at, say, five-year intervals. A useful device is a matrix, with vertical columns for books, stationery, materials, major and minor equipment; horizontal bands

for year groups and/or courses; and a five-point scale for assessment. This highlights areas of need.

2 What does each department need? This faces the head with policy considerations. Should he or she feed the department which has been run down, or whose performance is weak? Or should he channel funds to the energetic and successful heads of departments? To what extent should allocation be related to the personality of the heads of departments and their staff?

3 What system should be established to allocate capitation if the total requirement is greater than the resources available? (Which it always will be!) There are four main strategies available.

(a) Benevolent despotism, by some margin the most common system. It is flattering to the despot and involves some evaluation of departments. But it is very time-consuming, is open to prejudice and vulnerable to lobbying.

(b) Open market. Each department is invited to bid every year both for on-going expenditure and for new items. The problem is that departments inflate their estimates, and so the total is substantially more than the sum available, and has to be reduced either by method (a) or by departmental in-fighting or on a proportional basis. This approach also favours the aggressive at the expense of the modest.

(c) 'Creeping incrementalism'. This assesses the percentage increase available and then raises quotas by that proportion. It is time- saving but only perpetuates historical situations.

(d) Formula. This relates departmental quotas to the number of pupil periods taught each week, and a weighting factor according to the expensiveness of the department. This approach highlights the agonizing problem already encountered under (a) and (b): how much more expensive is science and CDT than English or Mathematics? However, the system automatically adjusts for changes in volume in subjects, and it is predictable for several years ahead, and so encourages forward planning. It is also time-saving.

Most schools operate a combination of these methods – most commonly despotism for the bulk of capitation, and open market for expensive or development items. Having met all four, I am personally convinced that the formula approach is the best by some margin.

There are some other questions. Should stationery be paid for centrally? (This seems to lead to greater waste.) Should expensive items be treated as a central category? (Possibly – but the smaller the category is, the better: departments look after their *own* money better.) Should there be a contingencies fund? (Not really necessary if the school can carry forward.)

Controlling expenditure

Preventing overspending

It is obviously important that the school should not overspend its funds. Control is not always easy, because a school's expenditure will not be regular during the year. It is important that potential overspending is detected early. A simple device to monitor spending is a bar chart, with a column for each month showing the cumulative total spent (i.e. April £3000, May £6000, June £9000 etc.) It is then relatively easy to extrapolate from these rising columns to the end of the financial year, particularly if one has similar graphs from previous years. Should overspending seem likely, an embargo can be imposed in say December and January. The embargo can be released in early February, as items ordered then will not normally get into that year's accounts.

Departmental overspending needs discussion with the head of department, to make sure that it's not going to become deep-rooted. Underspending is much less of a problem. If unspent balances can be rolled forward, then any department which under-spends is only robbing itself. It is actually making more money available for other departments.

Control of equipment

Purchase of equipment presents the head with a range of problems. The larger the item, the more care needed in purchasing. Audio-visual aids can be a problem. It is often better to have a learning resources fund from which such equipment is purchased on request and then lent out to departments on long loan. This ensures that there is no duplication of equipment and that when it has ceased to be used it can be taken back into store. All items of equipment should be entered immediately on inventories, with body number etc. Appropriate security measures should be taken, particularly with items like computers and videos.

Good housekeeping

Good housekeeping is dull, unexciting and time-consuming, but it does save money. Inventories and stock-taking are important. All local authorities require inventories for expensive items, and some require them for items such as textbooks and minor hand equipment. In fact, these are much more likely to be lost than are the expensive items. Pupils do not often walk off with lathes! Heads should require departments to keep full inventories for textbooks and other books, and for minor equipment, excluding totally consumable items. Stock-taking is time-consuming, but if departments are answerable for inventories, they do take much more trouble to track down missing books and equipment.

Common sense economies can often be made in items such as cleaning materials, paper towels. Economies in heating and lighting are possible by encouraging staff and pupils to switch off lights and to keep doors closed, by reducing draughts, controlling thermostats, removing obstructions in windows which reduce light etc. Maintenance of premises can include considerable expense from wear and tear and vandalism. Some internal policies can reduce these; for example, charging pupils for damages, encouraging pupils and staff to report defects, charging departments for damage of furniture on their patch, improving lighting or security systems. A handyman or caretaker can do minor repairs at a very much reduced cost. Many independent schools use a quite extensive direct labour force.

Preventing abuse

A number of minor abuses are common to many schools. These include theft of stationery (it should always be kept under lock and key), unpaid private photocopying (a signing-in system is needed), abuse of school postage (this can be checked by a postage book or franking machine), and abuse of the school's telephones (this can be checked by restricting the number of phoning-out points, barring calls out before 1 p.m., and installing the new equipment which monitors the calls from each extension). More serious abuses could include the purchase of private goods from school monies or misappropriation of school funds. Local authority financial systems ought to be proof against major abuse, but heads do need to be alert.

Abuse is more likely to arise in 'unofficial funds'. In a maintained school these will include all monies which did not originate from LEA rates and grants or from 'official' income. They can therefore include receipts from a tuck shop or vending machines, funds contributed by parents or raised for a special event, as well as funds raised or held by school clubs or societies. Most of these will be under the control of the bursar in independent schools. There are a few important rules. Such funds should not be kept in a number of separate accounts, like pots under the bed, and certainly should not be held in individual teachers' bank accounts. There should be two accounts only, current and deposit, both in the main school bank. The school then becomes the banker for each individual fund. Since most funds will be in credit, surplus in the current account can be shifted to deposit at frequent, even weekly, intervals and at the end of the year a 'dividend' declared. Receipts should be issued to children or parents wherever this is reasonably practicable. Large cash sums paid in, for example from a sponsored walk or raffle, should always be received and counted by two people together. Cheques should always require at least two signatures, and any withdrawal by a club etc. should only be on written authorization by the person responsible. Organizers of large expeditions and camps should produce a final balance sheet.

Auditors

In maintained schools, auditors have the right to come into a school at any time and check on official funds or equipment. In some authorities they make an annual visit. In others they come much less regularly, and in this case heads need to be more vigilant. Unofficial funds may be audited by the LEA. If not, the school should appoint its own auditor, obviously detached from the person running the account and preferably external to the school. Most independent schools are controlled by the Companies Act and have to submit their accounts annually. They are required by law to appoint auditors. Governors may have the same financial responsibilities as directors while as charities their funds may be used only for the benefit of education.

Premises and grounds

New buildings

With current demographic and financial trends, it will only be a small minority of heads who experience the pleasure and pain of building extensions. The process follows a logical sequence. Once approval has been given, a brief for the architect is drawn up, and this will normally be discussed with the school. It is important that the brief is right, because it is upon this statement about the purpose of the building that the architect will base his design. He first produces sketch plans which can be easily altered. Detailed plans are then produced. It pays the head to scrutinize these with a magnifying glass. It is worth marking out rooms in a large space so that their actual space and fittings can be imagined, or making a scale model. Details of the siting of points, cupboards, the spacing and positioning of doors, circulation areas etc. need care. Wall surfaces pay for careful examination; durability is important. A little anticipation at the detailed plan stage can save a lot of frustration later.

The project is then put out to tender and if tenders are too high there can be traumatic reduction and trimming. On the whole it is better to sacrifice fittings than square footage. Once the building commences, the head often has no responsibility, but it's worth keeping an eye on progress with the clerk of works to make sure items are not overlooked. Simultaneously a kitting-out fund will be set up to finance equipment, furnishings and fittings. Finally, once the building is complete it is important to note all initial defects so they are put right within the defects period.

Existing buildings

Alterations   Most existing buildings change their use gradually over the years. When a new need arises, there is a temptation for the head to say either that it can't be met or to push it into the first obvious space. However it can be valuable to sit down with one or two senior colleagues and study methodically a plan of the whole site room by room, testing whether the use of any rooms could be altered, or whether there are unused spaces that could be brought into use. It is often surprising how for a particular purpose there may be a small alcove that can be boxed in or a room whose use can be altered.

The process of alterations and additions is not as straightforward as it looks. In the case of external alterations, planning permission will usually be necessary. Internal alterations need immediate discussion with the specialist responsible for the upkeep of the buildings. There may be fire and safety requirements to be met, and even an innocent-looking wall may have electrical wiring or drainage lurking within it. If the school is going to carry out alterations itself through a handyman, parents or pupils, there will be a tendency to skimp on materials, which may create problems of sound insulation or durability later.

Maintenance   In some schools all maintenance is done by outside staff, in others the school's own staff are responsible for some items. The latter situation is often much happier because defects can be remedied quickly. In local authorities where the school is dependent on a central department either doing the work directly or sanctioning its completion by a contractor, frustration can set in because of long delays. It is worth cultivating the acquaintance of the person in charge, so that requests can be speeded up by personal contact. The most durable paint should be used in circulation areas.

Cleaning Cleaning will sometimes be the responsibility of the school itself through its team of cleaners, sometimes the responsibility of a cleaning department or firm. In either case, it is worth the school setting up systems to stack chairs and clear up mess at the end of the day, so that cleaners can work efficiently.

Playing fields and grounds Responsibility for maintenance varies between school and school. Some entirely maintain their own fields; some partly do so, but supported by a team; others depend entirely on a team provided by the education department or an outside department like estates or architects.

Some policy issues will arise.

1 Should a group system be welcomed, or resisted?
2 Do standards of maintenance need to be improved? If so, what can be done to achieve this?
3 Are the educational needs of the school being properly and conveniently met?
4 Are there any major improvement to the fields necessary, e.g. drainage?

Obviously responses will vary and solutions will often lie in personal discussions with the personnel involved. But heads would often be well advised to seek additional support from governors. Grounds are an area on which governors often have expertise.

School administration

The bursar

Happy is the school which has a bursar! He or she can be a tower of strength to head and to staff. Ideally the job specification should be cast as broadly as possible to include finance and catering services, transport, premises alterations and maintenance, and supervision, appointment, and welfare of non-teaching staff. The bursar should be seen as a senior member of the staff, responsible directly to the head or one of the deputies. It is essential that he or she has sufficient clerical support to carry out management duties properly.

Most independent schools will have a bursar who will normally be responsible for finance, building and catering. Frequently he will be directly accountable to the governors though enjoined to remember that at all times the head is head of the school.

By no means all schools will have a bursar, and with falling rolls such appointments may shrink. Schools without bursars will still have the same management functions to fulfil, and it is essential that the same tasks are identified and allocated to one or more members of staff.

Non-teaching staff

All schools will have an establishment of non-teaching staff, although it may not be called such, whether it is defined by the LEA in bodies or 'points', or cash as in an independent school's budget. If the establishment is clearly inadequate, the head must determine how he can attempt to enlarge it. Schools will often have flexibility in deploying staff within their establishment, particularly when staff leave. So it is particularly important that a vacant post is not filled automatically until the situation has been reviewed. Non-teaching staff commonly work less than a 52-week year, and often less than a full day. Careful scrutiny of such hours can often make savings which can be re-used.

The school office

Each school office will vary, depending on the type and size of school, the accommodation and staff available, and not least, on tradition. Each head will be wise at some stage to take stock, and to ask some general questions. What are the functions to be carried out? Are any of these unnecessary or out of proportion? Can they be simplified or reduced? How well does the present division of responsibilities fit those functions? To what extent would reorganization or increased use of new technology make the office more effective? Some of the more detailed issues are outlined below.

Reception and general layout   This gives the outside person his or her first impressions, so sign-posting to the office needs to be clear and the first impression welcoming. Equally, telephone reception needs to be friendly and welcoming. Some schools use pupils for reception but unless they are well trained, they can give a poor impression. Reception will also deal with innumerable queries from staff and students – and the more it can insulate the main office from these interruptions, the better.

The ideal layout is probably a reception counter opening from a large central office, housing all clerical staff except probably for an inner office for the head's secretary. A central office allows better cover for absence and equalizes work loads. These offices can shield the offices of the head, deputies and bursar. Nearby should be a central reprographics unit. It is wasteful to have some reprographics equipment in the office, and other elsewhere for school use, and undesirable to have school staff interrupting the office to use its equipment.

The head's office   Ideally this should include a conference area. The telephone should be able to dial out direct, but in a large school the head may prefer that most internal extensions can only reach him via his secretary. Some heads have a personal phone, separate from the school system, but this is often of doubtful value.

Correspondence and filing   It is worthwhile adopting a modern house-style for correspondence, with minimum punctuation and indenting. It does save clerical time. A reference system is necessary, commonly originator initials/typist's initials/file or subject reference.

Unless the head has a speedy dictating style, he or she will find a dictating machine more efficient than dictating to a secretary. Dictating drafts of long documents saves a lot of time and longhand should be avoided as much as possible. Shorthand is still valuable from a secretary for emergency letters and telephone messages.

Some heads insist on seeing or even signing all outgoing mail. Personally I think this is unnecessary and prefer staff to be responsible for their own mail, providing it is firmly understood that sensitive letters should be discussed with the head or another senior colleague. Incoming mail should be sieved heavily by the head's secretary. It can be helpful to have two in-trays – 'important/urgent' and 'less important/routine'.

Filing is always a potential hazard. The secretary will know where everything is – but if she is absent or resigns . . .! Theoretically there should be a central filing system, but most heads keep some files in their own office, as do the bursar, deputies and pastoral heads. A few commonsense rules are given here.

1 Copies relating to a pupil should be filed with that pupil's records.
2 Files in frequent use by the head, bursar (e.g. building repairs) or other senior staff, which relate to one of their main functions, can often be kept more conveniently in their rooms.
3 Letters (in or out) which are *important*, or difficult to classify, should have two copies made, to be filed separately.

Office files have ring clips and file everything in date order. Personally I find this unsuitable for files in heavy use, because it makes regrouping of papers difficult, and so I prefer to keep them loose in envelope files. But there is more risk of loss!

A useful office device is a circulation file, circulating from head to deputies, to house heads or year heads, bursar, community tutor, carrying copies of all outgoing letters, incoming letters, general memos, notices etc. generated by anyone on the circulation list. It's an easy way of keeping a lot of people in the picture.

Another useful device is a prompt file, alerting the head's secretary to prompt the head or other senior staff about jobs that need to be done, often annually.

Forms and returns   Maintained schools enjoy a rich harvest of weekly, monthly and annual forms. It is better if these can be concentrated on one clerk, or if not, split by areas. Copies must always be kept, and at least one other person must know how the system works. Most forms need the head's signature, but in practice the LEA can sometimes be persuaded to accept a nominated alternative – bursar or deputy – to reduce the head's workload.

Finance   This will be a major feature of any school office. Routine finance in large schools needs its own clerk, working under the bursar. Unofficial funds and receipt of income monies often generate as much work as capitation itself. Dinner money, in maintained schools, is a self-contained financial system, but often administered from the school office. Banking of monies needs care – visits can be frequent and coinage heavy. Large sums should not be kept in safes, and no cash should be kept elswhere. And, a point sometimes overlooked, the safe key should be on a key-ring not in a drawer!

Support for teaching staff   Typing of exam papers, worksheets and other materials, and some correspondence, needs to be provided. Teachers' time is better spent elsewhere, and the product looks better if the typing is professional. Such support can be separate from the main office, ideally close to the staffroom. But in practice it is often part of the main office, though this increases interruptions.

Duplicating and photocopying is best dealt with by a central reprographics unit, with a 24-hour turn-round, re-charging departments for copies.

Lettings of premises   Ideally in maintained schools this should be provided by a community tutor. If not, it will need to be handled by the main office – but the more successful it is, the more work is generated. LEA procedures are often excessively complicated. In some LEAs lettings are handled by an external community education office.

The use of new technology Word processors are still relatively expensive, but they are ideal for schools. They facilitate the reissuing, with minor changes, of letters about meetings, letters of various types to parents, options and parents' booklets etc. So they do save time – although they may encourage increased output!

Microcomputers are already used in many schools for some school administration and timetabling purposes. But for full development a hard disc system is necessary, to house full pupil, staff, timetable and buildings files. Only by enabling these to be inter-connected can the full benefits be gained. Access to the staff file should be limited with a password system.

3 Staff management I

John Sayer

Whether the head is to be considered as a chief executive or as the leading professional in a teaching community, the main responsibility will be to organize and enable a large number of colleagues to help pupils learn. That responsibility extends to an element of partnership in initial training of teachers; to staff appointments, whether of teachers or of non-teaching colleagues; to induction at all levels, including probation (again, also for non-teaching staff); to in-service education and training (INSET), not least for a school-focused approach; to staff appraisal and promotion; to matching staff skills to intended tasks; and to the whole pattern of staff relationships in the common room and in the community.

Staff relationships, indeed, are much more complex than all the complexities of reorganization put together. In my first week as a head, I was much better prepared for system change than for the testing of position and personality which is at the heart of school management. Quite simple incidents spring to mind. The first visit to a separate lower school staffroom: a smartly-presented man at the head of the coffee queue almost springs to attention, beckons the new head to the front as a matter of course. Accept or decline? The other thirty in the queue may have appreciated that my thirst was no greater than theirs; but was I ever forgiven by, as it turned out, my ex-Navy NCO colleague? The head of the lower school tells me I must make a decision about staff dogs: his had previously been parked on the outgoing head's home and garden, but another dozen or more were somehow secreted on to the school premises, in laboratory prep. rooms, home economics areas, and my deputy's room among others. While I was hesitating, the caretaker brought an example of the problem to show me from the staffroom carpet. So dog ban. What did that mean for teachers drawn from a 600-square-mile area? I gradually found out. Or, in those days, the deputy head (mistress) asked me to make a stand against an older senior colleague who had given notice that she intended to wear a trouser-suit to school, despite my deputy's insistence that this was a bad example for the girls. When I refused, could I have predicted the splendid gesture of the deputy herself being the first to come in trousers? All these incidents are examples of what the general principles are about in practice.

The staffroom

Industry does not have anything comparable to the school staffroom. That is one of the most valuable perceptions to have come from an industrial manager.[1] The staffroom is a workplace, a resting place, a meeting room and a social area, an asylum and a reception room, a hive of communication and a place of privacy. It both affects and reflects the spectrum of staff relationships, the degree of communality, the ethos of the school, morale of staff, and their corporate relationships with governors, parents, education networks beyond the school, and pupils. The management of a staffroom is first and foremost a matter of relationships and people.

The staffroom does not figure on most management courses, and very little thought has been given to it in general terms. It is all the more important for the head to ensure that it is a positive influence, and to be aware of its potential as well as of the way which teachers perceive it. First, who belongs there? Is the head a member or a visitor, in the eyes of colleagues? How fully welcome are non-teaching staff, language assistants, students engaged in teaching practice, visiting professionals, visiting parents, pupils with enquiries? What does the staffroom feel like to a governor? What does it feel like to a new colleague? What does it feel like to the families of staff members? Has it developed clique areas? Is it felt to be equally accessible by men and women? Does it include a professional library?

These are not just questions which could occupy the lifetime of a social anthropologist; they mean a great deal to teachers and non-teachers alike. The head will wish to ensure that the various functions of the staffroom as a physical resource are adequately provided for. There is a strong case for staffroom management to be a task for a sensitive senior colleague. The head has to take into account the developing role of staff governors, who may now be involved in the head's appointment, and are a part of the complex of influence and support in the staffroom.

A staffroom committee, distinct from the sectional meetings, which will reflect other aspects of school management, can be of great benefit not only in responding to some of the questions just raised, but also in articulating a balance of concerns which may not emerge in other contexts.

For teachers themselves, not forgetting those who are visiting for interview, the staffroom is the prime expression of the school as a professional place. Is it a happy staffroom, and what is meant by that very common question? If it is, then half the head's task of staff management has been accomplished. If it is not, the other half never will be.

Staff appointments

Procedures vary according to the guidelines of each local authority and according to the wishes of each governing body; but whatever the procedures, the head has a central role in the appointment of colleagues to the school. Local authorities are having to become somewhat more prescriptive in order to honour commitments to existing teachers at a time of falling rolls. The head must not just be on the receiving end of such constraints, but must clearly share the will to make sense of difficult times. Frequently, heads can work together in an area to encourage shared staffing or transfer of staff without the formalities of redeployment procedures and the delay which they can cause to staff management as a whole.

In a large school, a staffing plan for the following year is needed at latest by the end of January, taking account of decisions on curriculum, secondments, staffing reductions which might require redeployment from the school, bids for voluntary redundancy or enhanced premature retirement, and other known or predictable staffing changes. A sequence of appointments has then to be established and flexibly applied from February to May. Thereafter, the timetable will be under way, and last-minute movements out will have to be matched as far as possible by direct replacement. It must be emphasized that this aspect of school management has changed beyond recognition since the 1970s; the relative immobility of the profession has reduced the 'turnover' in conventional terms, but it has added to the need to relate internal and external redeployment, school and LEA procedures, secondments and temporary appointments, internal promotion and appointment to posts of responsibility from elsewhere. The tasks are more intricate, more sophisticated, and much more closely observed. It is increasingly important to have the whole staff aware of the issues and engaged in facing them.

Heads also have to make clear to local authorities what are the necessary time-sequences for careful staff planning. Rate-capping is just one more reason why local authorities may panic, delaying advertisements, vetting through personnel departments, leaving the whole operation too late to be related to timetabling and too late to prevent the best candidates from being snapped up elsewhere or being lost to the private sector. These pressures on local authorities make it all the more necessary to maintain a constant and open contact with the staffing section of the local authority, so that at least there is trust and understanding. It remains likely, however, that a sequence of events which should be taking place during the period March to May could be condensed into three weeks of crisis management from mid-May with the fear that a preferred candidate may be unable to offer his resignation from his current post by the statutory date of 31 May.

The nature of each post, a job description, and procedures for appointment have to be determined by the head after consultation with, or in conjunction with, those senior colleagues who will share responsibility for the person appointed. The head will have sought from governors a general framework for their involvement, and will have consulted the chairperson as appropriate. LEA advisers should be consulted according to the head's view of their ability to assist and according to any LEA procedures. It is particularly important for the head to signal to the LEA the precise wording, timing, and placement of advertisements: one of the curious features of current practice is the habit of those in local education offices to place prominent display advertisements for office appointments and to try to economize on much more responsible positions in schools. The head may well have to use powers of persuasion to add a few pounds to good advertisement for difficult posts, each of which could involve £500,000 in salary once the appointment is made. Where the school is able to place the advertisement direct, or where advertising and appointment expenses are part of a virement scheme for school management of finances, the head will have to use the same powers of persuasion with senior colleagues and governors. For an appropriate advertisement, the quality of job description, and care for the whole appointment procedure, necessary expenditure just has to be cleared. It is also increasingly important to recognize that a job description may be considered to have contractual significance. The head would be wise to set out expectations which may be binding, but to leave scope for reasonable modification of role after appointment.

On average, a sequence of about six weeks may be anticipated, or about ten weeks if LEA redeployment is first attempted without success. A six-week schedule might be as follows:

Week 1. Receive resignation; negotiate internally and externally nature of replacement; agree and send in advertisement, a fortnight before intended appearance; establish datelines and procedures for processing, long-listing, short-listing, and interview with all to be concerned.

Week 2. Advertise within the school in advance of public notice; prepare job descriptions and other school details for mailing to candidates and eventual referees.

Week 3. Immediate responses to requests for details; process applications for long-listing; seek reference at once for outstanding applications.

Week 4. Whittle down to short-list while still processing applications; chase references for good late applications by phone; seek supplementary reference as needed by phone; have letters of invitation ready.

Week 5. Conclude short-list; invite as soon as possible after latest date for application; prepare summaries of short-listed candidates for those concerned with interview etc.

Week 6. Interview proceedings; appointment; communication of result.

That is if everything goes to plan and if there is nothing else happening at the same time. It is as well to go for a tight schedule: the best candidates are being sought elsewhere at the same time.

Candidates should expect to be treated as they would be as members of staff. A head should have constantly in mind what it feels like to be applying and visiting a probably unknown school. All correspondence should be by first-class mail, with telephone back-up as necessary. Invitations to interview should include the arrangements to be expected, including those for board and accommodation.

At least a full school day will be needed for candidates to see the school and be seen by those directly concerned. That day is for mutual appraisal, not for one-sided selection. The ethos of a school is most clearly shown in the approach to interviewing. For the more senior appointments, in which more colleagues and governors may be involved, two days may be well worth the extra commitment. There should be opportunity for candidates to discuss the job, probably with the head; to see the school in general and working areas and colleagues with whom they will be involved in particular; to withdraw without fuss as soon as they have made up their minds that this is not the right job for them; to have both formal and informal discussion, in groups and individually; to be in a position to indicate whether they want the job, and then to be free to make their departure (having agreed later means of contact) rather than wait until the end of whatever formal procedures are being employed. Those sharing in the appointment should have agreed beforehand how they are to proceed at each stage, what each or all will be looking for, and how this is to be communicated in order that a decision can be made promptly. When possible, the head will want to telephone to invite the chosen candidate to take the job, and follow this with the written formalities. Phone messages to the other short-listed candidates on the same day should also be made if at all possible. A note of the decision should be posted to all applicants who have asked to be notified. From the moment of appointment, future colleagues should be posted with all staff communications, involved in discussions affecting their future work, and encouraged to visit and seek assistance with professional and personal upheavals. They are doing two jobs at once, and need support to manage that.

In principle, similar arrangements should be made for internal candidates, whether for posts which are for internal appointment only or for those in competition with a national field. The same facility should be accorded to teachers who come forward for redeployment from elsewhere in the LEA. In a dynamic staff, there may well be three times as many major changes of role in a year as there are staff replacements. In my own school of 130 staff, there were 46 such changes in 1983, despite a very low turnover. The task of managing all these concurrently between February and May is one which has to be subsumed in the normal running of a school. It has to be highly disciplined, and the discipline has to be shared across more than just the most senior colleagues. If one communication goes wrong or one participant fails to play the expected part, the effects can be disastrous. And this is the most important job for the head to get right in order to be able to sustain its rightness once the appointment has been made.

A final throwaway line: what goes for teaching appointments should also go for non-teaching posts. Does that really go without saying?

Induction and probation

If the first noun is ecclesiastically awesome, the second is criminally gruesome, and it is the main responsibility of the head to ensure that such overtones are eradicated. Those who have delegated responsibility for the work of an incoming teacher (heads of department, year tutors and the like) must take direct responsibility for introducing them to their new tasks and environment. In addition, it is often advisable to vest in the professional tutor or equivalent the responsibility to provide an induction programme of value to any newcomer at whatever level, and to be readily available to them, supplementing rather than replacing the responsibility of section heads; and perhaps in a less judgmental position towards the newcomer, and a somewhat more judgmental position towards the school's reception arrangements.

All who are new to the teaching profession require a training programme in their first year of teaching. Initial training institutions cannot prepare for particular situations, and as yet no assumptions can be made across all initial training in even the most general terms. As far as possible, this training programme should be for all incoming staff, whether experienced or not. It will probably be most systematically structured in the first term, and if possible will start before the beginning of that term. A day set aside in June or July for all due to arrive in September is particularly helpful. It will include explanation of the personal timetable, beginning of term routines, the new staff handbook, textbooks and materials to be used with classes to be taught, and above all reassurance that the decision to come was a right one. A day immediately before the outbreak of term in September may usefully include discussion with teachers who have just survived their first year as well as the more obvious welcomers. It is also a time for the head quietly to make sure that those new to teaching have made adequate arrangements to be fed and watered, and know how to survive without salary for the first month of contractual barbarity.

An induction programme will include formal and informal arrangements for teachers to discuss their work with those to whom they are responsible and with each other. It will include opportunities to study the context of staff responsibilities, from the practical 'where to go for what' to some appreciation of what others are trying to do. It will cover the local arrangements for communications, contacts with parents, assessment routines and documentation. It will give opportunities to discuss and comment on problems as they arise. It will enable incoming teachers to take a full and immediate share in decision-making affecting all parts of school life.

There may or may not be an LEA input for incoming teachers. If there is, it should be incorporated in the school programme. The head will wish to be personally involved at some stage, and will wish to have informal and probably formal discussion with each incoming teacher in the first half of the year.

For entrants to teaching, probation should be fitted naturally into such arrangements rather than have these arrangements seen as part of probation. Satisfactory completion of probation is a

INSET should always have been the priority; even in times of less rapid change, there was no prospect that initial training could equip a teacher for a whole career or that professional growth could just be left to happen. But in a period of falling rolls, the struggle to retain what has already been achieved, relative immobility and lack of career prospect in the same context, INSET becomes all-important. Heads have to get that accepted, along with a sharing of the underlying causes for frustration and disappointment, of which the immediate symptoms will be felt by all and which may result in bitterness in the school itself unless it can be seen as part of a major problem being faced for the first time in the history of this country's schools.

INSET is too often conceived as the additional opportunities specifically provided under a separately categorized activity, separately organized. It then becomes associated with courses out of the ordinary context, funded and provided by various bodies, from the Department of Education and Science to training institutions, local authorities and professional organizations. For some teachers, it is associated with additional qualification as a step to promotion; and that is the perception of those teachers who do not take part and sourly comment on others who do. Teachers are quite rightly scornful of national or local encouragement to take part in INSET programmes which are inadequately funded, and in particular which fail to provide for additional staff time; on the other hand, when a local authority gives such funding priority over maintenance or improvement of staffing levels at a time of falling rolls, teachers' associations are hardly likely to applaud on behalf of their beleaguered members. These sentiments are partly justified and demand proper solutions; partly they are aggravated by this view of INSET as an additive rather than inherent in professional activity. Heads need to work at both ends of the problem.

First, there is the task of establishing that there is an INSET ingredient to everything that teachers do in school. That is more than soft soap. A head who means business will be demonstrating that in every decision about who is to do what, there is not just the question of who will do it best but for whom is it best to do it. Learning is after all not confined to pupils in a classroom, and what applies to a classroom group has to apply to any group in the business of continuing to learn. Obviously, priority has to be given to the best service to pupils rather than the best interests of teachers; but it is very rarely that the best interests of pupils are served by decisions which are not beneficial to teachers as well. It is the head's job to marry the two in any decision, and to encourage that approach across the staff. If two people could both do a job, there are times

when the decision ought to go to the person for whom that job would
be a learning opportunity rather than to the person who has already
had that experience.

It is from that kind of attitude to staff development in the round
that the best sense can be made of added INSET opportunities. Here
again, rather than looking immediately to external agencies, the head
has to develop the view of the school itself as a provider. There are
many good reasons for this. One is that a school has a larger group of
professionals than most training institutions or most local authority
advisory services, and ought to be using that resource for INSET.
Another is that INSET is best planned and provided according to the
needs of teachers and schools, and is most likely to meet those needs
if it is initiated at source. Far from this being an insular approach, it is
the best means to enable other agencies to provide what is needed
beyond or in support of the school. This cannot be done without the
school having a major role in identifying needs and the best means to
meet them.

If a school is to be supported within LEA budgets for its contribution to INSET, needs and plans to meet them have to be
identified and agreed well in advance. For the school's sake, too,
advance planning is essential if INSET is to be built into the annual
organization and not be seen as a last-minute interruption to planned
and scheduled activity. A formal three-year cycle of programming is
valuable: a systematic annual review by each colleague individually
and by each section of the school should include an evaluation of
what has been found valuable in the past year's INSET activity; what
is the involvement in the current year; and what are the priorities for
individual and working groups for the near future. From these views,
which may best be requested in a standard formulation, a draft
programme can be drawn up for agreement among the staff and
then negotiated with the LEA if resources are required, and with
INSET agencies beyond the school where it is considered that provision can best be made with their involvement, or by them alone. At
the same time, the Head (or others designated) can use the individual staff returns to prompt further discussion or to respond with
information about INSET opportunities which may meet expressed
needs. The relationship with staff development as a whole cannot be
overlooked. In contexts of formal staff review, the INSET exploration
may be particularly beneficial; in a staff suspicious of formal
appraisal, the INSET review is unthreatening and probably more
necessary.

Longer in-service courses involving secondment will usually derive
from the same identification of individual and group needs and
priorities. There have been some very encouraging examples of

team secondment for purposes of school development or for developments across schools in a local authority. Such examples make even more patently obvious the need for a school to plan to make use of the training, experience and insights gained during a period of secondment. There are profound problems of re-entry anyway for anyone who has broken the school habit for a term or a year; and if that is combined with a sense of futility and wasted experience, a secondment can do more harm than good. So INSET planning has to include what to do with the products of INSET.

There is also a large management problem, which can be turned to advantage in an INSET context. A seconded teacher will be someone with considerable experience and probably in a post of responsibility. During the secondment, there is an opportunity for someone else to gain that experience, and perhaps to assume that responsibility. That person, in turn, may be replaced for the year either by a temporary incoming teacher or by yet another existing colleague. Or there may be a distribution of responsibilities across several colleagues, which if carefully planned makes for extended experience and enrichment. And when the seconded teacher returns, what is to happen to those who have been gaining that experience? For them too there are either problems of re-entry to their previous tasks, or the encouragement to share work with the person returning, or to go on to further qualification themselves. Looking at both ends of a secondment process, any one secondment could well have a profound effect on ten teachers. Either that effect is thought through as part of an INSET planning exercise, and made beneficial, or it can result in muddle. In schools with plenty of opportunity for secondment, that alternative is a challenge to good management by the head.

Staff and organizational review

By the time this volume is published, pressure for formal review of schools as organizations, of working groups within them, and of individual teachers may have resulted already in a decision to introduce into all local authorities a selection of the practices already to be found in some schools as required practice, and in some schools by choice. The pressure has not come from heads, but from the government, from employing authorities in the context of salaries, promotion and conditions of service, and from some teachers' associations.

Schools have run not on contractual obligation, which is minimal, but on professional expectation, goodwill and trust. Moves towards accountability, in all its very different manifestations, and towards formal review procedures according to the various models already developed outside the education service and in some schools, must in the long term result in a greater emphasis on conditions of service, and the inclusion within them of activities which are still voluntary and beyond the call of duty. Heads may well regret this; employing authorities and government must come to realize shortly, that they may no longer be able to expect without planned resourcing much which now happens in schools; teachers' associations will be under increasing pressure from their members to secure greater promotion prospects once it is clear that there will be many more openly recommended promotions than the present system can allow. Whatever the reservations, any head must now be prepared to manage formal staff appraisal, must be able to minimize the dangers and draw on the advantages which some heads are able to see.

Whatever such scheme is introduced, heads and their colleagues need to have thought through the implications, particularly in terms of staff relationships and power. A serious danger for the head is that such schemes may appear to increase the head's power over colleagues. That is not what most heads want, but it is what others most fear. The second danger is therefore that this apparent increase in power will be countered by vesting in local authority advisers the power to control the head. Just as a collegiate approach to responsibility and decision-making inside the school may be damaged by inappropriate appraisal procedures, so too the partnership and cooperation of heads and local authority officers and advisers may be damaged. The task is to avoid both these dangers. For some, they are more apparent than real, particularly for heads who have come to terms with local authorities in which line management is the prevalent reality. But so much can go wrong.

Let nobody believe that formal review procedures are a panacea. They can, on the other hand, be anodyne, and this is largely the experience of the civil service. Schools cannot afford to waste time on mere formalities. It has been well argued elsewhere that the appropriate model for staff appraisal in schools is one of openness and mutuality, rather than one which establishes hierarchies within or beyond the school.[3] Again, the question in a school is whether the mutual appraisal is between a teacher and the head, or more directly to a section or department head; whether the head is to conduct a hundred formal reviews of individuals each year, together with formal reviews of working groups and the organization as a whole. If that is the way it is to work, it leaves little time for much else or it will become superficial; for each such review demands thorough preparation and even more thorough follow-up. If it is to work indirectly, does that close the head's door to teachers? And however such schemes operate, time has to be allocated to them and budgeted by an employing authority.

Many of the same questions apply to school self-evaluation and organizational development reviews. Within the school, as many as possible should be drawn into contributing to assessment of the whole organization and its parts. Schools exist as partners in a service, and no review can properly be made of the school in isolation from the local authority. The accountability aspects must reflect mutuality. A condition for introducing such schemes might be schools' involvement in reviewing education departments; and again, strengths and weaknesses are part of a relationship and a shared responsibility. Properly applied, such schemes not only improve awareness of priority needs for planning purposes, but also have the makings of a fully professional approach to an education service viewed as a whole. But where they have been only superficially thought through, they are a prey to the personal weaknesses of those involved. Heads would do well to seek advice from their association and from colleagues with worthwhile experience of such reviews. The head should not take the whole thing as a personal responsibility from which others are to be sheltered.

Partnership in initial training

Following the recommendations[4] of the Advisory Committee for the Supply and Education of Teachers (ACSET), all courses of initial training will be required to demonstrate the good practice of partnership with schools which is already to be found in some training institutions. That partnership will include an involvement of schools in the selection of students for training. The head of any secondary school will wish to ensure that pupils with an interest in a future teaching career, especially those wishing to move from school to B.Ed. courses, have had ample opportunity to match themselves to future reality. One valuable feature of a general studies programme is the opportunity to help in local schools under the joint guidance of teachers there and of a course tutor. There is no reason why this should not in future be managed within the framework of the Certificate of Pre-vocational Education.

Heads collectively will have a major influence in determining what is the most appropriate school involvement in the selection of students applying for initial training courses. It is the responsibility of the head to ensure that a school's share in practical training of teachers is thoroughly discharged, and that those directly involved are aware of the whole initial training programme of which they are a part. The school responsibility is centred on teaching practice and school experience for students, but the relationship with training institutions is likely to grow much stronger. The school responsibility for assessing students and making their introduction to the teaching experience memorably positive flows into a bond of partnership with colleges and departments of education, not only in initial training but for in-service education too. It is not reasonable to expect all the approaches to be made by training institutions. The head has the responsibility for establishing valuable contacts, whether this is done in person or through designated senior colleagues in a professional tutoring role.

A danger and difficulty in the new proposals is that schools adjacent to training institutions could be more closely involved in this professional partnership than those at a distance, regardless of the strengths of skills and resources for students. It would be unfortunate if distinctions were to develop between training schools and others not involved. That problem has to be shared with local and regional professional committees as they grow in their proposed new role as funding brokers. Meanwhile, a consortium of schools at a distance can help to solve transport and communication problems, as well as being a source of mutual development.

Task-related staffing

If a genuine attempt is being made by society to define the expectations which schools ought to satisfy, and then to provide matching resources and conditions of service, the head has more than ever to identify what time and whose time is needed to complete tasks of all kinds, whether or not they are expressed on a timetable. Time for staff and organizational appraisal has just been mentioned. Time for equally regular and detailed assessment of pupils' progress and achievements has to be calculated and provided. So much has been added to the expected tasks of the secondary school in the last two decades that the whole framework of organization now requires remodelling according to what actually happens or is expected to happen as a result of teachers' work. In 1977 research[5] into what teachers actually did showed that whereas schools are staffed and organized as though only 20 per cent of a teacher's time were spent on professional activity other than classroom teaching, the reality was that only 21 per cent of professional activity took place in the classroom. By now, the added pressures of accountability, of external liaison, of planning response to even more rapid change, of one-to-one support for children and their families, of professional collaboration and interchange, will have widened still further the gap between reality and the myths which surround the school day and school year for teachers. This argument has particular force in the growing number of community schools. In them the 'school day' is blown wide open and it is no longer possible for people to perceive the school as nothing more than its timetable.

It is no longer accepted as good management to describe as extra-curricular, and therefore not to make allowance for, those many activities which are part of the school's intention for a pupil's experience. Part of the staff review exercise must be devoted to identifying more rigorously how time is spent, how it can best be spent, and how it should be budgeted. That exercise must in turn be the starting point for negotiation with the employing authority on staffing levels. The head today is having to manage staff and staffing in a context in which at one and the same time most things are taken for granted and nothing can be taken for granted. Staff time, whether contractually tied or freely given, is the most valuable commodity the school has to offer to pupils, and the most important one for the head to understand and to manage. Heads are far more likely to enable employing authorities to understand the nature of the problem if they make common cause with their colleagues in other secondary schools rather than appear to be making a single particular case.

4 Staff management II

John Sutton

Anyone can manage the kids, it's the staff who create all the problems.
– Anon (a head)

The context of staff management

The role of headteacher in secondary schools has changed significantly over the past twenty-five years. This has been due in part to the creation of larger and more complex schools and in part to the great increase in the demands imposed upon heads. The very term 'headteacher' once described fairly accurately the nature of the job as a senior professional with some responsibilities added to the central task of teaching. In secondary schools today, the title is a misnomer. Many heads do not teach at all and most teach only a little. Although proficiency and success in teaching played a major part in their movement up the promotion ladder, these qualities may be of little or no significance in their success or failure as heads.

Headship is now an executive managerial function and, as such, is more capable than hitherto of being compared with other executive functions outside the world of education. Heads have tended to resist these comparisons, believing that the nature of education and the way in which schools operate make their job unique. Those who have investigated the matter more closely, however, have concluded otherwise. Dr K. B. Everard, for example, in his Report commissioned by the Centre for the Study of Comprehensive Schools, 'Management in comprehensive schools – what can be learned from industry?', argued strongly that, 'The role similarities of the Head and the industrial manager far outweigh the differences.'

In no area is this more true than in that of staff management and the recent growth of senior management courses for schools reflects the growing awareness on the part of both providers and receivers that heads and other senior staff in secondary schools are engaged in managerial activities in which their performance may be enhanced by the acquisition of appropriate learnable skills. It should not be supposed that such skills have hitherto been entirely absent from schools. Many heads have possessed them instinctively, others developed them in a particular style from invaluable experience in the armed forces (a source which has now dried up) while others have learned from working under heads who possessed these skills and followed a deliberate policy of passing them on. Relying on serendipity, however, is not a sound basis for progress and the development of positive and structured management training for leadership in schools must be warmly welcomed.

There was an early tendency to assume that, because the industrial world was the repository of management skills, their transfer into schools would be a one-way process and much disappointment and disillusionment resulted, largely because the providers knew little about the real demands and pressures of the school environment. Not surprisingly, senior staff in schools, exposed to this kind of experience, concluded that there was little of relevance to be learned. Because schools have distinctive characteristics, the development of managerial skills must be related to the conditions which obtain in them and the particular management problems which they present.

The purpose of this chapter is to describe some of the ways in which staff management takes place in schools, to present what seems to be good, or at least effective, practice and to demonstrate that there is great scope for the acquisition of knowledge and skills which will enhance the effectiveness of the institution as well as the individual.

The management structure of a secondary school is different from other management structures in several important respects which relate both to the nature of the institution and to the people employed in it. The function of a school is to provide a service and the immediate consumers of that service, the pupils, are present in the school for most of the time. There are two groups of employees: the professionals, whose main task is to provide the service, namely to teach, and ancillary workers, who are employed either to enable the service to be provided in an acceptable environment or to enhance the efficiency of the service. The senior professionals also exercise, in varying degrees, management functions in relation to how the service is provided, to the organization and welfare of the consumers, to the work of fellow professionals, to the allocation of resources and to the relationship of the school to higher management and external pressures.

The important point is that, in contrast with the school structures of many other countries, the teaching functions and the managerial functions overlap almost totally, so that every teacher has some involvement in management and almost every manager has some involvement in teaching. Furthermore, a promotion structure has developed in modern times in which proficiency in the professional function of teaching has been the principal means of advancement to positions where managerial functions become more important and occupy an increasing proportion of time. This is not to argue, of course, that the teaching and management functions should be separated, as they are in other systems, because it is the British tradition that the successful fulfilment of the management role in schools can only be assured if those in management have the understanding of the consumers and the rapport with fellow professionals which derive from a measure of participation in the teaching process.

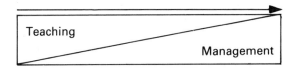

Fig. 4.1. Teaching management functions

From the management point of view, however, the career pattern of the professional staff, as summarized in fig.41, means that in contrast with most industrial situations, by far the greater part of the staff who work under a head see themselves to some extent as fellow managers and expect to play a part in the management of the school. Thus, the entire teaching force of a school is, in a sense, the managerial team and a head who fails to recognize this runs the risk of creating a substantial group of disaffected and discontented staff.

In what follows, attention is concentrated upon the teaching staff. It must be remembered, however, that the supporting and ancillary staff play a crucial role in the running of the school and that they deserve the same sort of consideration and involvement in all matters which concern them as do the teachers.

Styles of management

Students of management have observed, not surprisingly, that styles of management can be described in terms of a spectrum ranging from the totally autocratic at one end to completely democratic or participatory at the other. They have also noted that all managers need to vary their position on the spectrum in different circumstances. Putting it simply, in school terms, a decision to send an

injured pupil to hospital may be taken quite autocratically, a decision
to abolish detention might more wisely be reached by other means.

Heads, like managers in industry, find their own place on the
spectrum in accordance with their own personality and perception of
their role, but it is worth noting that research has indicated that
autocracy is not necessarily a sign of strength and that 'the
participative approach is by far the most efficient leadership style.' It
is possible to find schools where the style is quite rigidly hierarchical
and others where virtually every decision is taken by a 'moot' or
general meeting which everyone on the staff is entitled to attend.
What is most important here may not be so much the style itself as its
consistency. Whatever style a head adopts for decision-making and
for communication, it must be followed in all comparable situations.
Nothing is more confusing to a staff than not to be able to foresee
with reasonable certainty how a significant issue is likely to be resolved. By the same token, a change of style, if deliberately undertaken, should be clearly signalled, explained and adhered to with
equal consistency.

The management style is not simply a matter of effective staff
leadership. In schools, it has a wider significance because the way a
school is run and is seen to run is part of the 'hidden curriculum' for
pupils. Although it might be considered 'unprofessional' for teachers
to discuss such issues with pupils, there can be no doubt that the
frustration of disgruntled teachers can rub off on their pupils just as
their sense of being positively involved in the development of the
school can enhance their performance. Pupils, in any case, are not
blind. They are the most acute observers of the world about them.
They see and hear how their teachers relate to one another and to
their superiors, and they respond to the atmosphere which those
relationships generate. They also learn from this experience lessons
about the ways in which the adult world works and, if a school is to
fulfil its purposes fully, care must be taken that, in this area too, the
lessons learned are the ones the school intends to teach.

Staffing structures

In an earlier and simpler age, it was assumed that all teachers were
equal, if not in the sight of God at least in the sight of the Burnham
Committee. Apart from heads and their deputies, often called senior
masters and senior mistresses, the staff of a school shared the
teaching duties and other functions in a hierarchy which related to
age and experience rather than to salary structure. After the Second
World War, however, the Burnham Committee introduced a

structured salary system which provided additional allowances for additional responsibilities, confined in earlier stages to the running of particular subject areas in the school.

During the 1960s and 1970s, the rapid expansion of the education system, coupled in most parts of Britain with reorganization on comprehensive lines, led to a highly mobile teaching profession, as teachers competed for additional allowances and viewed their careers as a step-by-step progression up the scales in the quest for status and relative affluence. The Burnham Committee fine-tuned the system, first to create more grades and later to consolidate them into a pattern of graduated scales, the allocation of which was related in a direct way to the size and age-range of the school.

The development of comprehensive schools brought with it additional problems of size which could only be tackled with the extension of managerial functions beyond the confines of the head's study. In addition, schools took upon themselves a greater responsibility for pupil welfare than had hitherto been seen to be necessary and 'pastoral care' posts became a common feature of staffing structures.

It is necessary to go through this potted history in order to make the important point that there is a 'chicken and egg' relationship between the staffing structure which exists in schools and the salary structure has been created by the Burnham Committee. Because status and salary are inextricably interwoven, the way in which teachers are paid constrains the way in which any school develops a staffing structure.

By 1984, the salary structure was very hierarchical but increasingly unsatisfactory. A system which had been devised in a period of expansion proved wanting at a time of falling rolls, fewer schools and restricted opportunities for promotion. More and more good teachers, who might have expected speedy promotion in the 1970s, found themselves blocked on Scale 1 or, at best, on Scale 2, at salary levels which had steadily declined in relative terms. From the head's point of view, the opportunity to pick out and to recommend for promotion talented young colleagues and so to maintain a dynamic structure was severely constrained.

This semi-paralysis of the career structure coincided with a number of initiatives taken by the Secretary of State for Education and Science, Sir Keith Joseph, who had convinced himself that the quality of the teaching profession was in need of improvement. He believed that this could be achieved by introducing regular and systematic assessment of teachers and by finding ways of rewarding those who demonstrated excellence in the classroom.

These contrasting arguments for change were brought together in

a Working Party on Salary Structure set up by the Burnham Committee which debated a package of radical reforms which were
expected to be introduced in 1985. The proposals put before the
Working Party were fundamental and, in some ways, turned the
wheel full circle back to the stage when all teachers were equal. In
other respects, however, they broke new ground.

The principal criticism of the hierarchical structure was that it did
not appear to concentrate attention on the prime function of
teachers, namely teaching. In any large secondary school, a considerable number of functions have been developed, most of which
are closely related to good teaching, or help good teaching to take
place, but which are not actually teaching. Some, such as taking
charge of CSE project work in Social Studies, or taking charge of the
second year, carry administrative or pastoral duties which are
essential for the organization of teaching on the one hand or the
welfare and supervision of pupils on the other. Others, such as
looking after the school bank or running the school football teams,
have much to do with the 'hidden curriculum' of the school but little
directly to do with teaching.

The practice which has grown up is that teachers are employed
and paid a basic salary to teach and are then paid extra when they
undertake responsibility for tasks additional to the basic function.
Heads might well argue that they rewarded good teachers by giving
them additional duties, but this cannot obscure the awkward fact
that, the more additional duties a teacher acquired, the less he was
actually required to teach. A side effect of this system was the attitude
it fostered among many teachers that one ought not to take on
additional duties unless one was paid for doing them – or was likely
to be paid in the near future.

From the management point of view this system, regulated by a
fixed allocation of salary points to each school, made it essential for
the head to ensure that all the additional duties which he deemed to
be necessary were identified and suitably rewarded. At the same
time, an appropriate balance had to be maintained in the distribution
of posts over the four salary scales so as to ensure a reasonable
promotion ladder and to attract well-qualified applicants to key positions.

The proposals advanced in 1984 sought to sweep away most of
the concepts inherent in the existing system. The new philosophy
was that, if the prime function was teaching, then it was teaching that
should be rewarded, while most of the additional functions, however
necessary they might be, should be regarded as incidental. The new
system would achieve its aims, firstly by making entry to the profession more rigorous, secondly by increasing quite substantially the

highest salary level for teachers on what was christened the Main Professional Grade, and thirdly by regarding the majority of the tasks for which salary additions had previously been paid as duties to be allocated by consultation among the staff of the school, as an integral part of what might be expected of any and every teacher's work.

To allay the fear that such a method of handling all these essential duties might lead to their non-performance, the employers' side of the Burnham Working Party proposed that the allocation of these duties should have contractual force and that annual assessment of teachers should be introduced. The notion that the latter scheme should be associated with accelerated progression up the salary scale and with merit payments beyond it was greeted with scepticism by the teachers' unions.

That schools did need some hierarchy of management was, however, recognized and provision was made for additional allowances above the Main Professional Grade for those teachers who had responsibility for organizing, supervising or coordinating the work of teams of teachers. These would be fewer in number than in the previous system and would replace what had been the highest scales under it. The lower scales would disappear.

At the time of writing, the discussion of this new structure has not reached the negotiating stage and it is not possible, therefore, to do more than to speculate about its adoption or the management consequences which might follow. It must be said that most heads remain sceptical that the essential additional tasks of secondary school management will be effectively carried out under a system which relies upon contract as opposed to incentives. They foresee that mobility within the profession will be even more reduced than it had become under the constraints of falling rolls and they fear that good management within a collegiate system, which depends upon consultation, will be considerably more difficult. On the other hand, however, the definition of many tasks currently regarded as voluntary, such as attendance at staff meetings and parents' evenings, as an integral part of professional obligation will make it easier for heads to manage in those areas which have been disrupted in the past by the withdrawal of what is known as goodwill.

If, as is intended, the effect of the changes is also to enhance the value and the standard of classroom teaching, then the long-term interests of schools will be served. What is certain is that some changes in the existing system must come, if only because the frustration of so many teachers who are currently unable to progress, by way of promotion, to reasonable salary levels can only be harmful to those same long-term interests.

The head's approach to creating a management structure will

need to be adjusted to meet the new conditions, if the projected reforms go through. While it will still be possible to identify and to reward in financial terms those staff who take on a major responsibility, whether as faculty heads or in key pastoral roles, the remainder of the necessary tasks will have to be allocated among the remainder of the staff. How this will operate in practice remains to be seen. Clearly, it will still be in the interests of teachers who are ambitious to accept responsibilities, the succ. ssful execution of which may be viewed as accumulating credits towards later promotion into the remaining superstructure. For the less ambitious, however, the incentive to do so may be limited by the general requirement that all the Main Professional Grade teachers will take a fair share of those responsibilities and duties. Admittedly, the proposals give the head the ultimate power of direction, although the main thrust is that the allocation should be the outcome of consultation. The skills of consultation and persuasion are likely to be of even greater importance to heads in the future than they are already.

One of the most difficult aspects of this procedure, from the head's point of view, will be the question of fairness. If all the Main Professional Grade teachers must accept a fair share, the definition of 'fair' will become critical and inevitably open to conflicting interpretation. This will force all heads to be completely open in their dealings in this area, an approach which some will find easier than others, but there can be no guarantee that open management will be more acceptable.

The key factor in staff management will be the annual statement of his job given to each teacher. This will consist of three elements.

1 A job description, drawn up at the time of appointment to the Main Professional Grade at the school, with or without subsequent modification (e.g. Teacher in charge of German).
2 A statement of the general duties and responsibilities of all Main Professional Grade teachers.
3 A statement of particular duties and responsibilities allocated to that teacher specifically for the coming year (e.g. Form Teacher of Form 3B, 32 teaching periods per week, break duties on Tuesdays and Thursdays etc.)

It will be of the utmost importance that these statements should be full and complete in themselves and in aggregate so that all the tasks which the head sees as essential for the efficient running of the school are fully covered.

The new approach lays great emphasis on the job description. This is a relatively modern development for many schools. In times past it was assumed that everybody knew what the job entailed and so there was no need to write it down. The development of ideas on accountability and the introduction of management techniques into the educational world have changed that. Today, it is generally expected that responsibilities should be defined and most posts now carry a job description, although the quality and precision of these descriptions vary widely. A good job description should indicate the main areas for which the holder is responsible, to whom he is responsible for their execution, and who is under his authority. A description which is couched in very generalized terms will be too vague while too great an emphasis on detail will seem pernickety. A complaint which is sometimes heard from heads is of staff who hold posts but are not giving value for money. A good job description can form the basis of regular and systematic performance appraisal and thus contribute towards an improvement in performance. In the last resort, it can also be used to demonstrate the incapacity of the post-holder without the need for recourse to vague generalizations and subjective judgements.

Both the staffing structure and the job descriptions need to be generally known and understood within the school. This applies to all staff in that they can then identify their own roles within the overall scheme of things, and have a clear idea of who is responsible for what. Confusion and overlap can be avoided and the business of the school can run more smoothly. Although they do not need to know the detail, the pupils also need to know the nature of the structure and the place of individual teachers in it. If, for instance, a harassed teacher threatens to report a pupil to the head of department, it helps a lot if the pupil knows who the head of department is, how important he is in hierarchical terms and what the consequences of such referral might be.

The link between an effective structure and job descriptions with the making of appointments and the development of staff capability through training should be obvious and these themes have already been developed in the previous chapter.

Communications

The desirability of ensuring that the staffing structure and the place of each individual within it are both known and understood is just a small part of the general area of communications which poses problems in all organizations and not least in schools. The complexity of the daily life of any secondary school, makes good communication essential but hard to achieve. In large schools, particularly those occupying more than one building or with more than one staff base, the difficulties can be daunting. The main reason for this is that expectations are high. One teacher may be in contact with 100–150 pupils in one day or with 300 or more during a week. Any one of these pupils may present a personal problem which would be better handled if the teacher has foreknowledge of particular circumstances applicable to that pupil.

Arrangements of out-of-school visits, special lectures, school photographs, inspection by the 'nit-nurse', lessons from peripatetic musical instrument teachers, exeats for doctor's appointments and a thousand and one other events which occur in schools all impinge on the daily work in the classroom and there is nothing which irritates a teacher more than for such events to come as a surprise.

School rules and routines, not to mention occasional variations on these, arrangements for completing reports, examination entries, subject choices, ordering of books and materials, visits by LEA Inspectors or HMIs are all matters of concern to teachers, to pupils and sometimes to parents as well. Without an effective system of communication, the school can easily become disorganized and chaotic.

Devising a system of communications is a tricky business, or rather devising one that works is a tricky business. It is not too difficult to discover in almost any organization a system, which has been most lovingly and thoughtfully created with the object of communicating, totally failing to do anything of the kind. This may be because the system is too complicated and people have simply not bothered to use it; it may be because people are communicating more effectively by other means, making it superfluous; or it may mean that there are obstacles preventing the system from working.

Just to give a simple illustration of the point, consider the following situation:

Irate Head: Miss Smithers, why did you not send your class to the special assembly I called this morning?
Miss Smithers: I am very sorry, I did not know about it.
IH: Good Heavens, woman, there has been a notice on the staffroom board about it since Monday.
Miss S: I am terribly sorry; I didn't see it.
IH: Kindly be more attentive to these matters in future.

Poor Miss Smithers! She did not mention to the head that the small piece of paper on the board was buried in a collection of others, half of which were completely out of date. She also failed to point out that, because her classroom is a long way from the staffroom, she seldom goes in there, preferring to go directly to her class in the morning and taking her coffee break in the Science Prep. Room. We can hardly blame her, although the head did, when really he ought to have been taking a close look at his communications system.

To start with, the system should be set out and understood. It must then be monitored and assessed at regular intervals to ensure that it is working and, wherever any failure of communication comes to light, critical questions must be asked to ensure that it was not a system failure. The importance of these tasks is such that they should be specifically included in the job description of a senior member of the staff, probably a deputy head.

The first area to be tackled should be routines and this is closely linked with the concept of planning. A school which runs from day to day, staggering from one emergency or deadline to the next, can never have effective communication. The school year is the obvious starting point. Many activities and functions are predictable or planned well in advance. Examinations, parents' evenings, presentations, sports days, overseas journeys, school plays, field trips and so on are all likely to come into this category. A calendar for the school year can therefore be planned with all these items written in even before the year begins. It can be widely displayed and key entries from it can be circulated, for example to parents. Although widely displayed, it must be understood that only the senior member of staff in charge may insert new entries and it is then his/her task to see that these additions appear on all copies.

From the calendar comes the weekly diary, a device used in many schools both to remind staff and pupils of immediately impending events and to publish news and notices. It is a useful device in both respects but, most important, it concentrates as much information as possible into one place. Except for matters of emergency or instant importance, the need to post a constant succession of notices is overcome by accumulating them for a weekly bulletin which is widely circulated. It is important that this bulletin should be used by everybody and not just by senior management. All staff communication of general relevance should be channelled through it. It is also important that attention should be paid to the presentation of this bulletin to ensure that the reader's attention is attracted, particularly to vital matters.

If, in our example, the head had been able to say to Miss Smithers that the information about his special assembly was the top item in last week's bulletin of which she had been given a personal copy, he would have been on stronger ground. Even if he had been dependent on his notice-board, he would have had a better case if the display had been organized and if there had been a custom that all staff assembled in the staffroom to be briefed at regular fixed times. Keeping the notice-board well-organized and readable is always a chore and, once again, it is important enough to be somebody's explicit responsibility. The use of segregated sections for different purposes, the adoption of colour codings for important matters and regular purging of obsolete material are all methods of improving this aspect of communications.

Some large schools have public address systems connected to all rooms. These may be a blessing or a bane; a blessing if used sparingly and effectively in precisely defined ways; a bane if they are irritating interruptions to other activities and if three-quarters of the messages are irrelevant to the hearer. They do have the great advantage of solving one problem: communicating with pupils. Pupils are notoriously bad at reading notices and do respond better to oral communications, if they are effectively and authoritatively presented. Hence the practice of reading notices in assemblies which, in moderation and confined to important items, is both efficient and effective. Unfortunately, in large schools, not all pupils can attend the same assembly and, in some instances, may not meet more than once or twice a week. The public address system then comes into its own, because it is so much easier than circulating many copies of notices to be read out. Because it is easy, however, it encourages laziness and a careful censorship must be operated to weed out non-essential items and those which could and should be dealt with by other means.

One of the biggest problems in communication is over-kill and there are organizations everywhere, not only schools, which sink slowly under the weight of their own paper. In determining the circulation of documents, there are two questions to be answered. The first is: Who needs to know? Into this list must go all those whose work is directly related to the material which the document contains and whose actions may be affected by it. The second is: Who would like to know? This is a little more difficult because there are always people about who would like to know everything, informational magpies of insatiable curiosity. There are, however, those with known special interests for whom the information would be positively helpful and we should try to ensure that they receive the document. As a rule of thumb, the people who need to know should have a copy while those who would like to know may see one on the noticeboard.

One of the most sensitive areas of communication in schools is that of confidentiality. It has become more sensitive in recent years because it has become a matter of public debate and proposed legislation. Many LEAs and schools have reviewed their practices in the handling of sensitive material. The legal aspects of this are dealt with in chapter 6 but two points are relevant here. The first is that there is no justification for open access to confidential information whether supplied by parents or other professional agencies. Those who want to know, but do not need to, have no business here. The second is that those who need to know should have access to the information as and when they need it and this is best dealt with by placing a note in an open file that additional information is lodged elsewhere and may be seen subject to consultation with the custodian of it.

Returning to the broader question of circulating information, it is important to remember that it is the task of the office staff to put into effect the wishes of the originators of documents. These wishes need therefore to be clearly stated. A very helpful practice is to have a number of routine lists for reference which can save a great deal of time all round. A typical list might look like this:

List A: All teaching and ancillary staff
List B: Teaching staff only
List C: Ancillary staff only
List D: Heads of department
List E: Heads of year
List F: Management team
List G: Management team and governors
List H: Probationary teachers
List I: Members of PTA committee
List J: Form tutors

Communication is an institutional function but it is also a personal one. No amount of routine, no refinement of system can take the place of personal communication and no head can afford to neglect this vital aspect of his task. It is a curious feature of school organization that, in spite of an increasingly developed hierarchical structure, every teacher and ancillary assistant likes to relate, in certain matters, directly to the head. So, time-consuming though it is, the head needs to communicate directly and in person not only with the senior members of staff but also, though inevitably less frequently, with them all. Much of this communication will be informal and transitory but some of it will be significant for both sides and, occasionally, it will be formal.

Many heads have cultivated remarkable memories but none is infallible and it is a very valuable practice to record briefly the substance of important discussions with individual members of staff and to see that a copy of that record is supplied to the subject of it. Two examples may underline the importance of doing this:

30 June 1983
Mr X (Head of Science) saw me to discuss the integration of science teaching. His department is well forward with plans and is broadly agreed on the direction. We agreed that Mr X should raise the issue at the next meeting of heads of department, backed by a paper outlining the changes proposed. I should also need to use this paper in reporting to the governors. Mr X promised to report again on the way in which his department would evaluate the changes in operation.

10 March 1984
I saw Mr Y at my request to discuss with him the worries which his head of department had expressed to me about Mr Y's contribution to the work of the department this year. Mr Y said that he had discussed the issues with the head of department and accepted that he had had a difficult year, partly for personal reasons unconnected with the school. His circumstances had now improved and he was hoping to be able to pull his weight more effectively from now on.

Such notes are useful records to assist the memories of both parties about what was discussed and agreed. In certain circumstances, such as when disciplinary action may be contemplated, it is vital that such records should be kept and that both parties should agree upon their accuracy in matters of fact.

Consultation

Closely allied to communication is consultation and this, too, can prove a minefield for the unwary. The idea of consultation is very firmly rooted in our society today and particularly so in education, where one is dealing with a community of intelligent and communicative people. People want to be involved in decisions which affect them or the circumstances in which they work, they like to feel that their interests, and feelings, are taken into account when decisions are made and they tend to resent decisions which are made arbitrarily, even if they appear to be correct.

A wise head will therefore demonstrate his belief in consultation and will practise it systematically. However two important points need to be kept in mind. The first is that consultation should not be confused with majority voting. Most decisions in a school are made at a point within some sort of hierarchical structure and, for the purposes of this argument, it is more important to consider how they are made than where. This is because any decision, wherever taken, will be more acceptable if all those affected by it feel that proper consultation has preceded it. There are schools where endless staff meetings occur because they are trying to reach consensus or majority decisions where the first is unattainable and the second leaves a thoroughly disgruntled minority: often a better result can be achieved if the staff are encouraged and enabled to offer opinions which are taken into account when the decision is reached elsewhere. A head can then say to the staff: 'The management team listened carefully to the opinions expressed and decided to act as follows. We are aware, of course, that some of you are not happy with this but we felt the balance of the argument favoured this course. We shall see how it works and discuss it again in the light of experience.'

The second point is the need to keep consultation within limits. One is reminded here of the old advertisement for shaving soap (which dates the writer terribly): 'Not too little, not too much.' Here we are dealing with instinct and experience as much as with principles, because it is difficult to lay down hard and fast rules. A newly-appointed head will need to spend longer on consultation than one whom the staff has already learned to trust. The key here, as with communication, is having a system which is effective, accepted and consistent. If it is known that all decisions affecting the curriculum are arrived at in consultation with the regular heads of departments meeting, then decisions so reached will be accepted, especially where the members of that committee consult their departments about the stance they will adopt at the meetings. A structured procedure for arriving at such decisions is often much more effective than a general staff meeting. An extreme example of consultation erring on the side of 'too much' was the staff meeting which discussed earnestly for two hours the proposal that pupils be allowed to use correction fluid.

An even more significant test of good management is the effectiveness of delegation. A recent survey of heads conducted by the writer revealed that most of those surveyed (including himself) worked very long hours and felt constantly under pressure due as much to the volume of their work as to its inherently stressful nature. At least some of these problems are caused by inadequate delegation. For every overworked head, there may be underworked or badly used deputies; and for every overworked deputy, there may be underworked senior and junior staff. This is said with reservation, however, because the non-teaching tasks of modern secondary schools are inadequately recognized in staffing terms and especially in terms of support staff.

Heads in general have a fatal desire to be in touch with everything that goes on in their schools, although, in schools above a certain size, this becomes impossible to achieve. The impossibility of the task does not stop them trying, however, and this can have dangerous consequences for themselves, if not for the schools they manage. The answer can only lie in effective delegation because there is no other way in which the head can free himself to look at the general condition of his school and its long-term objectives. The fact is that top management, in this context, has more to do with looking, talking and thinking than with doing. Much of the doing must be delegated to others to create the time for these vital functions and heads whose time is too full of activity have to ask themselves how far this is serving their main objectives and how far it is hindering them.

Schools can learn in this area from the business world, where delegation is generally more accepted and better practised. It means the allocation to others not of tasks but of areas of responsibility and letting go of that responsibility oneself. It means monitoring the execution of that responsibility, not by checking on petty details, but in regular discussion and reporting and by the provision of support when needed. It means accepting that somebody else will do a job in a different way from oneself and, so long as it works, allowing that to happen. It means giving up tasks which one enjoys doing oneself and letting somebody else do them without interference. It means having confidence in the ability of others to carry out tasks for which one is oneself ultimately accountable.

It also means structure and system. A first principle of delegation is that the responsibilities and tasks delegated should be clearly set out on paper and understood on both sides as well as by others within the organization. Deputy heads and others with delegated functions need to have full job descriptions, which may be modified from time to time in the light of experience or the school's changing needs. These functions, once delegated, should stay with the recipient, and a head must have the courage and the will not to undermine the system by taking back arbitrarily or at random a function which he has delegated. It is not always easy to say to a teacher, parent or pupil who comes to the head with a problem, 'You must see the deputy about this' or, 'I must first discuss this with the deputy', but this is the essence of effective delegation. Once established in a school, however, such a system becomes readily accepted by all concerned and also spreads downwards through the system when heads of department and others see the need to delegate some of their functions in order to concentrate on the essential tasks entrusted to them.

A sound structure of delegated authority, clearly set out and properly applied, is also the basis for effective staff development because it is through the successful execution of one set of delegated tasks that a teacher seeking advancement is prepared to progress to a higher level. For this reason, among others, it is important not to allow a structure to ossify. Not only do those holding positions within the structure need to be appraised in their performance but the structure also needs to be reviewed from time to time to ensure that it is serving the needs of the school in the most effective manner. This is especially true at the senior level where deputy heads may need to gain a variety of experience both to keep them 'fresh' in their jobs and to broaden their experience for promotion to headship. For them, the 'cabinet reshuffle' has much to commend it.

This breadth of experience is also fostered by the institution of a management committee or team, a practice which, under a variety of guises, has become standard in most large secondary schools. The existence of such a team gives great support to a head and in-stitutionalizes the decision-making process in the school in a way which protects the head against any tendency to autocracy. The size of the team varies from place to place. In some schools, it consists of the head and deputies and is thus three or four strong. In others, senior teachers are included, enlarging the group to between five and seven members. The present writer has a prejudice towards the larger group on the grounds that it enables more senior staff to participate, brings in a greater diversity of opinion, enables the jobs to be more widely distributed and fosters the development of leadership potential among a larger number. Too small a group creates the risk of a 'junta' being formed which is out of touch with opinion within the school and does not spread the management load sufficiently widely.

Whatever the size of the team, its operation needs to be governed by four basic principles.

1 It should meet regularly, probably weekly, and should consider all policy decisions relating to the school.
2 It should have a written agenda and minutes of decisions taken, both of which are circulated to members.
3 The members should accept collective responsibility for decisions taken, even when they may have argued against them in the com-mittee.
4 It may sometimes be necessary to agree that some aspects of a

discussion are confidential so that an issue may be raised with total frankness.

All these points must be made explicit by the head in establishing the team and must be understood by any new recruit. They must also be understood by the rest of the staff as well and, lest the committee become too exclusive a group, it is a useful practice to invite an outsider to attend from time to time when an issue concerning him is discussed. If, for example, the head of science is not a member, his absence when the science curriculum is being discussed might be difficult to defend.

The control of the team's business is vital, if time is not to be wasted on trivia. It is important to remember that, if you gather together the most highly-paid members of the staff for an hour or two, their expensive time ought not to be wasted. The head's role as chairman, which includes ordering the agenda, steering the discussion and pinpointing decisions, is crucial. Decisions need to be based on the fullest information which can be made available and it is the head's task to see that such information is collected and presented. The meeting of the management team must not degenerate into a weekly chat session but must be business-like and supported by appropriate documentation. It is through the operation of the team that the head pulls together the responsibilities which have been delegated, reviews the operation of the structure and creates a common policy base within which all members operate.

The accusation most commonly levelled against the management team approach is that it creates an oligarchy which is in its way as unhealthy as old-fashioned dictatorship. This would be a fair accusation if the same principles which governed its operation were not extended throughout the organization of the school, and, in particular, through its committee structure.

While the ultimate responsibility for school policy rests with the management team, there are many decisions within that policy and in extensions of it which can and should be taken on a broader base. Most schools will feel a need to establish committees of heads of department, to coordinate the curriculum and the administration of it and to promote a common approach to pastoral care. Just as with delegation to individuals, it is important to spell out the terms of reference of such standing committees, to specify the membership and to institutionalize the preparation of agenda and minutes, both of which should be available to the staff as a whole. It must be clear when the committee is taking a decision, and when it is conveying its advice to the management team. The principal of representation should be clear, so that there is equity of treatment of interested parties, and alternates should be encouraged to ensure that full representation is preserved. Here, too, the professional conduct of business is an essential feature, if confidence is to be maintained, and it is not always necessary for the head to preside. Others need to learn the skills of chairmanship too.

This same professional practice should be extended to departments and to the units of pastoral care, whether year-groups or 'houses'. Those who lead these sub-groups within the school should have within their job-descriptions the responsibility for arranging regular meetings which should also be organized on professional lines. Indeed, a good school calendar should allocate specific times for these meetings to occur and their minutes should be available to the management committee. Last, but by no means least, the same style can be extended to include pupil and student participation through school councils and the like.

While a well-planned committee and consultative structure should meet most of the needs of school organization, there are three other modes of consultation which need to be mentioned: the ad hoc committee, the full staff meeting and the unions.

The use of ad hoc committees is a handy device for special purposes or detailed planning. The use of a special committee to plan for a 'one-off' event needs no elaboration but it can also be a useful instrument for developing an innovation. If, for instance, the school feels the need for a new staff development policy or a new system of pupil-profiling, a small group of staff who have a particular interest in the subject can do a lot of the detailed research and preparation before presenting to the appropriate standing committees or to the staff as a whole their report and recommendations.

The use of the full staff meeting is a difficult task in any school above a medium size. A large body does not generally lead to effective debate and yet all staff like to be involved. It is a useful forum for 'letting off steam' but ought not to be a focus for grumbling. It is not the appropriate place for decisions, other than those which affect staff welfare generally, but it is a good place for explaining and questioning. It is better to deal with a few specific and important issues rather than with a rag-bag of trivia, and it is better to run to a fixed and reasonable time of adjournment than to plod on to exhaustion. If the rest of the consultation structure and the communication system is working well, the full staff meeting can become a good debating chamber and it is this function which it is best suited to perform.

The presence of the unions is something which no head can afford to ignore, even at times when no industrial action is in the offing. The head has to deal with three or four different unions within the teaching staff, as well as perhaps NALGO, NUPE and GMWU among the support staff. The head should be aware of the relative strength of the various unions among the staff and know the names of their representatives. They should be consulted individually whenever any of their members runs into difficulties which might lead to disciplinary action, and such consultation can often be most helpful in dealing with the problem. They should be consulted collectively whenever changes are proposed which could properly be said to affect the conditions of service of their members, as opposed to their professional duties. Such things as a change in the timing of the school day, facilities in the staff room, increasing the contact ratio, and a new system of cover for absent colleagues, are all examples of matters which they might regard as their legitimate concern and where advance consultation may well serve to avoid difficulties later on. When industrial action is taken, the head would do well to consult the union representatives before determining his response to the situation.

Finally, a head may well wish to encourage the setting up of a staff room committee to look after the amenities available to the staff and to foster the social aspects of staff communal life which do so much to create a harmonious and happy atmosphere within the school.

It will be apparent that this chapter has been written against the background of a large school. But the principles set out are valid in any school, namely that the organization should provide a setting in which each member of staff is given the best possible opportunity and incentive to serve the pupils. The argument is that the likelihood of this will be significantly enhanced if he has appropriate opportunities of understanding and contributing to the processes whereby management decisions are made. It may be possible to achieve this with fewer formalities in a small school. On the other hand it may be easier for the head of such a school to persuade himself that 'he knows what they all think', and therefore to justify the making of decisions which are in fact autocratic.

It must also be said that, if the Burnham Committee decides upon a pattern of staff promotion which moves away from the 'managerial ladder', as being no longer appropriate at a time of contraction of the school system, this in no way means that the principles which have been set out here become less relevant, or that the tasks which teachers at present undertake will no longer need to be done. Ideally such a revision should lead to a wider sharing of responsibility and a tighter evaluation of performance.

5 Pupil management

David Williams

At least one education authority which has attempted to define the role of the Headteacher states firmly: 'The fundamental responsibility of the headteacher is to ensure that the school functions properly, in all its aspects, so that it contributes fully to each pupil's educational development, intellectually, physically, morally, spiritually and personally.' This at any rate puts first things first and reminds us that all the managerial tasks of the head are undertaken not for the benefit of the government, local authority, governors, parents, employees or teachers but for the benefit of the pupils for whom schools exist.

The great majority of heads came to their posts throught success in teaching and pastoral roles, so that it is always something of a shock to realize how limited their direct involvement with pupils is now likely to be. This is partly a function of size: heads of small schools of whatever kind will certainly, if they wish, be in a position to exert their influence much more directly on pupils than the heads of large comprehensives. Public opinion still sees the head of a school as something more than an administrator or managing director and the majority of heads do retain some teaching commitment and a position in the pastoral hierarchy which ensures that they do have day-to-day contact with pupils. Most feel that they can only get the true feel of a school by themselves engaging in its most important activity and that they will not have credibility with their colleagues unless they themselves are seen to be grappling with the problems of extracting homework from low-ability fourth formers. This emphasizes that the head's teaching load should not be confined to comfortable sessions of General Studies with the upper sixth or RE with a first form. And if it is to be convincing it has to be done well with high standards of preparation and marking. There will be crises and inevitable absences which probably make it inadvisable for the head to undertake examination work. A possible alternative to a regular teaching commitment is for the head to cover classes for absent colleagues up to an agreed maximum each week. Such periods if properly handled give plenty of opportunities for gaining insight into pupils' morale and attitudes but they are poor subsitutes for the shared experience of teaching and learning which comes from regular contact.

However dedicated to teaching heads may be, they will never be able to meet more than a small minority of pupils in the classroom. If they are not careful, they will find that in other contexts they get to know the very good and the very bad but remain only slightly acquainted with the mass in the middle. Most discipline systems, except in very small schools, will delegate routine procedures to heads of house or heads of year with more serious cases being handled by a deputy. The head is only likely to be formally involved where normal sanctions have failed, where parents have been brought in and where exclusion or suspension are real possibilities. This is not to say that there will not be many occasions when procedures are short-circuited and the head finds himself dealing with relatively trivial problems of uniform, litter or misbehaviour simply because he happens to be available at the right time. But it is easy to dissipate one of the head's great strengths, a certain air of remote authority, if he is invoked whenever a school rule is breached.

Inevitably the head will come to be aware of those pupils who give cause for concern. It is not always so easy to recognize those who are doing well. It is helpful if teachers are prepared to notify the head directly when pupils have done good work or distinguished themselves in any other way, and if there is an accepted system whereby such pupils can come to the head for congratulation. A formal system of 'merit marks' can provide a means for identifying those who have made some notable contribution and, if time is available, it is worth following up reports by interviews with those who have done very well as well as with those who deserve warning or reprimand. It can be particularly rewarding if Art and Craft Departments can be persuaded to send pupils with specimens of their work for praise, and assemblies can be useful opportunities for the presentation of certificates and the recognition of excellence on the games field.

Assemblies indeed are likely to be the main occasions when most members of the school gain an impression of the head as a person and therefore it is essential for him to use them to convey as effectively as he can his policies and aims. Nowadays a school will be fortunate if it is small enough or has a hall large enough to accommo-date all its members in reasonable comfort. Most large schools will hold assemblies by house or year groups and they will occur two or three times a week only. The head will usually wish to be present with each section of the school once a week at least, even if he does not always take the leading role. The organization of an assembly as a means of expressing the values of the school as a community, and not just a rather messy interlude between registration and first period, is not an easy task and it is not surprising that some schools have experimented with holding assemblies at the end of the day or at some other time when it may be easier to invest them with their proper importance. The religious content, which to the framers of the 1944 Act was the main justification for morning assembly, does not become any easier to manage convincingly as society becomes more and more secular and as more and more schools find themselves with multi-ethnic minorities. What is certain is that the religious or moral element needs to be clearly separated from the administrative and notice-giving function. Traditional school assemblies are all to easy to parody.

In conclusion, if the head wishes to make himself a noticeable personal presence in the life of his pupils – and not all heads will want this or think it desirable – he must take all the opportunities formal and informal, that he can. He will teach, he will take assemblies, he will see such pupils as his colleagues refer to him; he must also be prepared to walk around the school during lessons, at breaks, at lunch times; he must watch matches, attend plays and concerts, accept invitations to end-of-term form parties; he will entertain sixth-formers to coffee, endure fifth-year discos, patronize first-year charity jumble sales. If he is prepared to find time for pursuing his own special interests – producing a play, running a camp or taking a school trip abroad – he must realize that it will be at the expense of more routine but possibly more valuable commitments.

Like any senior manager, however, the head cannot hope to do the work of his colleagues and he will best fulfil his responsibilities to his pupils by making sure that he has set up systems which facilitate both the academic and the pastoral activities of the school.

The organization of learning

The main areas with which the head is concerned are, firstly, the curricular aims and objectives of the school; secondly, the curriculum which will best embody those aims and objectives; and thirdly, the implementation of this curriculum in terms of the actual organization of teaching programmes and the school day. The first two of these tasks will involve consultation with many interested groups including governors, parents, local employers as well as colleagues, and will also have to take account of the policies of national government and local authority. These specifically curricular problems are considered in another chapter. Some of the practical issues involved in translating the curriculum into an actual teaching programme are dealt with here.

Departments and faculties

Most parents, pupils and teachers continue to talk about traditional subjects and these remain enshrined both in timetables and in the school's administrative structure. This state of affairs comes under increasing attack on grounds both of curriculum irrelevance and of organizational inflexibility. Both of these issues are dealt with in other chapters of this book. The aims of such reforms as we are able to effect must be the improved motivation of both staff and pupils.

The school day

It is curious that there is no generally accepted length of the school day so that the amount of teaching time may vary by one or two hours per week between different schools. Attempts to change an existing pattern can often be frustrated by bus timetables, if the school relies substantially on public transport, or by the time needed for school dinners. In any case strong staff support will be necessary for any change which may appear to involve worsening of conditions of service. A common pattern consists of four 70-minute periods, two in the morning and two in the afternoon, although these may sometimes be subdivided to give eight 35-minute periods. There will usually be a break of 15 or 20 minutes in the morning and a shorter gap in mid-afternoon. Changeovers between periods are traditionally assumed to occur instantaneously – which is not in accordance with the facts. The 15–30 minutes set aside for reg- istration and assembly at the beginning of the day may or may not be seen as possible teaching time e.g. for tutorial work.

Heads will of course attempt to alter or modify any such pattern in accordance with their own needs but there are usually incompatible demands from different subjects. Modern languages prefer 'little and often' e.g. one 35-minute period a day; craft subjects and home economics and sixth-form science practicals call for complete sessions. All such requirements (not to speak of the problems of link courses, where such exist) present particular difficulties when option schemes are being considered. On the whole the amount of time wasted in movement between lessons suggests that the balance of advantage lies with the longer periods, however tiresome these may be for particular teachers with particular classes.

It is not surprising that the effort to squeeze a quart into a pint pot has led many schools to experiment with six-day or ten-day timetables. These create their own problems especially in accommodating part-time staff, and the complications need to be justified by some clearly-perceived advantage in terms of curricular flexibility.

Types of teaching groups

The number of teaching groups that a school can afford will ultimately be determined by the local authority's staffing policy, whether this is expressed in terms of a crude pupil–teacher ratio or by some more sophisticated formula based on curricular needs. It is unlikely that groups in the first three years will contain many fewer than 30, except for the craft subjects, which traditionally claim only 15 or 20, and remedial classes, if such exist. In the fourth and fifth years rather smaller groups of 20–25 are desirable but if the school's policy calls for the preservation of minority subjects such as Latin or music, some uneconomic groups may have to be compensated by larger groups elsewhere. The sixth form is usually staffed more generously and groups are unlikely to be larger than 15 but it is important to realize that a lot of very small sets will probably be subsidized from the staff of the main school.

Teaching groups may be organized on the basis of age, ability or, more rarely, sex. Grouping in terms of chronological age is widely accepted as the norm, (although there will almost certainly be a year's variation in the ages of a class). The exceptional, very able pupil may be transferred early from primary school or may be accelerated through secondary school but for social and pastoral (as well as administrative) reasons this is not common. At sixth-form level it is not unusual for both years of the sixth to be taught together for some subjects and in community schools, and some others, adults are successfully admitted to sixth form classes. It is a pity that there have not been more experiments with vertical groupings, however daunting to the organizer of the timetable; and English schools have never adopted the practice, common in other parts of Europe, of promoting or keeping pupils down for a year on the criterion of performance rather than age.

Similarly, in coeducational schools the emphasis has been on equality of treatment for boys and girls rather than on differentiation. The Equal Opportunities Act ensures that all must have access to the same curriculum so that craft subjects and home economics which were the last bastions of differentiation (apart from PE) are now taught to all, at least for the first three years. Option choices in the fourth year all too often reveal that sex-stereotyping has only been postponed. Nevertheless, while few would deny the value of mixed classes as a general rule, there is now accumulating evidence to suggest that, for instance, boys may perform better at languages and girls at physics in the absence of the opposite sex. Girls often seem to have a more mature response to English Literature at a younger age than boys. It is worth considering whether, for some periods in some subjects, parallel sets for boys and girls might not enable both to reach higher standards.

The bias, however, is always towards grouping by ability. Mixed ability groups are normal as pastoral units in the first year and often throughout the school. They are also likely to form the learning groups for most subjects in the first and second years but there is usually increasing pressure for setting by ability in particular subjects, most often mathematics and languages. Some schools preserve mixed ability groups throughout up to 16, even in mathematics. Much will depend upon the style of teaching and the willingness of teachers to develop new methods. Some schools have concentrated on individualized resource-based learning, have developed effective resource centres and carried out careful INSET programmes to prepare teachers for their new rôle as teachers of a mixed ability group. Any group, no matter how homogeneous, is in fact a mixed ability group but most teachers are understandably uncertain of their capacity to cope with a wide range of pupils. Setting by ability lessens the scale of the problem although it can create problems of its own, especially in bottom sets. Unless the school operates a blocked timetable it will be impossible to set over the whole year group and it becomes necessary to divide into two or three bands. Within a band there are variations possible such as the extraction of a top set with the others equal in status. Although with any such system departments or faculties can have discretion to use their own preferred systems, it is probable that, sooner or later, there will be need to define an overall school policy. Since parents, employers and the media are very far from being convinced of the feasibility or desirability of mixed ability teaching in secondary schools, it is very important to win public support before introducing it on a large scale.

Special provision

Most schools accept the necessity of making special provision for pupils with learning difficulties, particularly in the areas of reading and number work. Some schools may possess special units for pupils with particular forms of handicap, whether mental or physical, and who possess 'statements' under the 1980 Act, and every effort is usually made to integrate such pupils as fully as possible with the main school within the limits of their disabilities. But as the Warnock Report reminded us, in addition to the 3 per cent who will receive statements there are 20 per cent who will need some form of special provision during their school careers. In the past such provision was often under the aegis of a remedial department which was responsible for special remedial classes in the first two and sometimes the first three years. Such classes had favourable staffing ratios and were taught as a separate group for much of the time with special emphasis on reading skills, although some integration was often attempted for games and the practical subjects. For some pupils, whose problems were due to faulty early teaching or illness at a crucial time, learning difficulties could indeed be remedied quickly and they could be integrated into the main school, but there always remained a hard core whose progress was limited. When at some stage, often in the third or fourth year, it was felt that such pupils could no longer be protected in special classes, very considerable difficulties could be created if they were introduced into existing stable form groupings. The tendency nowadays is to have a special needs department with an emphasis on dealing with learning difficulties by a withdrawal system. Some pupils may be withdrawn for most of their lessons, others only for a few lessons for a limited time to deal with a specific problem. This system has the advantages of allowing all pupils to be placed in mixed ability pastoral groups and enables the specialist teachers in the department to give help to a much wider range of pupils with problems. In the short term it is possible that some would make greater progress in a sheltered environment but in the long term this cannot be a preparation for the 'real world'.

If schools are conscious of their duty to provide adequately for children with learning difficulties, they are sometimes less ready to cater for the special needs of the gifted or exceptionally able. Stimulus, encouragement, suitable resources and learning materials are necessary if such pupils are not to coast through their school life, unstretched and under-achieving. Definition and identification are not easy: standardized tests, primary school reports, the classroom teachers' impressions can all play a part. Individualized learning is the ideal but at the least teachers should be ready with extra tasks, suggestions for reading and more demanding homework. It is sometimes possible to operate a withdrawal system for the very able so that they can have the stimulus of working with their peers and many out-of-school clubs can offer opportunities for enthusiasts of different ages to meet together. It is important for the head to make sure that his colleagues realize that the needs of the gifted should not be neglected.

Options and guidance

For the first three years of the secondary school all pupils are likely to follow a common curriculum, with the exception of a minority who may start the study of a second foreign language. In the fourth and fifth years, however, pupils will be presented with a range of option choices. These choices, which have to be made by most pupils at the age of 14, mark a crucial stage in their school careers and schools will do their best to provide guidance so that the choices are informed ones which do not lead to future problems (e.g. a potential engineer who drops physics or a potential Oxbridge candidate who drops his only foreign language). The grouping of the options can ensure a degree of breadth and it is important this is made clear in the documentation sent to parents. It is helpful for the head to explain the school's practices and intentions to a meeting of parents well before the actual choices have to be made but neither he nor heads of year or house heads are in a position to give the detailed guidance that will be needed. This must be delegated to the form tutor, using the reports from his subject teacher colleagues, and this will come more naturally if proper use has been made of tutorial time to discuss the bearing of subject choices on career possibilities and the need to balance the subject which is enjoyed against the subject which may be seen as necessary. Some pupils will have to be discouraged from over- ambitious or over-academic choices; ex-remedial pupils may need to be guided towards non-examination courses; the able but idle must be steered away from soft options; the implications of new subjects like computer studies must be explained.

Whatever the system, it will be impossible to satisfy everybody. It is worth remembering that any system, however enlightened, which fails to permit the ablest pupils to tackle three sciences and two foreign languages is unlikely to satisfy many of the most articulate parents.

Homework

Most schools demand some form of homework from all their pupils. Ideally it enables pupils to develop the important skills of working on their own; it provides time and opportunity for the reinforcement and consolidation of work done in class; it offers opportunities for wider reading and study in depth. All pupils should be able to profit from regular, quiet study on their own in their own time but, for those hoping for success in external examinations, a serious commitment to homework is absolutely essential. Homework should not be a burden or a chore but it does need to be seen as a priority and as an integral part of education.

In practice there are problems. Not all parents, nor indeed all teachers, are convinced of the value of homework; pupils may have many conflicting demands on their time; family circumstances may not allow the provision of a separate, warm room. Yet on the whole, parents are supportive and the head is likely to receive many more complaints about too little homework than too much. The school policy needs to be clearly stated and departments need to face up to the difficulties of setting suitable homework for mixed-ability classes. All pupils should have a homework timetable and a homework notebook can avoid many of the arguments about what was set and when. Parents should be encouraged to check homework, at any rate for junior pupils, and to contact the school if the load seems either too heavy or too light. It is helpful if a room can be set aside for supervised study and homework, either in the lunch-hour or after school so that pupils with problems at home have at least the opportunity to work in peace.

The head will need to satisfy himself that homework is being adequately set and assessed but this is essentially the responsibility of heads of departments. All teachers must be aware that pupils need instruction and guidance in study skills and how to make the best use of their homework time.

Assessment

Some sort of assessment is essential to the whole process of education. Every teacher is engaged in a continual monitoring of the progress of his pupils and this, to be effective, must be combined with a system of record-keeping which provides the evidence on which judgements can be based. Here we are concerned with the head's responsibility to set up systems for the assessment of academic progress. The more general question of records of achievement is discussed later.

Initially some information is likely to be available on transfer from primary school or middle school. This may include information about graded test scores (e.g. in mathematics) or standardized scores for verbal and non-verbal ability, although it is all too likely that different primary schools will provide quite different material. Such information is useful for those concerned with setting or establishing well-balanced mixed-ability groups but it needs to be used with caution and there are disadvantages in making it publicly available. Children are entitled to a fresh start in a new school and it is easy to be influenced by the apparent objectivity of standardized test scores. Nevertheless standardized tests, such as those produced by the National Foundation for Educational Research (NFER), do provide a useful way of helping to identify the under-achievers or over-achievers, as well as those with special learning difficulties, and there is value in testing all pupils at some stage during their first term, and possibly again in the third year.

As long as external examinations retain their importance most schools will find it necessary to hold formal internal examinations at regular intervals, probably at least once or twice a year. The timing and frequency will be the concern of the academic committee: the organization of examinations can be a major task and has a considerable disruptive effect on the whole school so that there is much to be said for the traditional 'exam week' towards the end of the summer term. The marking burden, however, can be a great strain and if, as is now usual, examinations are tied to reports and parents' meetings, the pressures can become unmanageable. 'Mock' exams for 'A–level, O–level and CSE must in any case be held in December or January and, by taking an overall view of a pupil's school career from the first year to the fifth year it is possible to devise patterns which allow examinations for different year groups to be spaced out during the school year. The justification for examinations is that they provide practice in 'exam technique', they provide feed-back on progress for both teacher and taught, and they provide motivation for learning and revision. In addition, 'mocks' are intended to throw light on examination potential and hence help to determine entry policy. Internal exams and tests do indeed have their value but they are no substitutes for continuous assessment. In particular, internal exams are often set in a very amateurish way and have low reliability and validity. Within a group they are probably more or less successful in arranging candidates in an order of merit but they rarely make use of the full range of marks, especially for arts subjects, so that quite unreal significance can be attached to particular percentage scores. When exams are to be used for grading purposes it is essential for departments to set common papers across a year group but, even so, crude marks on their own may simply reflect different teaching techniques. In a mixed ability group there are serious problems in setting papers which will do justice to the whole ability range and enable all pupils to show what they can do rather than what they can not. Overall assessment needs to be based on classwork and homework as well as on examinations.

Reports

The results of assessment have to be communicated to parents, employers and institutions of higher or further education. Communication with parents is usually by means of a written report or directly at official parents' evenings. Ideally one would hope that a school could provide some sort of report at least once a term and the pattern of two written reports and one meeting in the course of a year is still common. Pressures on staff, however, particularly on those who teach a large number of groups for two or three periods a week, is such that many schools provide only one full-length annual report with perhaps some interim statement of exam positions or grades. If, as many will feel desirable, the formal report is closely linked with personal interviews at a parents' meeting, there is a real danger that parents may only become aware of problems or lack of progress after an unacceptably long interval. Even if the school has some system for alerting parents in cases of special concern, a single annual report must be a very minimal way of fulfilling its responsibility to the majority of its pupils.

In any case written reports can cause much confusion and misunderstanding. The art of writing clear, full, jargon-free and constructive comments is not one that all teachers find easy and the head is well advised to make sure that instructions are available and to read a representative sample of reports, whether or not he contributes to 'head's comments'. The traditional standard report form with little boxes and narrow columns leads to the brief, dismissive remark and many schools now prefer the report booklet made up of separate sheets clipped or stapled together. This encourages longer, interpretative comments and enables teachers to complete reports without having to wait until the set of forms becomes available. If NCR paper is used a duplicate report can easily be retained and the inclusion of a slip for 'parents' comments' gives the opportunity for useful dialogue. Few schools can now afford to send reports by post and the parents' reply slip can also act as an essential receipt. Some schools, however, prefer to hand out reports at parents' evenings so that discussion and feed-back can be immediate. This certainly has the effect of increasing attendance.

Very often the significance of marks and grades is not properly explained. Few parents will be fully aware of the setting or streaming system in operation and a good report on performance in a lowly set may arouse unjustified expectations. It is often quite unclear whether children are being assessed in relation to the group or to the year as a whole and the difficulty is not removed by the use of a five-point scale rather than marks, although a grade does have less of an appearance of objective accuracy. If separate grades are given for different aspects of performance (e.g. attainment and effort), the written report must explain any apparent discrepancies, such as A for attainment and E for effort. It is not easy to ensure that all teachers pursue a common policy or indeed attach a common meaning to grades, even where they are defined. For the benefit of parents some explanation of the coding must be attached to the report. The school must examine its reporting procedures to make sure that parent and pupil are fully informed about how the pupil is performing in relation to his ability and potential, how he stands in relation to his contemporaries, what are his likely examination objectives, what can be done to bring about improvement, and what useful help can be offered by parents themselves.

Pastoral organization

English schools have always seen themselves as having a responsibility for the education of the whole child and have seen this responsibility as involving concern for moral, spiritual, aesthetic and physical development as well as for the cognitive development which is the most obvious objective of education. To a large extent this springs from the realization that a child who is unhappy or faced with unresolved problems is unlikely to make much progress with learning, and from the age-old dictum that a good teacher teaches people not subjects, so that the right sort of relationship between teacher and taught is fundamental to the whole educational process. The growth of large schools in the last twenty years has made the need for a defined system of pastoral care more apparent: problems which in a small school can be recognized and handled in an ad hoc way may be overlooked in a large organization unless specific arrangements are made to ensure that all pupils have access to help and guidance.

Structures

Most heads would agree that the separation of the academic and pastoral rôles of the teacher is artificial. Nevertheless, just as the academic work of the school is organized around departments and faculties, so in the majority of large schools there is a pastoral organization with its own parallel hierarchy. The form of this organization tends to be determined by the buildings available and the head often must accept that there is only limited scope for modification. Since the independent public schools were based on a house system, it was perhaps inevitable that the early comprehensive schools should be structured around house blocks, often with their own social and dining areas and with provision for housemasters and housemistresses. Frequently the sixth form, where it existed, was housed as a separate unit and, more rarely, a separate house for first

year pupils was provided. This vertical system of grouping has its problems. Houses are generally too large, with 200–300 pupils, to exist as very meaningful entities and the sort of close unity fostered in a boarding school where pupils eat, sleep and spend their leisure time together is just not attainable in a day school, where the natural unit is the teaching group. The situation can be improved if all the members of a particular form or tutor group are automatically assigned to the same house and there are certainly advantages in the continuity of pastoral care and guidance that can be achieved when a housemaster and his team of tutors have responsibility for the same pupils throughout their school careers. A house system also provides a ready-made framework for games and other competitive activities and offers opportunities for giving responsibilities to senior pupils.

With the growth of comprehensive reorganization in the 1960s and 1970s, schools were often faced with buildings, often on split sites, which were very difficult to adapt to house units. Under these circumstances horizontal patterns, based on year groups or school sections became much more common. Sometimes the divisions consist of upper, middle and lower schools, with separate heads of school and deputies; sometimes each year group forms an autonomous unit with its own year tutor working with a team of form tutors. The actual pattern is often dictated by bricks and mortar: lower school may contain the first two or the first three years; upper school may or may not include the sixth year; not infrequently the sectional division manages to split the fourth and fifth years, which are the most closely-linked in curricular terms. Where possible each year group or school section will have its own geographical social area. The main advantage of the horizontal pattern is that it recognizes that a pupil's main links are likely to be with his contemporaries in the same teaching group. Their broadly-similar interests and needs can be recognized in assemblies and in organized social activities; many of their problems (e.g. in relation to careers guidance) are likely to be similar; the tutor group provides a useful and realistic basis for games and other competitions. To provide continuity of pastoral care it is desirable that each year tutor stays with the year group for more than one year: ideally the tutor may remain with the same group from the first year to the fifth year, although there are those who will claim that a change at some stage may be valuable. It is certainly true that individual form tutors may acquire considerable specialized expertise (e.g. in advising on fourth year options) and may wish to remain as tutors in a particular school section.

Many schools, of course, work out some sort of compromise in practice. In a vertical system, the sixth form may be separate and there will be many occasions when the fifth form needs to be seen as a separate group; in a horizontal system, there are often vestigial house groupings to facilitate a wider spread of competitive activities.

Group tutors and tutorial work

The individual teacher acting as group tutor must be the lynch-pin of any pastoral system. Only the tutor is in a position to have anything like a full picture of each of the 20–30 pupils in his tutor-group and only through him can the school hope to substantiate the claim so often made that there is at least one person who is in a position to give an in-depth report on any child. In practice, however, this is a claim hard to verify. Simple arithmetic ensures that the great majority of staff have to act as tutors and some of those will see the pastoral rôle neither as one for which they are trained nor as one which they find rewarding. Except in the first and second years when the form may be taught as a mixed ability group it is rare for the tutor to teach his group as a whole and, at worst, his contact with them may be limited to a few minutes formal registration before the morning and afternoon sessions. Even when the registration time expands to something like half an hour, as it may on several mornings a week if there is no formal assembly, or when there is a timetabled tutorial period, many teachers find difficulty in using this time profitably and it easily degenerates into idle chat, games-playing or belated homework. In consequence many schools have introduced pro- grammes of active tutorial work on the lines made familiar by Leslie Button and Douglas Hamblin. Often these will incorporate elements of social and personal education, in addition to study skills, careers guidance and health education. Such programmes can be very successful when they have been introduced in response to demand from the staff concerned and when there has been proper provision for in-service training and an adequate supply of resources. When imposed from above on unwilling or unenthusiastic teachers, they quickly run into the sand. The head must encourage house or year heads to work with their tutors to develop their own schemes of work in response to what they see as the needs of their own pupils – and to accept that different teachers will have different priorities. Tutorial work can make great demands on a teacher who is perfectly happy and successful as a specialist mathematician or modern linguist.

If increasing demands are to be made on group tutors, it is vital that the importance of their rôle be recognized and that they be given real responsibility for the members of their groups. Tutors should, for instance, have full access to their pupils' files and should be the first people consulted when subject teachers have problems. Although they should, of course, refer serious difficulties to their head of house

or year, they should be able to contact parents on their own initiative and should, as of right, be invited to attend all meetings or interviews concerning any of their pupils. If senior staff show that they value the tutor's opinions and expect him to provide information in depth about the members of his group, they are much more likely to obtain the committed response which makes a pastoral system really effective.

Much will depend on the overall school climate. If pupils trust and have confidence in the teaching staff as a whole, the task of the group tutor will be enormously eased. The head and his senior colleagues have to set the example by their own attitude to and treatment of their pupils.

Rules and discipline

All heads would like their schools to be well-ordered communities where those who learn and those who teach can pursue common objectives in harmony. The reality is often quite different and in most schools an altogether disproportionate amount of time is devoted to trying to discipline pupils whose behaviour is considered un-acceptable. School brochures and staff handbooks give much space to rules and sanctions and the state of school discipline is a source of constant concern to parents, governors and the media.

It is probably helpful to have a set of school rules, or a code of conduct, to cover basic behaviour around the school but its usefulness is limited and it will never cover every eventuality. The head will inevitably make clear by his pronouncements in assembly, his letters to parents and his stance at staff meetings the sort of things which he considers really important. He will probably stress that pupils should show commonsense, courtesy and respect for other people at all times but it is essential that his colleagues share his concern and are prepared to take notice of breaches of both the letter and the spirit of the rules.

Good discipline, however, is not just a matter of rules and pun-ishments. Schools generally make much too little use of praise and rewards as inducements to good behaviour. At a very simple level a system of commendations or merit marks for positive achievements can be surprisingly successful in motivating pupils – and not only those fresh from primary school. Teachers need to be encouraged to praise as well as criticize, and to watch for opportunities to take a positive line.

Some bad behaviour, both in and out of the classroom, certainly arises from boredom and lack of understanding. It may well be appropriate to call for a review of curriculum, teaching methods and the effectiveness of teachers, in connection with disciplinary problems. Similarly a full range of activities available during the lunch break can reduce the risk of violence and vandalism.

However positive the attitude of the school, there will always be the need for sanctions. Teachers properly expect support when serious difficulties arise and the head must ensure that there is a clearly defined and clearly understood system for coping both with the sudden emergency and the long-standing problem. Where needed, action should be taken at as low a level as possible. For instance, in the case of a classroom problem, the subject teacher may set extra work or impose a break or lunchtime detention which he supervises himself. Minor offences may be punished by chores such as collecting litter. If there is recurrent trouble, the form tutor and probably the head of department will be involved. This may lead to further official detention, or contact and interview with parents, (often the most effective sanction of all), probably after consultation with the head of house or year. A pupil whose work or behaviour is persistently unacceptable may be placed 'on report', which means that a signed note must be obtained after each lesson which will then be submitted to a senior member of staff. Corporal punishment must be seen to be on the way out. Its use in mixed schools has always been anomalous and recent decisions by the European Court make it clear that its complete abolition can only be a matter of time. Heads will be well advised to anticipate this by establishing systems which rely on other methods of control and by pressing the local authority to establish special units to which the hard core of persistent offenders may be referred, if only on a temporary basis.

To deal with the sudden crisis some schools maintain a permanently-staffed 'isolation room' to which pupils can be sent to cool down and work under supervision while the matter is sorted out. The head may well find himself involved in such cases but in general he will prefer to be used as support and back-up only in the most serious eventualities. When these occur, however, he must be seen to be capable of taking a strong line if he wishes to maintain his credibility both with his colleagues and his pupils.

Uniform

Apart from corporal punishment, there is probably no topic capable of causing more unnecessary argument than school uniform. Many expected that the advent of comprehensive education would more or less rapidly lead to the disappearance of traditional uniform and certainly there are plenty of schools which seem able to tolerate jeans and T-shirts without any very obvious decline in moral or academic

standards. But these are probably a minority: there is a firm con-nexion in the public mind between uniform and high standards and a conviction that blazers and ties, however scruffy, are educationally preferable to informal dress, however neat. Any Head who wants to abolish uniform, or even to make changes, must bear in mind that he will have to carry with him not only his pupils and colleagues but also parents, governors and indeed the whole local community. This is particularly important if there is competition with other schools, for the school without official uniform is likely to find itself at the bottom of the pecking order.

There are of course good arguments in favour of uniform. It can be a source of pride and contribute towards a sense of community; it minimizes social differences; it prevents the wearing of the tribal gear of punks and skinheads; it provides a means of identification off school premises; it provides a channel for financial assistance to poorer families where uniform grants are available. For some pupils at least it is a relief to have no choice about what to wear and to be freed from peer-group competition. The trouble is that, however strong the majority feeling, there will always be a sizeable minority who for a variety of reasons object to uniform and either refuse to wear it or wear it in a way designed to provoke. Since there is little point in a uniform which is not compulsory, form tutors, heads of house and heads of year can find themselves devoting a high pro-portion of their time to dealing with infringements of uniform reg-ulations. Perhaps it is useful to give young people some relatively unimportant rules to rebel against; but the consequences can certainly be time-consuming.

There are various possible compromises. Most schools allow sixth formers freedom from uniform rules in line with their contemporaries in further education or employment. Sometimes uniform is com-pulsory for junior pupils but the regulations are relaxed as they progress up the school, possibly by allowing free choice of styles within the school colours. If there has to be a uniform there is much to be said for having it as simple as possible with the main items readily available from the large suppliers. Cost can be a serious problem for many families, especially now that many local authorities have reduced or even abolished uniform grants.

Nevertheless, whatever his own attitudes, a head will be lucky to avoid trouble over uniform. Should boys be allowed earrings? Or girls trousers? What sorts of shoes, or outer garments, are permissible? And, even if not strictly uniform, what about all the multifarious conflicts possible over hair? The head can only cultivate tolerance, understanding and a sense of humour.

Pupil responsibilities

If one of the aims of the school is to equip its pupils to act as responsible citizens, then its organization must allow them opportunities to act responsibly. Traditionally in an 11–18 school this has been the privilege of the sixth form and the familiar hierarchy of head boys and girls, senior pupils, prefects and monitors still exists and flourishes in many schools. Increasingly, however, their functions have been modified. Rather than appoint an elite group, it is common now for the whole sixth form, or at least the upper sixth, to be accorded privileges and responsibilities. Although there is still scope for some supervision and monitorial duties, sixth formers themselves are often reluctant to be placed in this sort of role and, in today's circumstances, they may well find themselves faced with disciplinary problems with which they are unable to cope. The emphasis increasingly is on giving senior pupils opportunities to exercise pastoral responsibility. They may volunteer to be attached to junior forms as assistants to the tutor and in this role may help to organize group activities and games, or accompany their form on weekend visits and camps. They may listen to remedial pupils reading; organize fund-raising events for charity; help with drama or music competitions; referee house matches; take a morning assembly. In addition they will have the opportunity to take a lead in running clubs and societies and in organizing their own common-room and social activities. Some of these responsibilities may be more easily assumed under the umbrella of a house system but it is important for the head and senior staff to make sure that all are encouraged to play their part.

One of the weaknesses of many 11–18 schools is that they give only limited opportunities for pupils below the sixth to show what they can do, so that many who leave at 16 may never have had a chance to develop properly their sense of responsibility in the school context. By contrast, heads of 11–16 schools can often point with pride to the maturity and leadership displayed by their senior pupils. The fifth-year tutor needs to discover ways in which these pupils can be given responsible tasks appropriate to their abilities, whether by running a disco or arranging a 6-a-side hockey tournament.

One favoured way of offering responsibility is through the mechanism of a school council. Although attractive in theory this is not easy to organize successfully and exaggerated expectations often lead to disillusionment. The question of its powers needs careful definition: to what extent, if at all, does the head consider himself bound by its decisions? All too often it becomes a not very effective talking-shop, with agenda devoted to minor points of uniform, school dinners and the state of the toilets. It is indeed difficult to find

matters that can be usefully discussed by a body with representatives from all levels of the school, and separate year councils appear to work better in many cases. It is easier to identify topics of concern or interest – and possibly easier for the year tutor to initiate action. It is a great incentive to any such group if it can be allocated some funds for which it has complete responsibility. In all cases it is essential to make proper provision for the elected representatives to report back to their forms or tutor groups.

Schools are not democratic institutions but they can seek to make as many pupils as possible feel that they have a stake in the organization and some responsibility for the way it functions. This will not happen by chance and the head will need to encourage and persuade his colleagues to make it a reality.

Guidance

Individual counselling and guidance will have an important part in every school's pastoral system. On the whole schools have preferred to see this as an integral part of every teacher's job and there are now relatively few counsellors, whether full or part-time, specially trained for the purpose and with little in the way of teaching commitments.

Although most of the formal responsibility for guidance in connexion with academic or behavioural problems for a particular pupil is likely to be delegated to the form tutor or an equivalent member of staff, it needs to be remembered that much counselling is of an informal nature and individual subject teachers may have just as important a rôle to play. Indeed sometimes a non-teaching member of staff, whether school nurse, secretary, technician or caretaker, may prove to be the most effective counsellor. What matters is the existence of a relationship with the child of sufficient trust and understanding for advice and criticism to be seen as acceptable and helpful.

A particularly important area is that of careers guidance. There is no doubt that a majority of young people and their parents value education primarily as a preparation for the world of work. While it is desirable that some realization of the importance of commerce and industry should be a natural element in the teaching of many school subjects, most schools will incorporate some specific careers teaching as part of the curriculum, probably from the third year and certainly in the fourth and fifth years, often as part of the common core. Such courses are usually designed not so much to provide detailed vocational information as to widen horizons and examine prejudices, since many pupils have very limited ideas and ambitions derived from their families and friends. They will involve self-assessment, study of 'vocational families', methods of application, information about qualifications and the sort of qualities looked for by employers. Very often some work experience is built in to the course and this seems to be greatly valued by pupils and employers alike. All of this can only be a preparation for choice and the information provided needs to be backed by careful individual counselling.

Many schools have a separate careers department with a head of careers who has responsibility for organizing the teaching and counselling programme and for liaison with the local authority careers service, local business and industry, and institutions of further and higher education. He will also need to run a careers room, where books and pamphlets can be displayed, to organize work experience and factory visits, to arrange for visiting speakers and probably an annual careers convention. In all these ways he will act as essential coordinator but he cannot do everything himself and in practical terms every teacher must have some knowledge and responsibility. This is particularly important for form tutors in the third year who have to give academic guidance in connexion with option choices.

Records of achievement

In 1963 the Newsom Report stated: 'Boys and girls who stay at school until they are 16 may reasonably look for some record of achievement when they leave'. Many schools do indeed now provide some sort of leaving testimonial to supplement the bare record of examination grades but it is only recently that strong interest has developed in the idea of systematic profile-reporting as a means for encouraging the development of good personal qualities and fostering opportunities for social development. There have been a number of local initiatives, often based on the practices of further education, but the implementation of a national scheme for all school leavers would certainly present a considerable additional challenge to heads and school staffs.

A record of achievement would not be a substitute for a confidential reference: it would be the property of the pupil to whom it related but the school would bear the main responsibility for its completion, although there should be an element of negotiation between pupils and teachers. The aim should be to provide information which throws light on qualities such as enthusiasm, effort, persistence and willingness to accept responsibility and this is most likely to be achieved by concentrating on concrete examples. It would be possible to give weight to experiences and achievements outside the school environment as well as to activities such as school games and clubs. Attempts to grade personal qualities by ticks or letters are not to be recommended, mainly because of the difficulty of attaching real meaning to the grade descriptions.

In addition to information about personal qualities and achievements, a record of achievement would contain details of public examination results, including any graded tests, and where possible other evidence of academic attainment. Such a document might be based on a pupil's whole secondary career or, more realistically, on the results of the last one or two years of secondary education.

The project is attractive but heads will realize that there are very considerable resource implications in introducing such records for all pupils. The compilation of the records will be demanding on teachers' time and management skills – and both teachers and pupils will have to be convinced that such records are accepted and valued by employers and other potential users.

6 Legal issues

Florence Kirkby

Whenever the training of heads is discussed and their views or the views of their deputies are sought on what training they would most wish to receive, there is almost always a request for more information about legal obligations. Because of the increased emphasis on parental rights, the importance now attached to health and safety regulations, the greater prominence of legislation dealing with industrial relations and much else, heads feel much more conscious of the limitations imposed by law and their liabilities under it.

Nevertheless, it is important to keep a sense of perspective in such matters, particularly when one considers the importance of precedent in the interpretation of English law, since no head could ever hope to have personal knowledge or even access to information about all the previous cases which may influence a decision. It is also important to realize that knowledge of the law, though highly desirable, is not in itself any guarantee that a head will never find himself a party to a legal matter. Indeed, any long-serving head who has not found himself at some time in such a position should count himself fortunate, since no one can cover every eventuality and too detailed a knowledge of law can create in the layman a false sense of security. As in motoring, the head is likely to be affected not only by what he does himself but by the actions of his colleagues, the governing body, the LEA, and parents. A matter which might be expected to be settled on an informal basis may well escalate into a major conflict if one of the parties proves unreasonable and the motivation for this, as heads often find, may lie not within the incident itself but in attitudes generated many years ago in one of the parties concerned. The attitudes, for instance, of many parents are generated for good or ill by what happened in their own school days as well as by the experience of their children in schools today. Equally it may sometimes be salutary to examine one's own instinctive reactions and judge their respectability. 'Going to law' should always be a last resort.

This chapter is intended to give practical guidance under broad headings. In particular situations a head is likely to need reference books on his shelves. These should include an annotated copy of the 1944 Education Act with its amendments and one of the reliable commercial publications on teachers and the law. If there is any likelihood that the difficulty which has arisen may become serious or complicated, he would be well-advised to inform his professional association at an early stage and to keep them informed about developments. A head who does not seek advice until he is in real difficulties can create problems not only for himself but for his association. A good case can often seem less convincing if the initial actions taken to present it are not appropriate. A head may put himself in a wrong position by acting impulsively or intuitively before consulting his association, and the association, even if at that late stage they agree to give their support, may have difficulty in retrieving a position which need not have been lost.

There are two aspects of law which concern the head in varying degrees, first the law as it relates specifically to education and secondly the law as a whole which governs the relationships of all citizens both to each other and to the state. At first one might be tempted to assume that the first law is the most important, but frequently it is the law in general which is invoked.

Education Acts

The basis of law governing schools is the 1944 Education Act, a comprehensive piece of legislation which has stood the test of time well and proved capable of flexible adjustment to differing situations. It has of course been supported by amending legislation designed to extend its scope and to adjust to changing circumstances. Taylor and Saunders have pointed out in their book *The new law of education* that the act was born of the idealism apparent towards the end of the Second World War and sought to make sure that children were not deprived of educational opportunities because of the circumstances of their parents.

The Act lays upon the Education Authorities many duties ranging from the need to provide sufficient schools offering such variety of instruction and training as may be desirable considering the ages, abilities and aptitudes of the children, to more specifically determined duties such as 'to secure that the school premises maintained by them conform to such standards as may be prescribed by the Secretary of State' (Ed. Act 1944 S.10), to appoint a fit person to be chief education officer (S.88) and to keep separate account of the sums received and expended by them in the exercise of any functions under the Act (S.34). In addition to their duties the Local Education Authorities also have certain powers which they may exercise, though these powers are often guided by regulations made by the Secretary of State.

Matters arising from the Education Acts

The powers of the Local Authority are shared between the elected members and the chief education officer to whom they traditionally turn for professional advice. It is hardly surprising that with the division between duties and powers and the various forces which operate locally in implementing them there should exist considerable diversity between the practices of various LEAs. It is fortunate that teachers have a national salary scale, though even this is capable of different interpretation.

The Act does, however, require the LEAs to act reasonably. Parents cannot for instance claim a place at a specific school if that would require extensive building operations, and normally the LEA can expect the support of the Secretary of State for Education if they have acted reasonably and can so prove when any appeal is made to him.

Some powers the LEA must delegate to others, on occasion the governors, in some instances the head. In such situations the ultimate responsibility lies with the LEA, but the blame may be placed elsewhere. It is, for instance, the responsibility of the LEA to require of parents to cause their children of compulsory school age to receive suitable efficient full-time education (S.31) and to enforce the regular attendance of the children (S.40). It might in the past have been considered sufficient for schools to offer education suitable for the age and aptitude of the child and to notify the representatives of the LEA, usually the welfare officers, of any children in non-attendance. In practice most schools do a great deal more to ensure regular attendance and this seems increasingly to be expected of them even to the extent that it is sometimes suggested that the curriculum is to blame for non-attendance and that it is as much the schools' duty to make themselves attractive so that pupils will want to come, as the parents' duty to see that the children are educated. Fortunately most people take a reasonable attitude but there will always be some exceptions; and indeed despite most people's reasonableness a marked change of attitude has taken place over the years. A head can no longer safely assume that what seems to him a reasonable interpretation of his LEA's regulations will receive official backing, and there is sometimes a need for agreed guidelines. Heads collectively have striven for the right to make decisions in the light of the situation in their individual schools and in the light of the actual resources they have been given to enable them to fulfil their responsibilities.

One of the responsibilities of the head is to see that staff have easy access to such regulations of the authority as it is appropriate for them to know. In many instances there are such detailed regulations that the head may have difficulty in keeping a record of all of them and their various amendments. Apart from the code of practice on health and safety and the guidance notes on it, there will be regulations relating to sick pay, and maternity regulations, and probably on such matters as leave of absence, dates of appointment, salary, re-deployment and redundancy, assaults on teachers, assaults on pupils, compensation both under the Workmen's Compensation Act and on redundancy, damage to personal property, and regulations often of several kinds concerning out of school activities, disciplinary procedures, grievance procedures, insurance, retirement, race relations, and sex discrimination. Sick leave and pay alone can be considered under thirty three different headings. Many authorities have within their organization people who are experts on one section or another whom the head may consult.

Parental choice   This is a matter which has received increased attention in recent years. Parents have the right of choice, subject to the Act's provisions as to age, ability and aptitude. As stated earlier, the parent cannot exercise his or her right of choice if this would result in extensive building operations, but a head has no right to refuse admission to a pupil if a place is available which is suitable nor can a head refuse a right of transfer to a pupil already within his school. A head therefore has no absolute right to refuse a place to a pupil because he has a bad record of attendance in a previous school or a record of misbehaviour. Any case for refusal must be made in the light of particular circumstances. A head may expect successfully to refuse entry if he has already in the age group the full number he is expected to take or if the child's needs constitute a special requirement which he does not have facilities to meet. The last situation cannot be applied dogmatically. One might refuse a pupil in a wheelchair if the school was on several levels and the LEA refused to make appropriate building adjustments but a partially sighted child would be a different matter as such children have often been educated in normal schools. Cases of transfer are notoriously difficult when examination courses have begun. Whatever the situation, a head is well advised to outline clearly what can be provided and what cannot, supplying any evidence available. Attention may also be drawn to the school's rules and regulations, for by accepting a place at a school the parent enters into an implied contract to adhere to them. If it is likely that the head will be required to accept a pupil it is better to do so with a good grace rather than to be forced to do so when the atmosphere has become one of confrontation. In some cases the staff may hold strong views which both head and LEA must take into account.

In the case of withdrawal the parents again are in a strong position. It is not only the right but also the duty of a school to advise as to whether a transfer is in the child's best interests. The school may refuse to remove a pupil's name from the books until the parent can be sure of a place in another school, but these are merely delaying tactics as are some of the regulations which LEA's may impose such as transfers only at half term, zoning, transfer notes etc. All are of doubtful legal validity even though the LEA may find them expedient in order to maintain efficient education in all its schools.

Non-attendance Though the Act lays upon parents the responsibility to see that their children attend school, the LEA's have for many years instituted fairly elaborate procedures to encourage and finally enforce attendance. In order to do so they rely on the schools to keep accurate records of attendance and to supply information about absences. Since the onus for ensuring attendance is placed on the parents, legal matters lie between them and the LEA. As far as the school is concerned, it is the duty of staff to do all they can to encourage regular attendance and in particular to fulfil the regulations the Authority lays down with regard to attendance. These will normally give indications of allowable absence such as absence for family holidays. On the day-to-day basis the right to grant leave of absence is delegated to the head.

Legally speaking, a parent does not have to ensure that his child attends school. The obligation is to see that the child receives education suitable to age, aptitude and ability. This has recently led to several cases of parents insisting on educating their children at home and in some cases the law has sanctioned this even against the advice of the LEA. Often one of the parents is a trained teacher. As the difficulty of providing suitable education grows greater with the child's age such home tuition often entails a combined effort of several parents or the bringing in of paid teachers for certain subjects – a situation not unlike that of the nineteenth century before the state took responsibility for education. The difficulties are likely to prevent attempts being widespread and inhibit the development of the so-called 'free schools'. Many educational experiments are conducted in unusual circumstances and rarely survive for long in their original form.

Of more importance to the head is the problem of the absentee whose parents are inclined to lay the blame on the school rather than on the home. A head should take care to be as fully informed as is possible of the home circumstances and should be circumspect in any statements made about a child not attending school. The LEA when prosecuting for non-attendance will require a statement from the head. This is often not read in court but it is not strictly confidential; the parents have a right to see it and everything stated as a fact should be capable of proof. If opinions are expressed it must be made plain they are opinions not fact and they should be stated with moderation and some reasons adduced in their support.

Exclusion or suspension of pupils

An independent school head may expel a pupil (providing he has the backing of his governors). The head of an LEA school would find it difficult to do so (even with governors' backing) since the LEA must still be responsible for the child's education, although when circumstances are very difficult an LEA will endeavour to provide suitable alternative education or even home tuition.

There are of course official reasons for exclusion, primarily on health grounds, but the most common reason seems to be bad behaviour. Some heads will attempt to differentiate between exclusion until a specific event has taken place (for example, until the parent has visited the school, or until assurances have been given of future conduct), and the more far-reaching suspension which may be for a specific or indefinite period. Not all LEA's will recognize such distinctions, however, and most lay down procedures which include a full statement of the reason, notification of the parents and of the chairman of governors and subsequently the whole governing body and frequently the education committee.

With the removal of some traditional sanctions, for example corporal punishment, and with the increase of various pressures in society, suspensions are becoming more common and increasingly a problem for heads since they are not infrequently challenged by the parent who may well have legal assistance. It is necessary therefore to stress again the need for strict adherence to LEA guidelines and for seeking the advice of professional associations, and above all the need for accurate recording. It is unwise to say categorically that a pupil cannot return under any circumstances. If through legal process or pressure from governors, politicians or the LEA the pupil is taken back, the original statement will not have enhanced the school's authority and will have created the wrong atmosphere for future relationships between parent and school. In the case of a hearing, a head may be well advised to be represented by his professional association.

In loco parentis

In matters of education the strict letter of the law is sometimes an inadequate guide, for it lays down at most only general principles, and even less reliable is the concept that the teacher's attitude can be guided by reference to what might be expected of 'a careful parent'. Apart from the ambiguity of 'careful' which might bear a different interpretation in almost every circumstance and which is certainly likely to be interpreted differently now than it would have been twenty or thirty years ago, the fact is that teachers are not in the relationship of parents to most of their pupils. There may be instances in an emergency when that concept acts as a useful guide but generally speaking a teacher cannot use the freedom of action which a parent may use. The teacher is a professional who lays claim to expertise in handling the age group for which he or she is trained; the teacher can be expected to exercise a degree or impartiality which a parent might not desire to pursue; the teacher must see an action in relationship to the teaching situation and the welfare of pupils as a whole whereas the parent will be primarily concerned with his own child. The authority will have a policy on matters such as school attendance and corporal punishment which needs to be known and observed by every teacher. The school too will have its own rules, some the result of collective staff decisions, and these must be respected by teachers who wish to be on good terms with colleagues. The head of a school cannot support the freedom of interpretation which such a definition as 'a careful parent' may encourage, but by taking it as a starting point the head should assist staff to see the idea in relation to the regulations of the authority and the rules of the school.

Teachers' contracts and industrial action

Industrial legislation, like other aspects of the law, imposes upon the head conditions which do not come naturally in the teaching situation. Schools find it difficult to equate themselves with industry and indeed there are great differences. In the comparability exercise undertaken by Imbucon for the Clegg committee, it emerged clearly that the common structure in industry is that of line management. Each member of the organization knows for whom and to whom he is responsible and unless very high in the hierarchy has limited responsibilities which are to be exercised in clearly defined ways. Any decisions taken may involve considerable sums of money and influence many people, but they are usually taken in a defined situation in which the objectives are clear-cut.

By contrast teachers have far more autonomy and their decisions are always made in the context of human relationships. Mutual respect and cooperation within both the staffroom and the classroom are the essence of the educational enterprise. Yet this cannot be embodied in a contract of service. A school is soon in difficulties if teachers decide to interpret their in a strictly legal sense. All heads are aware of the problems which arise in times of industrial action. The greatest damage may not be the actual situation but the tensions which it creates and the aftermath of disturbed feeling within the staff which results. The tensions are very often because many staff are as unhappy about the action they are taking as the head, and it may depend on the union representative within the school as to how strictly sanctions are enforced; whether for instance 'totting up' of supervision is acceptable or not. Heads can therefore face a tremendous difference of response from both staff and LEAs, and it is they who must bear the brunt. It is they who must decide whether it is safe to keep the school open, sometimes in the face of political pressures from their employers. They need strong professional support in situations where the legal position is often unclear.

Disciplinary procedures

Regrettably there are occasions when a teacher's conduct or competence is called into question. The same considerations may arise in relation to non-teaching staff. Most LEA's formulate agreed procedures. Any cause of dissatisfaction must be pointed out to the person concerned and advice and assistance, if necessary, should be given to remedy matters. All action taken should be carefully recorded and should be proportionate to the degree of inefficiency or misconduct. If no improvement is forthcoming, the action taken must be reported to the LEA. The head may give advice or a reproof informally, or may formally warn and record the warning given. If it is a formal warning the member of staff is entitled to be accompanied by a friend who may be a union representative. The procedures will be repeated by the LEA who may record an interview, issue a first warning, or a final warning, or a first and final warning together. In some LEAs these powers will be delegated to the governors and there is always a right of appeal to them and to the education committee who are the employers. A board of govenors may hold a disciplinary hearing and recommend dismissal in cases of a serious offence but this must always be confirmed by the education committee. A teacher who is called to a disciplinary hearing must be given notice in writing setting out the action to be taken and its possible outcome and must also be supplied with copies of all the relevant documents.

In reporting any serious incidents to the LEA a head should remember that a copy of his letter can be supplied to the people concerned and should be careful not to include in it statements which cannot be substantiated. Most LEAs will require statements from witnesses when dealing with a matter of any importance and will normally give guidelines on this. In all cases of assault or accident, statements should be taken from any witnesses and as far as possible from the people concerned.

LEA regulations

Regulations come into existence after being approved by the education committee, and/or the full council. They are normally generated after consultation with teachers. This can take place nationally between the Council of Local Education Authorities and the Teacher Unions, whose joint decisions are accepted by all the LEAs, or between individual LEAs and local union representatives. In general this works well, although some minor matters, like the fixing of holiday dates, seem inevitably to lead to compromise decisions which cannot please everybody. It also of course leads to variations between one LEA and another, for example in the format of school prospectuses.

Corporal punishment

This emotive issue illustrates very well the variety of practices. Until recently it was decided by local practice or the decision of the individual school. Recent legislation carried as far as the European court has upheld the parents' right to opt out of such punishment (though normally a parent in deciding to accept a place at a school is held to have entered into a contract with the school to accept its regulations). Some LEAs forbid corporal punishment, others permit it if administered in a particular way, some make it a matter for the decision of individual governing bodies. As many schools have phased out corporal punishments already, the actual decision may be less important to the head than the way in which it is taken, since a decision which originates from the staff is much easier to implement than one which disregards staff opinion.

Leave of absence

LEAs have national regulations on leave of absence for periods of sickness and for union activities, but variable provision for what is popularly called compassionate leave, for example illness in the family. They also have varying provisions for replacing absent staff, usually fairly effective for long absence. Frequent short absences can constitute a severe strain on staff resources and absence is a matter in which the interests of staff and children may conflict, as when it is difficult to cover for in-service training. Although a head is normally given discretion to release staff or not, and even withdraw permission if circumstances change, it is difficult to collate requests well in advance and estimate last minute demands. Heads and staff must face these problems together and seek procedures which give optimum satisfaction to the legitimate needs of both staff and pupils.

Redeployment and redundancy

Falling rolls have recently created problems unknown in the past. In order to ease the situation LEAs have at their disposal various devices. Within their power lies 'the ring fence system' and 'redeployment'. Both of these will have been negotiated locally with teachers' associations. The ring fence policy however greatly inhibits the head's role in choosing staff and building a team. The terms of the local agreement may transfer the power of appointment almost completely from the head or governors to Local Authority staff. Like maternity leave, this may not operate as originally intended but once agreed provisions are difficult to alter. In redeployment the LEA will be technically responsible for nominating a teacher, but staff will be aware that the head has a duty, after appropriate consultation, to advise on the curricular needs of the school. In addition LEAs have discretion within national rules to offer premature retirement to teachers who have reached their fiftieth birthday and also to offer some enhancement of pension. It is the duty of the head to see that staff are fully informed of all facilities and that no unfair pressure is put upon them. He must also see that the LEA and governors are aware of the likely effect on the school.

The government of schools

The DES, the LEAs, the school governors and the head all play their part. The DES through Form 7 demands annual information about each school. It defines teacher status and heavily influences teacher pay. Through the inspectorate it gathers information and promotes good practice, notably through in-service training.

The LEAs mirror the DES in their own territories, and in recent years have greatly strengthened their own teams of advisers/ inspectors. Recently also they have become answerable to the DES with regard to their policies on curriculum.

Recent legislation has also instituted a national pattern of governing bodies which must now include representation of parents and of the teaching staff and must offer full membership to the head. The Instruments and Articles of Government are prepared by the LEA but subject to DES approval. The traditional distribution of function has been for the LEA to determine the general educational character of the school; for the governors, in consultation with the head, to have the general direction of the conduct and curriculum of the school; and for the head to be responsible for the internal organization, management and discipline of the school.

Governors and head have to operate within a budget over the size of which they have almost no control. Ideally the governors will respect the professional expertise of the head, and the head will respect the knowledge, understanding and influence of representatives of the local community. The head will look for a genuine commitment to the welfare of the school and should be grateful for constructive criticism. He will fear the possible effects of political polarization. He will hope to deserve and to be given a proper degree of freedom in the running of the school, not least in the appointment of its staff. A head who is not given genuine powers of decision can have little genuine commitment to the success of the school.

A similar degree of partnership and mutual trust is desirable between heads and the LEA's professional staff. The individual school must take its place in the family of local schools. Published prospectuses and HMI reports must be seen in the context of LEA provision and of local variations in the catchment areas of the schools. Nothing can be more demoralizing than the playing off of one school against another, particularly where the terms of 'competition' are unfair.

General legislation

General legislation affects all aspects of school life and since usually it has not been framed with education in mind it may have unintended results for schools. One anomaly is that staff of all kinds are protected by legislation governing things like minimum working temperature or first aid regulations. These are not applicable to children or only indirectly through staff.

Health and safety

The health and safety regulations have, for instance, made much more formal the duties and obligations of the head, and of other members of staff. Ironically these regulations were originally intended for workers, not pupils and it is galling that, at a time of education cuts, money can be found for matters related to health and safety even though they may not appear to members of staff to be of major importance.

Many LEAs have now issued guidelines to headteachers. Typically these outline the procedure for the setting up of a health and safety committee with representatives of teachers' associations, the school's safety representative, and selected staff who have an immediate concern with such matters, for example, teachers of science subjects and metalwork. The school needs to have a written safety policy which will set out not only the membership of the health and safety committee but also the frequency of meetings. The minutes of the meetings will normally be available to all staff and will be forwarded to the LEA. Non-teaching staff will be involved in this process also. From the head's point of view the advantage of this legislation is that it does point to a shared responsibility with staff. The fact that a matter may be referred to the health and safety committee in no way obviates the need for any matter of concern to be reported immediately to the head, nor does it automatically follow that if a matter is reported to the LEA action will follow. In such a situation it is still the head's responsibility to decide for instance whether the degree of danger is such that a piece of equipment should cease to be used, with or without the advice of the LEA adviser, the factory inspector, the LEA health and safety officer, or the appropriate member of the teaching staff. A head would need very strong grounds on which to challenge the decision of any of these people where health and safety matters are concerned. The school's health and safety committee needs to be chaired by a senior member of staff, if not the head, and it is one of the problems of the present moment that such an Act calls for training of personnel which the Local Authority may not have the resources to provide.

Industrial relations

Teachers are not the only workers in the school. All other staff are
entitled to protection under Acts governing industrial relations and to
union representation. They represent a wide diversity of interests,
and are represented by different associations. In many LEAs the
head may have little control over appointments, though dependent
on the goodwill of the appointees for the effective running of the
school. To a large extent the non-teaching staff represent the school
to the public: the first contact with a school is often through the
secretary or the caretakers. Their good-will is vital to the school's
wellbeing.

Divorce law

Recent alterations in the law of divorce have had a major impact on
schools. Single parent families are now quite common and, as well as
the reduction in standard of living and the psychological problems
which can arise, there are legal considerations. Discretion may have
to be exercised in the giving of information to divorced or separated
parents. In such cases the head needs to be kept informed by the
parent who has custody of what the court has decreed and what the
rights of each parent are. It is wise to be courteous but cautious in
supplying information of other than a general nature, particularly in
answer to solicitors' letters, although it will rarely be necessary to
deny all communication to a parent who makes an informal approach. Information however is to be distinguished from access.

It is always advisable to seek proof of identity from anyone seeking
to communicate with a child unless the person is known to the
school. Those who have a legitimate need to communicate are
unlikely to be offended by such a display of prudence.

The law of libel

Putting on paper judgements about people is an occupational risk of
headship. At a time when greater freedom of access to personal
records is being demanded, it must be wise to make sure that
anything stated as fact can be proved and that opinions are expressed with moderation and in a way which suggests freedom from bias.
School reports which are open to parents and which they can dispute
at the time they are written are the safest records to keep. Court
reports should be written in the knowledge that they may be shown
to parents. Nor is there any absolute guarantee that references for
further education or for jobs may not be shown to the applicants.

What is true of pupil records is even more true of staff records. Cases have been brought against heads on the grounds that unfair comments have impaired career prospects. When that happens it must be possible to produce reasonable evidence for the opinions expressed.

From time to time heads may be incensed by newspaper reporting upon their schools and may strongly wish to bring charges of libel against the newspaper involved. Very rarely is this wise. Newspapers know just how far they can go so that the outcome of any such case is always unpredictable. In the meantime the school is subjected to prolonged adverse publicity, which is the very thing it is trying to avoid.

Race relations

This important subject may concern schools in their treatment of both children and staff. Though equality is guaranteed legally, it is not easily achieved in practice nor clearly defined. Many heads have been challenged on matters such as suspension, with the implication that their decisions have been influenced by considerations of race. If a school's ruling is challenged, the LEA should be prepared to offer advice and support but in an appeal where the parents may be legally represented a head may choose to be similarly represented through his professional association. It can distress a head to feel that his staff's good intentions to any pupil have been called into question. An effort of the imagination is required to look at the situation in an impartial way. Careful factual information and records are needed to demonstrate that every effort has been made not just to treat all pupils equally but to see that every child is treated according to individual needs. High expectations and ambitions are not the prerogative of any particular race but they need to be treated with particular care in dealing with pupils from different backgrounds.

As far as staff are concerned consideration of race should not enter into appointments and equal opportunities for promotion are a self-evident requirement. There is, as yet, no legal obligation to provide positive discrimination, but as a spread of opportunities through all levels of society is desirable, not only as a form of justice to the individual but as a model for our pupils, particular care should be taken to avoid any possible suggestion of prejudice. Cases of alleged discrimination can be referred to the Race Relations Board.

Sex discrimination

The same principles apply as to race relations. Again both pupils and staff will be affected. Cases can be referred to the Equal Opportunities Commission. A parent may complain or threaten action if there is a refusal to provide teaching in certain subjects which can be shown to stem from sexual stereotyping. Increasingly it is also being realized that discrimination, whether sexual or racial, can be unconsciously and unintentionally brought about by the implicit values and attitudes conveyed through school textbooks. There may be no immediate remedy for this but awareness is important. Only rarely may staff advertisements specify the sex of applicants. Nor is it permissible at interview to ask questions about marital status or children.

Civil law

This is most likely to be invoked in relation to accidents either to pupils or teachers. Most LEAs have accident forms which should be filled in for any injury, however trivial. The effect of accidents is not always obvious at the time and there is a three-year period during which claims can be made. Detailed records are essential, together with accounts from any witnesses. Settlement may be deferred until the extent of permanent injury is known. The LEA will deal with such matters through its insurance company if there are allegations of negligence.

Claims can also arise for loss of or damage to property of either staff or children, but these rarely go to court. School rules should make plain that valuables should not be brought into school. If the school, for example, does take watches etc. into safekeeping, the system should be foolproof.

Most people will have read of recent cases concerned with the law governing copying from books or music and the use of tape recordings. It is the head's duty to see that staff know what the law is.

Many of the LEA regulations, for example those governing the information supplied about school visits abroad, are basically concerned with insurance cover and the implications for civil law if adequate safeguards are not provided. Most LEAs now insist on separate insurance cover for holidays abroad and some distressing situations have arisen when insurance cover has been inadequate or where there have been financial difficulties because of delays etc.

All school money must be kept according to LEA instructions as must any money held on behalf of pupils.

A school, or a school fund, or a PTA may be registered as a charity and accept covenants. What schools must not do is to act as if they or their funds were a charity without being so registered.

Criminal law

Care should be taken to protect the rights of a child who seems in danger of being involved in court proceedings for whatever reason. Evidence should normally be given when the parents are present and members of staff should think very carefully before acting *in loco parentis* in such circumstances. In disputes which involve two children and where the parents of both may be involved, for instance if two children have had a fight and one is even slightly injured, the legal position needs careful consideration. The LEA must be informed of the nature and extent of the injury but nothing should be done to prejudice the issue until the views and intentions of both sets of parents are known. In serious matters, however, an over-riding duty to maintain the law of the community may necessitate informing the police immediately and a head is entitled to take this decision and indeed may have no justifiable alternative.

Knowledge of the law is increasingly a part of general education for many careers in business and industry; no doubt it will also become more important in training for headship. But it is to be hoped that for most of the time schools will continue to function on the basis of good human relationships and common sense, and that the law will need to be involved only marginally.

7 The Curriculum

Michael Duffy

James Callaghan's Ruskin speech of 1976 focused rather than initiated the great curriculum debate. But he was the first Prime Minis-
ter publicly to claim that the Government had a duty to exercise an
overt influence on the content of the school curriculum. This debate
was carried on without reference to schools, most of which at that
time were concerned less with the question 'What should we do
about curriculum?' than with its corollary, 'How on earth can we do
it?' In any case, schools were well aware that the new curriculum
orthodoxy, with its quadripartite creed of coherence, balance and
breadth, practical relevance, and differentiation, was rather easier to
preach than to practise. But with Circulars 6/81 and 8/83 it began to
look as though orthodoxy would be imposed, and 16 plus criteria
and TVEI are making bids to become its instruments. In a speech at
Sheffield in 1984, The Secretary of State for Education, Sir Keith
Joseph, nailed his colours to the mast: 'We need to make certain
changes in . . . the primary and secondary curriculum . . . and the
examinations at 16 plus . . . There is now no serious dispute that the
school curriculum is a concern not only of teachers but also of
parents, governing bodies, LEAs and the Government, each
performing their proper role . . .'

Now in most schools there is considerable willingness to rise to the
challenge of the curriculum debate. In all schools, however, there are
real constraints which seriously inhibit the process of curriculum
development.

1 The status quo The most immediate constraint is that schools
have to start from where they are. They have an established
curriculum and an established structure for its delivery. Pupils are in
the middle of existing courses, and the courses have staffing and
financial resources locked into them and reflect long-held curriculum

assumptions and priorities. Any change of curricula is a long-term process.

2 The problem of resources   New courses need new resources. It is an obvious truism, yet one that the education service as a whole has failed to exploit. Perhaps it has concentrated too much on present difficulties and not enough on future need. We should perhaps look to industry for an analogy, and talk to parents, governors and the public about 'tooling-up' for educational change. Two crucial resources are in particularly short supply: time and confidence. Curriculum development happens most easily when staff have the time to discuss change and the confidence to carry it out; and government policy has sometimes seemed perversely determined on the attenuation of both.

3 The examinations system   The existing pattern of public examinations affects curriculum in two ways. Directly, it determines the content of most syllabuses and has a major and often malignant effect on the way that content is taught. Current proposals for the establishment of syllabus and assessment criteria may make examinations more amenable and responsive to change in curriculum content and process. Indirectly, however, their effect is greater, for they impose restrictions on the curriculum that have nothing to do with the curriculum itself. Many of our fundamental assumptions – about curriculum objectives, or the boundaries between subjects, or the length of an 'examination course' – are based on the pattern of public examinations. Most schools are beginning to recognize the present examinations system as profoundly inhibiting to the sort of changes to the curriculum that are required, but public opinion is not yet ready for the radical review that is needed.

4 Public opinion   Public expectations of schools are often conventional and simplistic. Parents lay great stress on academic values but are often more concerned with examination results than with the content of what is taught and learnt. Many schools and most employers (who still specify as 'qualifications' examination results that have little or no relevance to the job in question) encourage them in this. Parental choice and statutory publication of examination results makes it diffcult to confront this sort of wrong-headedness (to which, in any case, schools themselves have contributed) with the realities of economic change.

5 School attitudes and organization   It may well be, however, that the greatest obstacle to curriculum change lies inside the schools themselves. The traditional autonomy of subject departments, re-flected as it is both in the organization of the school and in the salary scales of the profession, makes it very difficult for teachers to see the curriculum as a whole, and the concept of subject status is pervasive. School rules and rituals also may be of subtle importance, to the extent that the hidden or pastoral curriculum they embody either reinforces or undermines the more explicit objectives of the formal curriculum.

So planned curriculum change is not easy to achieve. Opportunity does exist, however; to some extent each of the constraints contains an opportunity for change. Falling rolls, for example, curriculum-led staffing policies and ad hoc staffing reductions demand curriculum review, if only to establish which parts may have to go. The national argument about the examinations system and the place of profiling and achievement recording focuses debate on assessment pro-cedures and therefore by extension on what has to be assesed. The part played by industry in this argument[6] is particularly welcome. Inside schools both the search for improved pupil motivation and the development of improved techniques for the identification and teaching of pupils with special needs have acted as catalysts for curriculum review. The overwhelming stimulus, however, has been the sheer pace of economic and technological change. The impact of both pre-vocational education and micro-technology has been con-siderable, and has been absorbed with considerable success, The effect of YTS is not so easy to assess: some of its implications for curriculum 14-16 may, like those of TVEI, still be taking shape.

Teachers, preoccupied with their syllabuses and the coming ex-aminations, can often insulate themselves from such developments. Heads and deputies, however, cannot: whatever the proponents of 'partnership' may suggest, they carry the responsibility for actually making the changes, and for making them work. They have to consider the responses available to them in their schools, and the mechanism by which they may be put into effect.

Curriculum policy

Participation

Shaping curriculum policy, and making it work, means winning understanding and support from the staff as a whole and from governors, LEA and parents. Staff support is the most important, and may be the most difficult. It involves the exercise of a participative style of decision-making for which as yet few heads have either training or experience. It involves also certain complex management skills, for the opening up of curriculum issues is for many staff an uncomfortable process, threatening to their sense of subject territory and prestige, and often to their personal security. The winning-over of these colleagues especially will be a matter of relationships quite as much as of information and ideas.

Effective curriculum policy has to be flexible. It certainly will not emerge fully fledged from mere exposure to the debate. It is more likely to develop gradually from the involvement of the whole staff in a particular curriculum issue and from a growing awareness of its context and implications. The issue itself will be that which is most germane to the needs of the individual school as staff perceive them at a particular moment. Whatever issue it is (and some possible issues are briefly outlined in the pages that follow) its discussion will be most productive in a school where informed discussion is seen to be part of the decision-making process. Staff news sheets (with a weekly slot for curriculum affairs), staff working parties (with a specific and attainable brief), report-back from INSET courses, week-end staff conferences (which should be a priority for LEA INSET resourcing) all have their part to play, and will be the more effective if they are seen to be inspired by the staff rather than by the headteacher.

Aims and objectives

The review of curriculum aims required by Circular 6/81 may be a useful starting point. Most schools will have used the checklists contained in *The school curriculum*[7] and *The practical curriculum*[8] and will have produced an unexceptionable general statement as to the purpose of schools. The difficulty with this approach is that it does not easily permit the evaluation of the curriculum against its stated aims, which is necessary if any curriculum change is to come about. A more specific approach is needed, using a common terminology for the analysis of curriculum objectives (i.e. the learning that individual syllabuses are designed to achieve) as against the aims of the curriculum as a whole. The most familiar categorization (the eight 'areas of experience' argued by HMI in *Curriculum 11-16*)[9] has the disadvantage that it fits too comfortably the traditional assumptions of autonomous subject departments and takes huge liberties with the nature of knowledge. Hargreaves, however, has shown that the concept of curriculum principles can be very useful and Neville Stewart has put forward a valuable alternative in the CAVES model which describes curriculum and syllabus in terms of

the concepts, attitudes, values, experiences and skills that it is
designed to develop or transmit.[10] The Schools Council's list of the
values and attitudes that schools may wish to include among their
curriculum objectives is also a helpful framework for discussion.[11]
The advantage of the CAVES model is that no department can claim
any part of it as exclusively its own, and the subject teacher's
monopoly of expertise about his or her subject is no longer quite so
deadening to curriculum rethinking. If aims and objectives can be
described in the same terms, individual syllabuses are less likely to be
confined to the limited range of learning objectives assessed in public
examinations, and the rethinking of the curriculum as a whole is
more likely to occur.

Whole-curriculum thinking

Two approaches have proved particularly helpful. The first is to draw
attention specifically to those areas of curriculum which most clearly
do not 'belong' to an individual subject, yet which are recognized as
being important to all. The teaching of study skills is an obvious
example, and a staff working group in this area can be, irrespective of
its recommendations, a useful catalyst for more general curriculum
thinking. Working groups on health education, computing across the
curriculum, the improvement of pupil motivation etc. can have the
same effect. What such groups say is sometimes less important than
the manner in which they work, and the implications for continued
curriculum discussion and wider staff involvement will usually be
clear.

The second approach is to open for discussion the whole area of
what Marland calls the pastoral curriculum – the complex fabric of
assumptions and rituals that is woven unthinkingly into the day-to-
day organization of the school and the effect this has on what pupils
learn and the way they learn it. This is more difficult and more
threatening; it may challenge fundamentally the psychological
security of the staff and, indeed, of the head as well. The question of
negotiation, for example (to what extent should the pupil/student
negotiate his or her learning with the teacher and be involved with
the teacher in its assessment) may produce a profoundly emotive
response among staff conditioned to the relative certainties of autocracy. But the issue is important: the hidden curriculum can inhibit
learning. The best resolution of the problem may lie in the management structure of the school. The false antithesis between
'pastoral care' and 'the curriculum' has bedevilled schools since, with
reorganization, they invented it. When the opportunity arises many
heads will wish to create management responsibility, whether for

house groups, years groups, or divisions, over both aspects of the school's work.

Management responsibility, however, may leave the subject teacher in the classroom quite unaffected. Most heads will want to create a framework for curriculum overview that will carry involvement to the staff as a whole. The traditional forum, the heads of department committee, is usually unsuitable: it is too big, and too concerned with individual subject interest. The most usual alternative is some sort of faculty grouping, but this has drawbacks, too. It can appear to staff more like a cabinet than a standing committee; like cabinet ministers its members can be ruthless in the pursuit of departmental interest and it may compartmentalize the curriculum. But if it grows out of a consensus on curriculum principle, so that its members represent the curriculum components of which each pupil's learning is to be constituted, it may acquire a different connotation. A structure comprising, for example, faculties of language, mathematics, science and technology, creative and expressive arts, humanities and business and vocational education may be valuable not only as a framework for participation and policy-making, but also as a basis for timetabling and evaluation. With the addition of a seventh faculty, responsible for cross-curricular and extra-curricular learning, it can be a genuine and responsive instrument for whole curriculum planning.

Special needs

The failures of 'remedial' provision in secondary schools (and in primary and special schools as well) were sharply highlighted by the Schools Council research project on slow learners[12] and by the Warnock Report[13]. Since then there has been in many schools (often identifiable by their reluctance to use the word 'remedial' in any but its narrowest sense) a major reassessment of curriculum provision for pupils with special needs. To the extent that this has shown the importance of clearly defined objectives and appropriate teaching styles and has emphasized the concept of learning capacity as a continuum rather than as a series of categories, it has often acted as a valuable catalyst for more general curriculum review. It certainly throws up the curriculum issues that have to be faced, and because children with learning difficulties are less subject to the eternal constraints of the examinations system and less likely to find motivation and reward in their schooling, it is often easier initially to identify the issues in this context.

Defining the issues

Wherever it starts, curriculum review is likely to identify the areas where explicit decisions need to be taken, and though the decisions themselves and the order in which they are taken will depend on individual circumstances, the broad issues will be substantially the same in all schools. They will include most or all of the following questions.

1 What are the overall aims that the curriculum is designed to achieve?

2 Through what subjects or courses can these aims best be met?

3 What should be the balance of these subjects or courses for pupils of the age and ability range with which the school deals? Should it be the same for all pupils, or should it be differentiated?

4 What should be the specific objectives of each subject or course? Should they be the same for all pupils, or should they be differentiated?

5 To what extent may individual subjects or courses overlap each other?

6 In each subject or course, what should be the relationship between subject matter and the modes of teaching through which it is transmitted?

7 What is the nature of the class grouping required for the successful operation of each course? Should it be determined by age or by ability, or by a combination of the two?

8 How is the curriculum and its constituent subjects and courses to be monitored and evaluated?

9 What is the relationship between the pastoral curriculum and the taught curriculum? How can the two be harmonized?

10 What provision is to be made for pupils with special learning needs?

The most immediate expression of curriculum policy in a school, and the framework against which many of the above decisions will be made, is the school timetable. Here, as all heads will know, curriculum policy is sometimes modified by curriculum constraint. Constraint is not always, however, as immovable as the organiser of the timetable would have us believe and schools that have opened up curriculum policy may want to consider opening up also some of the carefully contrived mystique of the timetable. A standard curriculum notation, used both in preliminary discussion and analysis and in the timetable itself, is very helpful in this context.[14] So is the 'blocking' of the timetable by faculties, briefly referred to in the final pages of this chapter.

Putting policy into practice

Three is general agreement that pupils of 11+ and 12+ should follow a broadly common curriculum: English, a foreign language, mathematics, science, the humanities, the creative and practical arts, religious education, and physical education. The school curriculum policy will be concerned with the appropriate time allocation for these areas, the degree to which each area constitutes itself as a body of coherent and integrated knowledge and experience, and the relationship in each teaching/learning group between content and process.

On the first issue, schools have achieved a substantial consensus. On a 40-period timetable, for example, an allocation of six periods for each of English, a foreign language, mathematics, science, and the humanities and religious education, leaves ten periods for the creative and practical arts and physical education. With minor modifications most schools follow this model with most of their pupils. But curriculum policy now has to decide whether it is a suitable model for all pupils at this stage. If (as it surely ought to be) it is decided that it is suitable for all pupils, then the teachers of the different curriculum areas must be responsible for making appropriate provision, in subject matter and teaching techniques, across the whole of the ability range, and this implies a sophisticated system of support, diagnosis and referral if special needs are to be identified and met. In other words, the policy has to be agreed before the timetable is constructed. (It is widely assumed by teachers of foreign languages that in this aspect, as in so many others, they are a special case. It may be so, though experience suggests that a course for slow learners that deals exclusively with spoken language may help them to surmount the hurdles of incomprehensibility created in so many of their lessons by the primacy of reading and writing as learning modes. Certainly, if withdrawal from lessons is necessary for specific remedial work it would be sensible to choose foreign language lessons for this purpose.)

How the time allocation is used, department by department, will remain to be settled. There will be a tendency to sub-divide by subjects, so that six periods of humanities become two each of history, geography, RE and six periods of science become two each of physics, chemistry and biology. It is helpful, in the argument that ensues, to be clear about the positions that are being taken up. Teachers will argue, sometimes quite rightly, for the integrity of their subject and will fail to see the tension between this and the integrity of the curriculum as a whole. Individual schools will make their own dispositions. The pragmatically inclined, and those who have observed at first hand the day-to-day experiences of individual pupils, will look for a reduction in the subject/timetable fragmentation that often appears at this stage. Many departments of creative and practical arts have, indeed, already achieved it. Faced with the arithmetical complexity of fitting their four or five subjects into a six-period allocation they have devised a modular, cyclical provision that combines an adequate total allocation (i.e. x hours for two years) with access to the maximum number of subjects. In the process they may have invented two principles (that of total time allocation, as opposed to weekly allocation, and that of linking adjacent age groups) that will in future free the secondary timetable from its most insistent constraints.

Departmental flexibility over the allocation of time can of course be extended to the composition of teaching groups. The school that is large enough to timetable four forms simultaneously for creative and practical arts is normally large enough to do the same for science, mathematics, English and humanities. The timetabler will immediately point to the constraints that this allocation will create elsewhere in the timetable. He or she will either know or will very soon learn that 'blocking' by faculties in one year group almost invariably means blocking by faculty in all year groups, and this can create real difficulties, especially at sixth form level. Nonetheless, the faculty team may decide that the advantages of greater flexibility in the composition of the teaching group – whether by age or by ability, or from time to time by both – outweigh the disadvantages of less flexibility in the allocation of specific teachers elsewhere in the timetable.

The most important issues remain: the relationship of the subject syllabus to the overall curriculum aims for the age range; and, within the syllabus, the relationship between content and process. Faculty groups have a major responsibility for determining these issues and for monitoring the degree to which their policy is implemented. A check list of CAVES for every teaching group/session is a useful tool for evaluation; and a sympathetic understanding of the nature of the pupil's primary school experience, too often discounted by secondary teachers, is an essential prerequisite.

Year 3

As long as present assumptions hold true and pupils continue to begin two-year specialist exam courses at 14+, the 13+ year – the transitional year – is going to be as crucial in curriculum terms as it is for many pupils in terms of their physiological and social development. Many schools do not tackle the issues involved.

The 13+ year is the last year in which pupils will follow a largely common curriculum. However ingeniously we construct our 14+

option choices the pupils will end their formal education, over a substantial area of the curriculum, at the point where these choices take effect. At this point, in 1980, 7 per cent of boys and 4 per cent of girls were taking no science at all, and 39 per cent of girls were taking only one science (almost invariably biology) against 27 per cent of boys.[15] Similar finality of choice occurs in history/geography, and very often in foreign languages as well, where the 90 per cent of 11-year-olds who start a foreign language becomes the 30 per cent of 15-year-olds who continue with it.[16] The 13+ year is not, therefore, a foundation year: it is much more like a 'topping-out' year, and it is one of the mysteries of English educational provision that there is no machinery for the assessment and certification of attainment at this stage. The tendency in schools to treat the 13+ year as the first year of a 3–year course to examinations at 16+ is therefore under-standable, but it remains indefensible.

Yet in one sense the year *is* a preparatory year. If 'pupils' are to make the transition to 'students' – if, indeed, they are to become competent adults – they have to move from dependent learning towards independent learning. Schools do not always help them to do this: examination syllabuses are packed too full of content that has to be 'covered' for teachers to feel comfortable in the en-couragement of autonomy. The 13+ year is an opportunity to make good this deficiency by identifying across the curriculum the skills and processes whose mastery is necessary for future learning. At present many third-year pupils 'switch-off' in the subjects they're not going to pursue in years 4 and 5: a skills-based approach is likely to counteract this early and damaging tendency to de-motivation.

Too often the 13+ year is treated by schools as a sort of curriculum bazaar. All the subjects have to be on show, so that pupils can make an 'informed choice' of fourth-year options. Occasionally – when a second foreign language or a classical language is intro-duced for instance – this involves a pre-option choice, i.e. a choice made at the end of the first or second year. The fissile subject curriculum that is created can be confusing to many pupils, and the pressure it exerts on the timetable makes it very difficult to incorpor-ate important cross-curriculum issues such as health education, com-puter awareness and career education.

Certain subjects highlight sharply the nature of the problems that have to be resolved. In languages, the second language must take time from, or become an option against, something else. In science, the department must look at its policy in the light of the opting patterns for boys and girls in the fourth year. If science options are included in the fourth year that do not figure in the third-year course – geology, perhaps, or rural science – the reasons and implications must be examined. The timetable relationship between science and technology (profoundly confused in schools because of the extraordinary polarity we have created between the 'academic' and the 'practical' and the equally extraordinary hybrid we have invented in Craft, Design and Technology has to be made more specific. The relationship between history and geography and economics and social studies has to be considered.

Complex as they are, most of these problems are suitable for faculty consideration and resolution. It is not unreasonable, for example, to suggest that the departments of English and foreign languages might dispose of the second language problem among themselves, on the basis that pupils good enough to tackle a second foreign language should be capable of mastering their native language and a first foreign language on a slightly lower time allocation. In science, both the philosophy of the Secondary Science Curriculum Review and its regional structure render it particularly accessible to science teachers who are increasingly concerned at the content-inflation of single-subject science syllabuses. Here also, faculty blocking gives a flexibility (for example, for the running of third-year science syllabuses in terms of interlocking modules) which could allow a committed team to teach both science and its applications without threatening its future examination successes. With appropriate timetable support from home economics teachers, whose potential contribution to the curriculum is frequently undervalued, the PE department could incorporate a rounded health education module into the programme of all pupils.

The details of timetabling will vary with the details of policy. What is important is that the latter should dictate the former. It may be that a faculty-based allocation of ten periods to English and foreign languages, ten to science (including computing and technology) and six each to mathematics, humanities and social studies, and creative and practical arts, and four to physical and health education, would come closer to what schools wish to provide in Year 3 than does the conventional subject-loaded timetable.

Years 4 and 5

The national argument for a predominantly common curriculum to sixteen, and the high degree of dissatisfaction among many 15 and 16-year-old pupils that many schools report, have concentrated attention on these year groups. The options system is under particular attack: it is held that it produces a narrow and unbalanced curriculum, leads to premature specialization, constrains vocational opportunity, involves little real choice for most pupils, and so on.

Schools are anxious to meet these criticisms, but are aware of three particular dangers.

1 The danger of removing choice altogether. Properly handled, choice works: it motivates, it acknowledges the immense variety of individual need, and it is a means of allocating scarce specialist time and resources. The making of informed choice is central to our curriculum aims.
2 The danger of providing separate curricula for different groups of pupils. There are strong pressures on schools to stratify the curriculum and to provide a tripartite system inside the school walls. The current vogue for pre-vocational education, for instance, has significant implications, and two major providers of such courses have already indicated their intention of creating 'a new curriculum pathway for that majority of those between the ages of 14 and 18 for whom the traditional academic curriculum is unsuitable'.[17] This pressure is complemented by the current political arguments for a return to selection. In operation, TVEI curricula, however bravely comprehensive their launching fanfare sounded, may come to occupy the middle ground, and we will have recreated the grammar, grammar technical and secondary modern provision of the 1944 Act.
3 The danger of ignoring process in the search for an appropriate structure of content. The Hargreaves Report is particularly helpful here. It suggests that it is not the subject but the way that it is taught that causes pupils to lose interest. With certain teachers, the Hargreaves team noted, even the most disruptive pupils will 'settle down to the task in hand . . . Their enthusiasms seem to arise from being given the opportunity to elect to pace themselves and to elect to change activity . . .'[18]

One framework that avoids these dangers and enables schools to meet the external expectations that impinge upon them, uses a combination of three curricular elements: compulsory courses; courses allowing a degree of choice within prescribed areas (i.e. constrained options); and courses allowing free choice within the range that the individual school can offer (i.e. open options). In its simple form this allows for English, maths, physical education and the statutory RE period for all pupils, and requires all pupils to take one constrained option from each of three groups: the science group, the humanities/social studies group, and a group containing creative and practical arts subjects. On a 40-period timetable this provision would require 25/28 periods; the remaining time is available for three more choices from subjects and courses grouped so as to produce maximum flexibility. The 'flexi-groups' will permit, for example, two more science choices and/or two foreign language choices, a further choice of humanities and of creative and practical arts, and a choice of courses with specific vocational or more general pre-vocational value.

Even in this simple form this framework is not without its difficulties. They are most immediately apparent in the constrained option blocks where many schools will report parental opposition to the creative/practical arts requirement. Schools cannot avoid this: they have to be clear about their policy and the reasons for espousing it, and outside the immediate circle of their parents they can find strong support for the decisions they make.[19] More important in the long run may be the implication contained in the constrained science option that any one science course will provide an adequate minimum science education to the age of sixteen. In present conditions this will mean that a large number of pupils will follow an unbalanced science course to the age of sixteen, and that for many girls this course will be biology. A school that is clear about the importance of science for all its pupils will be led by this and by some of the constraints inevitably present in the open options (see below) to look very carefully at the objectives and implications of the Secondary Science Curriculum Review (SSCR), with its blunt recommendation that all pupils should spend 20 per cent of their timetabled time (and no more!) on science courses.

The number of open option choices will be determined by the content of the compulsory core. At its minimum this will include English and mathematics, physical education and the statutory RE provision, and here also difficulties will arise. The time allocation in English and mathematics at this age is traditionally greater than the allocation to the optional subjects and courses. Whatever the allocation, it needs to be justified by curriculum policy and not by force of habit. If the teaching of the skills of literacy and numeracy is reinforced in the remainder of the curriculum, there might be a case for some reduction here. A second difficulty concerns the provision of a course in 'life and social skills' or 'personal education'. It is clear that a large proportion of schools, aware of the omissions of the conventional subject-based curriculum, want to make some explicit provision at the fourth and fifth year stage, but where such provision is made (e.g. for careers education and work experience) it is commonly confined to the lower ability range.[20] Curriculum policy cannot possibly justify this limitation. Experience suggests that pupils respond positively to well-thought-out courses in this area, particularly if they are linked with the recording of personal achievement, and this argues for the expansion of such provision to the whole ability range. This means a significant extension of the common core, but it carries with it the exciting possibility of designing modular courses free of both the external constraints of public examinations and the internal constraints of departmental and faculty boundaries.

In practice, schools usually choose a modular structure because of the economy and flexibility it permits, and the experience that is being gained here may come to have an important effect on the way that courses in the rest of the curriculum are designed, assessed and certificated. It may also lead to the incorporation into the personal education modules of the school's religious education and physical education programmes, both areas of extreme importance that are increasingly seen to be handicapped by the limitation of the 'weekly dose' approach. If this can be achieved schools will have demonstrated that personal education, unexamined though it is, is central to their curriculum provision.

A core of English, mathematics and personal education will require some 40 per cent of the time available, or 16/40 of the timetable week. Constrained options will require a further 30 per cent, or 12 periods a week. The remaining 12 periods will be available for open options, and in this area some flexibility can be created.

The academic option   This has been the traditional approach, calling for the inclusion of two further science choices, two language choices, and further choices of humanities or of creative arts. O-level sets have usually taken priority and in smaller schools the non-O-level sets often have to cater for a wide ability range. The inbuilt tension between the demands of the two sciences on the one hand and languages and humanities on the other has contributed to the relative decline of the latter, especially among boys. To whole-curriculum planners it is a powerful argument in favour of the SSCR ambition to develop a two-option science course that is an adequate foundation for subsequent A-level work.

The Pre-vocational option   Conscious of the built-in failure factor of most CSE courses for most pupils and of the undeniable pupil-appeal that work-related courses offer, many schools have substantially increased the provision they make in this area. The syllabuses of the City and Guilds Foundation Courses have been found particularly valuable and the Stage 1 examinations in office and clerical skills of the Royal Society of Arts are well established. There is growing interest in the full-programme syllabuses such as the RSA vocational preparation awards, and City and Guilds 365, and schools using these use both core and constrained option time to complete the time allocation that they require. In many respects these are excellent courses: their stress on progressive and formative assessment is particularly valuable. Schools do need to check, however, that they meet all the objectives of the school's curriculum policy. There is a tendency, in the well-meaning proselytizing of the course providers, to recreate the academic/practical dualism that has done so much harm in the past.

The TVEI option TVEI affects only 3 per cent of secondary pupils directly: indirectly it is likely to be more influential. Larger schools, particularly, may consider the possibility of using the open choices to create a specific range of technical options including design, technology and computer applications, particularly in design and control engineering. Once again, curriculum policy needs to be specific. If it dictates 'three sciences for all clever enough to tackle them', neither technology nor computing will win the support or status they need. If it dictates 'at least one science and one applied science for every pupil', a significant change in curriculum emphasis is likely to result.

Coda

The analysis of what schools will want to provide in the open option element of their fourth and fifth year curricula neatly illustrates the schools' dilemma. At this level the ratio of teaching sets provided to the number of forms of intake is rarely greater than 3:2. Effectively, therefore, it is impossible in all but the largest schools to make the whole range of choice described available to the whole ability group. In practice the open option becomes an option that is constrained by the ability level of the pupil who makes it. In present circumstances the demand for more curriculum flexibility is really a demand for more staffing in schools, and it is surely one of our more important curriculum tasks to get this message across at the political level. One further alternative remains, however, and that is the creation of some curriculum flexibility by the deliberate removal of some part of the open-option area – to begin with, perhaps, 4 periods a week – from the straitjacket of GCE/CSE examinations. The 16+ examinations system is predicated upon two-year courses: schools need (and many pupils need) shorter courses carrying a recognized credit-rating for entry to further education/training at 16+. The universal interest in profile and achievement-recording systems of assessment may make the design and timetabling of such 'units of study' very much more straightforward than it is at present, and schools that are willing, for this small part of the total timetabled week, to teach fourth and fifth year pupils together may find it possible as a result to offer a range of half-year or 25-hour courses designed to extend or where necessary to reinforce the remainder of the individual's curriculum.[21]

Traditional timetabling assumptions argue strongly against this development, but traditional timetabling assumptions are being very widely questioned. As Hargreaves has shown, they do not always meet the needs of the pupils in our schools.[22] In curriculum as in all else, habit is a potent force.

Curriculum in the sixth form

Curriculum principle and policy are as important at sixth-form level as they are from years one to five. Unfortunately it is even more difficult to put them into practice. The simultaneous publications in the spring of 1984 of details of the government's intentions for A/S-level examinations and of the structure of the new Certificate of Pre-Vocational Education (CPVE), neatly illustrated the nature of the problem. These initiatives face schools and sixth form colleges with decisions not only of principle, but also of priority; decisions that have to be taken, as it were, in the dark. Below the sixth form, in spite of all the curriculum constraints that exist, there is one significant certainty: by and large the head and the deputies know the number of pupils year by year for whom they must provide, and they know too (though usually much later) the staffing entitlement on which they may draw. Beyond the statutory leaving age, however, these small certainties suddenly dissolve. In any year, how many students will continue into the sixth form is a matter of guesswork, where the outcome is affected by national and local policy decisions as well as by such imponderables as examination results and the availability of job and training opportunities. As staffing tends to be allocated on the basis of how many students 'stayed on' last year, and as there is no equivalent at sixth-form level of the broad agreement on curriculum content and structure that exists at 11-16 (the concept of 'curriculum-led' resourcing rarely exists at this stage), many schools are effectively discouraged from risking curriculum innovation. The danger that carefully prepared courses, staffed often to the detriment of younger age groups, will fail to attract a viable number of students is a powerful disincentive – especially in schools where post-16 students are few and the sixth form is threatened with rationalization.

This is doubly unfortunate, both because our present sixth-form provision does not obviously meet any of the Sheffield criteria (breadth and balance, coherence, practical applicability, differentiation) except the last, and also because the assumptions that underpin it (about the relationship between employment, training and education, for instance, or about 'the school-leaving age') are rapidly being overtaken by events.

Four particular issues focus these concerns, with a sharpness that varies from school to school and from college to college. The first is the problem, recognized for over twenty years but as intractable as ever, of the narrowness of the typical A-level course in both content and process. The second, almost as long-standing and just as far from solution, is the problem posed by the pupil of modest O-level attainment who should not properly be advised to embark on A-level courses. The third, of course, is that of the new sixth former of the 1980s, who has acquired few if any grade 1 passes at CSE but who sees the possibility of materially improving his or her qualification hand with a year of further study at school – encouraged, perhaps, by the local reputation of the Youth Training Scheme and, if the CEO is complaisant, by the possibilities of the DHSS 15- and 21-hour rules. In most schools and in many sixth form colleges all three groups exist and they pose three sets of curriculum problems. The groups do overlap, however, and what they have in common is as important, in the comprehensive school, as what divides them. Hence the fourth issue, which is that of recognizing, in curriculum terms, the commonality of experience of sixth-form students. To what extent is the principle of the common core applicable post-16?

The A-level conundrum

It is too easy to regard the students of three A-levels (and, even more, the students of four A-levels) as the only 'real' sixth formers. Few teachers would deny the intellectual satisfaction (and perhaps the self-esteem) that their teaching involves, and A-level groups are sometimes protected to an extent that is in pure curriculum terms undesirable. The narrowness of many syllabuses and of most subject combinations is realized, but is regarded as 'part of the system', beyond the control of the school. And, of course, there is a great deal of truth in this point of view. Schools do have it in their power, however, to broaden the A-level experience of their students, partly by reviewing the teaching styles they use and choosing the syllabuses that encourage genuine enquiry and in-subject breadth; and partly by making better use of their students' 'minority time'. Too often, because non A-level provision in the sixth form is geared to the assumed demand for O and even CSE re-sit opportunity, the A-level student's minority time is described as private study, and much of it, as we know, is misused. Schools need to reconsider their priorities. A small reduction in the number of A-level subjects on offer is not necessarily narrowing, in curriculum terms, if it permits the establishment of a range of A-level 'support' courses. Such a range might include statistics for non-scientists, computing, and foreign language for business and personal use – courses that justify themselves, and do not need the certification of the examining boards.[23] It might include also some of the more recent O and A/O offerings, such as industrial studies, or science in society, or modern communications, chosen for their obvious relevance to post-school experience. One of the odder aspects of the proposed A/S examination is that it is likely in practice to cancel out this sort of broadening.

The sub-A-level student

A second oddity of the A/S proposal is that it will offer nothing at all to the group of students who want a two-year sixth form course but who will be out of their depth at A-level in any subject which does not call for an essentially practical expertise. Over the years there have been many proposals designed wholly or in part to meet their needs but they have all failed to be adopted. What has tended to happen is that students have either been directed into what are regarded as 'easier' A-level options (not always those which carry weight with selectors for employment and higher education) or have been offered a piecemeal course of Certificate of Extended Education (CEEs) and repeat O levels. Given that CEEs have predictably failed to achieve national credibility, that repeat O levels have a depressingly low success rate, and that both have tended to involve a good deal of repetition of fifth-year work, suitable provision for this group must remain a major concern of sixth-form curriculum planners and providers. In the short term many schools will want to give more careful consideration to the FE alternatives or to the advantages that may accrue if they withdraw all re-sit provision except for English and mathematics and plan instead a limited but balanced range from the sort of 'new' (i.e. not normally offered below sixth form) O level courses mentioned above. In the long term, it may be that the success in schools of the new one-year pre-vocational courses may lead inevitably to the development in schools of the two-year National Diploma Courses that have hitherto been the preserve of the FE colleges.

The one-year pre-vocational student

Integrated one-year pre-vocational courses developed by RSA, City and Guilds and BTEC, and strongly supported by the Further Education Unit of the DES, have been a considerable success in schools and have proved acceptable to students, teachers and employers.[24] Many of their features – the modular construction, the emphasis on progressive assessment and on the practical applicability of course content, and the setting of realistic and recognized attainment objectives – have relevance in a wider curriculum context, and many schools have found the outlay of time and resources that they require more than worthwhile. The new CPVE to be available nationally from 1985/6, is both a recognition of the value of a course built round a common core and based on vocational studies, and a welcome attempt to rationalize the confusing and overlapping provision that has grown up in this area. There are indications, however, that CPVE will attempt to certificate far too wide a range of attainment, like the CEE before it, and in far too many contexts. In pre-vocational education, as perhaps elsewhere, schools will need to concentrate on the curriculum principles and processes involved, and not be unduly distracted by the difficulties of national certification.

A sixth-form common core?

The Schools Council Working Paper 45, which first identified the different needs described above, saw neither case nor need for a common core. 'For such a variety of needs, a common curriculum would be absurd.'[25] The groups, however, clearly overlap. To what extent should the organization of the curriculum reflect this fact?

The answer depends partly on timetabling. Some areas of need are common to all three groups. Re-sit English language and mathematics, for example, should be timetabled to be available simultaneously to all three groups; so should some 'support' courses, for example in computing. It depends also on the school's tutorial style. Traditionally, the A-level students and the one-year sixth have been in separate tutor groups, and here schools and colleges will want to weigh carefully the balance of advantage, for there are strong arguments in favour of wide-based grouping and the active tutorial approach that this permits. Mostly, however, it depends on the approach that the school or college takes to the widening of its A-level studies. A school that opts for an A-level general studies course – timetabled, taught, perhaps examined – will have little staffing to spare for a wider and perhaps more flexible general studies programme, designed to involve all sixth formers regardless of their examination objectives. Provision for physical recreation, in its wider sense, is an obvious component of such a programme; so is provision for all students of some element of direct experience of the business/industrial environment. Many schools would argue that planned involvement with the local community (and experience of that sort of work which is of its nature unremunerated) is an important ingredient as well. And many would make available to sixth formers the widest range of creative and aesthetic opportunity that their accommodation and timetable would allow. What clearly matters is that such a programme should require the student to exercise a genuine element of choice and should require him or her to take responsibility for that choice. The argument comes back to process: to the belief that *how* a student learns may be as important as what a student learns. As yet those who resource our schools and colleges are unconvinced. Students, however, are more responsive, and their willingness to enrol for school and college programmes constructed on the principles here outlined may prove to be the catalyst for the rethinking of our curriculum assumptions 16–19 (and, indeed, 14–19) that the changes of this decade are likely to demand.

8 Sources of support

Peter Snape

The romantic view of headship in England stems, inevitably I suppose, from the famous description of Arnold as 'The man who will change the face of English Education'. This assumed a solitary role, and indeed the folk memories of the greatest of English headmasters concern themselves with his relations not with staff or governors, and certainly not with parents or townspeople, but with his sixth formers, those acolytes who implemented his wishes, and in due course went out into the world to preach the gospel of solitary leadership, the unique view of the task, the isolation of the man in charge, and above all the loneliness of command.

How different from us! And yet how long a time it took for the change to take place. It is only in the last twenty years that headship has been seen not as a matter primarily of a unique vision backed by the resolution and determination to carry it out, legitimized by the willing assent of an admiring set of inferiors, and applauded by an uncomprehending and distant public, but as the approachable, human and often inadequate management of a complex set of relationships. But in the realization of this personal weakness lies the strength of the new position. If a head is now doing everything himself, and relying solely on the resources of his own personality, he is probably not achieving what he ought to be achieving, and what society would want him to achieve. Charisma is not a committee skill, and in a democratic society the effective chairman is far more valuable than the storm trooper. If leadership is no longer a matter of command, there are other qualities that must be summoned to take advantage of whatever resources are available. The effective head will study to take advantage of whatever is available to him in his task. This unglamorous view of school leadership will not be immediately attractive to everyone. Most mortal men would want to be larger than life, and headteachers are no exception to this. Speeches before the seige of Honfleur are far more attractive than the patient summing up of opposing views on the problem before the committee and the soft compromise that enables a highly heterogeneous body to make a little progress to the resolution of a pressing problem. Our history teaches us to applaud the man of action before the man of consensus, Cromwell rather than Pitt, Lloyd George rather than Asquith, Churchill rather than Attlee, but the historian looks to outcomes for his judgement. So heads, too, must look to what can be achieved rather than the grand gesture, and take satisfaction from their achievements rather than their postures. The effective use of what resources are available is one of the measures of success, and in many ways more difficult and dangerous than the splendid attitude and the solitary way.

Resources available are frequently a mess of unpromising material. In looking around for people to help in the task it is not unknown for heads to utter sighs of longing, though it is not always clear exactly what they may be longing for. Here is one unprepossessing group, without an original thought between them, lacking in initiative, their aspirations cast firmly backwards towards the ideal situation enshrined in their imperfect and deceptive memories. The wise head detects their valuable qualities of loyalty and industry, exploits their patience, and in due course is gratified by the intelligence of the contribution which they make. Here is another group, filled with naive idealism and short-term enthusiasms, forever suggesting unrealistic projects and making criticisms that reveal only their lack of understanding of the nature of the true world. The wise head encourages their energy, learns from their unsystematic rehearsal of half-understood ideas, and in the end, and after a year or so of patient management, is delighted by their increase in wisdom and their ability to persevere with a difficult task.

What must be firmly in the forefront of the mind, however, is that the direction of the school remains the responsibility of the head, and that in the end he must use the resources available in the way that is most relevant to his view of the school's needs. Groups will often seek undue influence as a price for cooperation, and in the midst of such pressures the head must make sure that he is charting the course and not drifting with various ebbs and flows of whatever current his boat is navigating.

Professional help

Colleagues

One, perhaps the only, advantage of our strange dualistic system of education as a national service, locally administered, is that there are very many and very different sources of professional help, each with their different strengths and qualities. The first and most important of these, which is only now beginning to be exploited in any serious way, is the professional expertise within one's own school. Heads have been forced, mainly for political reasons about how to achieve change within a highly unionized organization, to establish consultative committees of varying kinds. There is a limit, however, to what can be achieved by the staff meeting in concert. Stances adopted at staff meetings sometimes have little to do with the welfare of the children or of the school generally. A more effective way is by individual consultation, and especially nowadays with more junior members of staff, whose ideas are frequently both refreshing and pertinent. Some problems occasionally arise about this, since teachers are, as the saying has it, 'wondrous fond of place'; but part of the management task is the quietening of unreasonable fears about the revolutionary ideas of the Young Turks fresh from the intellectual hot-beds of the colleges of education. Working parties, often used by more traditional heads in the same way as a reluctant government sets up a Royal Commission to delay legislation, are an excellent source of ideas. Many a head whose ideas have been strongly challenged because they emanated from him has found the same proposals welcomed when they came from a working party of staff. Essentially, though, working parties of colleagues can be relied upon to generate new ideas, rather than to legitimize old ones, and many heads have noticed the improvement in the school's functioning that originated from ideas that surfaced in a staff working party. And of course, it is very pleasant to counter objections to change by the statement that 'this is what colleagues want', which gives pleasure to the initiators as well as diverting some of the flak.

Crucial figures in the running of the school are the deputies. In many ways it is time that the word 'deputy', with all its implications of second string and standby, was discarded. In the larger schools particularly, the title 'assistant head' would be far more accurate, since these members of staff have their own responsibilities which have to be carried out whether the head is there or not. What is clear is that deputies know more about what is actually going on in the school than most people, and their views are therefore central to any decision-making. The establishment of an effective management team, with regular meetings to review the school's working in all its aspects, is essential if the day to day decisions are to be correct, relevant and acceptable to all concerned.

Advisers

It is essential, though, to look outside the school for help. In times like the present, especially, when members of staff and heads are having to reconcile themselves to very long stays in the same institution, there is a great danger that schools will become introverted and unaware of what is possible with different approaches. At a local level, the county adviser can often be a source of new ideas and approaches, and even, on rare occasions, new money. The problem for the secondary head is that local advisers are almost exclusively promoted heads of department, without first-hand knowledge of either administration or of pastoral care; they are employed to advise on subject teaching, and subject teaching is almost the whole of their knowledge. It is rare, for instance, for an adviser to be appointed from the ranks of pastoral staff or deputy heads, and few heads are willing, except under the threat of redeployment, to accept the lower salary and job frustration that advisory jobs usually bring. Naturally, the credibility of advisers short on essential relevant experience is a little suspect, and often too the personality of the people concerned does not commend itself to the head who has to keep the school as a going concern. We all know the difficulties heads experience with the occasional talented and dedicated music or drama teacher before a public performance; the narrow view of the gifted physics teacher who sees only the scientific needs of children as important; the devoted PE teacher who cannot bear to lose a match. It is therefore unsurprising that when these diverse and engaging characters turn up in the head's room with silver-headed cane, *New Scientist* or muddy boots as the case may be, to advise on the curriculum, staffing and examination problems of the whole school, there is an irresistible tendency to look the other way. But we should resist as much as possible. Provided all the necessary reservations are made, the outsider's look at current proposals is often illuminating and almost always refreshing. 'Why,' says the drama adviser, in his carefully modulated voice, 'does one have all those tedious maths lessons, and only two for drama?' The question has to be faced, and a convincing answer given.

    Advisers, as they continually complain, move around, and this is a great blessing to heads since they also bring news of other schools with an objectivity that their heads might not possess. If we believe that others can have good ideas too, the adviser must be useful in conveying them. And of course the adviser has a most important role with the classroom teacher.

One particular aspect of the adviser's role is a comparatively new one, and that is his part in the 'performance review'. The term is taken from management literature, and is much favoured in counties where members are convinced managerialists, or where the officers have visited America. During a performance review, various aspects of the school are examined, advisers visit classes, talk to assistant staff, or even to pupils, examine the staff handbook, ask about the school log, and spend a good deal of time with the head discussing problems, solutions and ways forward. There are great advantages for a head in the examination of his school in this way, and it is often a prudent move to ask for a review, especially in the early months of appointment, when a quick snapshot of the school can be very useful indeed.

Most advisers are extremely helpful and friendly people, whose visits to a school are a welcome event, and whose influence is usually very positive. The current centralist tendencies in our education system, however, presage a much more interventionist role, where the adviser become the authority's hit man, with a rather unclear line of accountability, and no responsibility for the consequence of his actions. Heads have to be aware of this, and study their articles of government to establish the limits of power.

Officers

It is a great pity that nowadays one of the best sources of local help for heads, the education officers, have largely disappeared from the school scene into the mists of corporate management and so are rarely available for support or help. The days when the CEO of the largest authority could find time every week to visit a school or college are unfortunately past, and yet their wisdom and experience is of the utmost value. Some do maintain some sort of pastoral rôle for heads, and where this is divorced from a disciplinary or evaluative rôle, it can be useful. Education officers have the job most akin to that of a head: they deal with the public, with elected members, with professional staff, and with manual workers, and to have achieved their eminence, they must have been reasonably successful. Frequently, too, somewhere in the bureaucratic ragbag of their offices, there is that shred of educational concern that guided them to their present job, and the head who can extract it and put it to use will find himself with excellent material indeed. A useful rule in dealing with education officers is to avoid always asking for something, even his opinions – though of course those are the readiest gifts.

Neighbours

Nowadays schools are seen as being in competition with each other, as a result of the government's view of the importance of choice in education. In some ways this has made it more difficult to learn from the experience of colleagues than it used to be. One hesitates to seek advice from one's nearest rival, or indeed to share with him the secrets of success. Nevertheless, over the years useful contacts can be developed, and between old friends most things are possible. Most authorities now have Associations of Secondary Heads (ASH). Prefaced by the county's initial these provide not only useful forums for discussion but interesting acronyms, conveying perhaps the flavour of the counties concerned. It might be a useful test for education officers to nominate the most appropriate counties for words such as DASH, CASH, HASH, MASH etc. County associations have the advantage of being close to the authority, and therefore not likely to lose heads in clouds of speculation. The drawbacks are obvious – minor domestic issues tend to pre-dominate: sterile debate on the level of meal time assistance is an old and continuing favourite. A further disadvantage is, of course, that the county association does not have the benefit of the experience of other places, which is always a useful lever in improving conditions.

Professional associations

For a wider local view of educational issues, most heads will belong to one of the teacher associations, which deal with matters of current educational concern as well as with the problems of individual members. The Secondary Heads Association has the advantage of admitting into membership both heads and deputies of secondary schools, and so has a wide overview indeed of what is happening in the area. The National Association of Headteachers has most of the country's primary school heads as members, as well as a substantial number of secondary heads, and has therefore a special rôle in linking the phases. The associations do tend to stress their educational rather than their trade union rôle. SHA particularly value their involvement in Wales, Scotland and Northern Ireland which brings a cosmopolitan approach that can be of great value.

HMI

Her Majesty's Inspectors of Schools have changed beyond all recog-nition in the past twenty years. At one time they were almost all ex-teachers from the independent schools, who preserved their anonymity, measured their opinions, revealed little and influenced nothing.

In twenty years has come a massive change: many inspectors now will know what it is like to teach a group of low ability fourth years on a Friday afternoon; many of them have actual experience of headship; all of them *see* a large number of schools, and watch an even larger number of lessons. Their opinions are often both shrewd and pointed. Much has been achieved by publication. First of all came HMI papers on schools, on mixed ability teaching, on modern language teaching, and then the famous documents on the curriculum, which have had a significant national effect. Their latest task, however, the publication of school reports, and the periodic analyses of those reports will probably become very much more influential. It is worthwhile for all engaged in schools to send for reports of inspections, to see what is being approved or disapproved of currently.

Most heads welcome the visits of HMI, and some sympathy for them in their disagreeable task is not inappropriate. A moment's understanding of the plight of an HMI, closeted in the bedroom of an ageing two-star hotel in a small provincial town, in the silence of a wintery night, scribbling reports across the inhospitable surface of a stained and pitted dressing-table should transform this into an agreeable evening in the comfort of the home with some relaxed and amusing conversation about important educational issues. This is not bribery, though it may be enlightened self-interest.

Conferences

The professional associations hold annual or periodic conferences at which the major educational issues of the day are discussed. It is fairly rare for headteacher groups to spend much time discussing pay and conditions (assistants will probably take a cynical view of the reasons for that), but they will talk freely about what concerns them most, and one can be sure that those will be the vital issues as far as the children are concerned. The associations publish, too; and many of their discussion papers have eventually left their mark upon legislation or on current practices.

Lay help

Governors

As HMI have changed in the past few years, so governors have begun to take on a fundamentally different rôle. At governors' meetings of 30 years ago the business was really to find out what the head had been up to during the past four months, to hear of his appointments and promotions and to receive with the tea and cakes a brief oral report on the health of the school as perceived by the person in charge. Governors are rather more interventionist than that nowadays. Political appointments have been matched by the involvement of staff and parents, the two bodies with the keenest interests in the welfare of the school. Local authorities want to have an articulate presence in all debates on curriculum as well as on appointments and building maintenance. Yet it is important to remember that strange English alchemy whereby a body appointed to see that a local authority's wishes are implemented can be transformed, irrespective of political belief, into a bastion of defence against unwarranted interference. The head's first job is to realize that, and then involve the governors in as many ways as possible. Many of them want to do more than attend interviews and come to plays and speech days. Some will have a keen interest in a particular aspect of the school – the parent of a handicapped child may be extremely anxious to contribute something, and can be used to specialize in all remedial work on behalf of the governors; or perhaps a businessman governor will want to contribute to the commercial department or the careers work. There are sensitivities to acknowledge on the part of staff, and pupils, too, and one must always beware of the political careerist, whose passion is for publicity rather than quiet support. Heads can easily detect this particular kind of motivation and act accordingly. Far better for such a man to espouse the cause of a new playing field than to shine a spotlight on an area of the curriculum where quiet endeavour over a long passage of time is required for improvement.

The position of teacher and parent governors has given rise to some initial anxiety. Questions are asked about their eligibility to serve on appointment committees or disciplinary bodies of various sorts, but it is difficult to see why there should be any reservation whatsoever. Both teacher and parent governors have a far more lively stake in the school than political governors and there is nothing unusual in the practice of Jack having a say in the appointment of his masters, in Western democracies anyway. The 1980 Act makes no distinction between governors, and heads must learn to trust their own people. Some heads fail to realize what an asset a properly constituted governing body can be. Clearly, governors must be involved in all policy decisions, and especially in controversial ones; they will usually support the head where the case is clear. Where it is not there is a good argument for taking advice and acting on it. When once governors have reached a decision, a good deal of pressure is taken off the head, who can simply refer complainants to the minutes of the properly constituted body. This is not only the correct way of proceeding, but it also happens to be the easiest. Frequent contact with the chairman is the one sure way of avoiding conflict; heads who regard their governors as some sort of official inquisition are destined for strife.

The Press

It was once said of a famous headmaster of Eton that he did all that could be expected of a head by keeping his school out of the newspapers. We will all have a good deal of sympathy with that view of headship, but unfortunately those days are past. Education generally and schools in particular have an immense fascination for newspapers, because the great majority of their readers have some involvement with the system and will therefore pay money to read about something that is very close to them.

This is the first and most important point to remember. Journalists are interested in writing saleable copy, and rarely in much else, though they have their own careers to promote too. So scepticism about the motives of newspapermen is the first requirement of the skilled media-manipulating head. Newspapers are almost always chronically short of copy, if not for today, then for tomorrow, and they will readily accept articles, letters and interviews if they are asked. Local papers are especially useful to schools, and many heads will make a regular practice of inviting the reporters to visit the school once a month, or more frequently, to talk over events and give advance warning of events. When a friendly relationship has been built up over the months, there is less likelihood of damaging stories being run before the school's point of view is presented. And it is a great pity if success stories do not achieve the same coverage as the other sort, even making allowances for the editor's preference for bad news. Local papers are usually friendly and, with the caveats mentioned, can help a school and its head a great deal.

National newspapers are rather different. The educational correspondent of a national daily is not likely to concern himself with events in a single school, unless they are really of a disastrous kind, but the greater menace is the freelance, purporting to represent the London Press. 'I'm writing for the Daily—' (usually on the phone) does not justify a comprehensive response, since the caller may well be a housewife trying a self-study journalism course, or someone who hopes to earn twenty pounds with a saleable story. Such people frequently do not have the same awareness of the need for balanced reporting as their full time professional colleagues.

However, keeping one's school out of the newspapers is no longer a satisfactory achievement; the resourceful head wants to have his school in the newspapers, but always with an admiring and favourable mention. Unfortunately, this is not easy to achieve.

Television and radio

An effective head will encourage almost anything on television or radio. The medium is ephemeral, and people's attention so lackadaisical, that it is difficult to envisage that any harm can be done. The delight with which parents and pupils will say 'I saw you on television last night' is equalled only by their complete forgetfulness of what you said, and so whenever possible heads should encourage visits by the camera or the microphone. Unfortunately, this little truth has now been discovered by chief education officers and others, and many authorities ask heads not to appear, reserving the privilege for themselves and their chairmen.

Worthies

All towns and cities have worthy bodies, imbued with a sincere desire to help their fellows: Rotary, Round Table, trades councils, chambers of commerce, churches and political parties of differing views all pronounce frequently on schools and education, and it is only right that a head should be able to make use of them when he can see the opportunity. There are drawbacks. Associations of this sort tend to attract the most successful citizens, some of whom will ascribe that success to their imperfect memory of what happened in their own schooldays. This is not always the best basis for participation in today's comprehensives. The other drawback is that few people can be totally disinterested, and support and help from any group will have the interest of that group in mind, even if they are thinking only in terms of a *quid pro quo* in the shape of new members.

Rotary clubs have a great deal of experience of successful business life combined with a sense of civic responsibility, and they can be used most effectively in any work concerning careers. They can provide mock interviews for young men and women, can advise about the real nature of a job, and if they are familiar enough with the school, can promote its interests in the wider community. The school in its turn can help Rotary by speaking regularly on educational issues, and trying to persuade local leaders of the community to take a positive and supportive interest in what is happening on the educational scene. Round Table, with its younger age range, is characterized by its energy and enthusiasm, and usually by its efficiency too, so they can provide not only help but example.

Churches can have not only a curricular contribution to make, by conducting assemblies or giving talks, but are vastly under-used as a source of counselling, especially for older pupils. It is remarkable that so many independent schools employ chaplains for this very purpose, while maintained schools fail to give town clergy the much needed opportunity for regular contact with young people. The head must, of course, select his clergy with some care.

Heads will often be invited to join some of these bodies of worthies, and may be tempted to do so for the outside contacts that they bring. The head must expect that in these circumstances tensions will arise between his membership and his loyalty to his school, in a way that is unique to his job. The detail of most peoples' work is private, and not subject to public scrutiny. For a head everything, from exam results to the behaviour of the most disobedient fourth-form girl, can be the subject of a quiet and odious word in a relaxed social moment.

The move towards community policing in some parts of the country has provided a number of opportunities. The most obvious ways of using the police are not necessarily the most effective, and certainly lectures about vandalism before the beginning of the summer holiday are not necessarily the most effective way to combat it. Traffic and driving education are far more productive ways of involving the police, and of producing helpful attitudes of mind in young people. Magistrates are useful too; it is fascinating to observe in some tourist areas of the country, where English language schools proliferate during the summer months, how crowded the courts are with uncomprehending young foreigners, while our own children sit in the classrooms learning about the English legal system from a textbook.

Parents

The most consistently neglected source of support is the one on which we could place the most reliance. Parents have the most significant stake in the school and many of them take it very seriously indeed. Nowadays, too, many of them will have chosen one school rather than another, and, in maintained as in independent schools, will want to demonstrate that act of faith not only by their initial choice, but by their continuing support. For many, involvement in school either through the parents' association or otherwise is an important phase of life, bringing with it opportunities for service and leadership that our modern specialized society does not provide elsewhere; so in some sense it may be true that a school has a duty to parents as to children, to offer opportunities for growth and responsibility.

It is a pity that for many parents, the major, if not the only, rôle is that of fund raising. Parents can do this very well, but it is interesting that the largest contribution to school finances has usually come not from fund-raising events – the sales, raffles, sponsored walks and all the rest – but from the systematic organization of covenanted direct giving. And of course if parents give directly their energies can be diverted to other things. Schools generally nowadays lack good, stage-managed, formal occasions, whose rituals have a great deal to contribute to the development of esprit de corps, and there are good grounds for thinking that a return to formality might improve the academic image. Many parents would welcome the chance, not only to help with refreshments but with the general organization of formal events, and to be involved in a meaningful way with arts festivals, musical evenings and all the other events which enrich school life.

An elected parents' committee can keep open lines of communication between parents and the senior management of the school. It is frequently the case that representation on the committee is arranged on a geographical basis, and in rural schools especially contact with outlying villages is all the easier when a parent is known to be the local representative. The parents' committee must be seen to have an effective and audible voice, complementing that of the governors. It is not unknown for such a body to make its view clearly heard on matters as fundamental as the appointment of a new head, for instance, and cases have occurred where selection procedures have been changed to accommodate parental wishes for greater involvement. But the communication need not be only one way. A skilful head can carry the parents' committee with him on controversial issues, and be confident that his side of the argument will be put when school matters are discussed in the remoter parts of the catchment area.

Parents can be an effective political force, too. Numbers of local authorities, deaf to every educational argument against the reduction of the numbers of teachers, or the proposed closure of a school, have shown a remarkable improvement in hearing as a result of a sustained campaign by a determined group of parents. The immense advantage to a head of this is that he can play a subdued and unobtrusive part, allowing the parents to exercise their democratic rights in an enjoyable and prolonged fight against petty dictatorship or impenetrable bureaucracy, or whatever the political catchword of the day happens to be.

Heads should not be afraid of using parents in a less dramatic but just as serious rôle, as a sounding board for new ideas. Most educational ideas are not conceptually difficult, and while every parent would not want to be a curriculum specialist, many are

fascinated by the theories. Many a head has avoided serious problems by the judicious use of the phrase 'I wonder what you would
think' in one context, which has led him to be able to say firmly 'The
parents wouldn't stand for' in another.

Naturally, the involvement of parents in the central issues of school
life is fraught with difficulty. Like everyone else, they have their
imperfect memories of what school was (and therefore should still
be) like. The typical active committee parent will almost certainly be
the middle-class mother of a brightish child destined for the sixth
form, and perhaps further, and therefore by no means typical in
either demands or expectations. Heads must bear this in mind, while
recognizing the sincerity of their participation in the school. It would
be a waste of resources not to make use of all the skills and energies
that they offer.

Other help

The demands made on a head to make use of what other people can
offer lead him to make equal demands on his own inner resources of
judgement, resourcefulness and knowledge, and these must be continually refreshed. A wise head will make use of the many agencies
and associations of specific kinds. The Educational Year Book for
instance, lists more than 40 pages of societies and groups, each with
some particular task or function, and many of these produce
pamphlets and books of real value. The agency of greatest value was,
of course, the Schools Council, the high quality of whose curriculum
work was matched only by its comparative failure to penetrate the
country's classrooms. The time for central intervention seems more
appropriate now, so it will be interesting to see whether its successors,
the Secondary Examinations Council and School Curriculum Council
turn out to be more effective. They certainly seem at present to enjoy
more effective backing from the Secretary of State.

And while agencies are important, we must not overlook the
influence and importance of books and reading; one cannot imagine
that a head would want to be without his copy of 'Education' or the
'Times Educational Supplement', the careful reading of which will
keep his adrenalin flowing, his imagination lively, and his knowledge
fairly up-to-date. Every school, too, has its link with the university
institute of education library, and guided by the review in the
weeklies, the conscientious head can keep abreast of essential
reading. A growing resource for the sharing of ideas is the Centre for
the Study of Comprehensive Schools at York University, with its
computerized data-bank which draws from a wide range of schools
and other relevant agencies.

The Open University is one of the most persuasive and effective sources of help; many of their courses, for governors as well as for senior school administrators, have a great deal to say in the way of useful practical advice and theoretical speculation. Heads should not despise private study during school hours in the same way that some sixth formers do. Much of the day-to-day work is a matter of interviews, committees, discussion and confrontation of one sort or another. An occasional spell with a book is both nourishing and refreshing. The more traditional of our schools still speak of the headteacher's room as the Study, even though what goes on there most of the time gives little justification for that title. Schools might be better if it did.

Finally we must mention attendance at courses and conferences. Most heads enjoy these, in spite of the feelings of guilt that are often projected on to them by colleagues and parents who think the head's proper place is in the trenches with the troops. Enjoyment is not all, however. The sharing of experience, the exchange of ideas, and the input, however controversial, all help to develop the sense of perspective that makes for wise judgement and a calm approach. Fortunately, the present emphasis on training and retraining for heads indicates that there is a general recognition of the importance of regular in-service training.

It must be clear from what has been said that there is no shortage of support in running the complex machinery of a large secondary school, and there should be no sense of inadequacy in the realization that a head cannot and should not rely on himself alone as the source of all wisdom, initiative and judgement. There remains, though, that central kernel that makes the job so uniquely important in a school, the kernel of vision of where the school is going, the kind of community it should aim to be, its long-term aims, its short-term objectives, and the quality of its life as its moves towards their achievement. As an artist selects not only his materials but also the viewpoint of his painting, so the head must do the same. Many may help to develop that vision, and many others will be needed to accomplish it, but the head's task in shaping and selecting is unique. The final decisions are always his, and with all the responsibility and isolation that that may carry, few would wish it otherwise.

9 Clients

Michael Smith

Most business and professional enterprises are single-minded. They exist to serve their clients with a readily identifiable product or service. The fruit seller, the aircraft manufacturer, the architect and the doctor may serve many customers but their clients' needs are easily described – quality fruit, efficient aircraft, sensible plans and effective medical care. However complex the enterprise may be, the object of the exercise has recognizable form or function and only varies between fairly well defined parameters.

This is a luxury denied to education. Not only are there many clients from different backgrounds and representing a variety of interests, but they rarely speak with a common voice. Parents and their children, industrialists, academics in institutions of higher education and the community at large look at secondary education from their own partisan standpoint and register their conflicting demands.

'I want him to be happy!'
'I want her to go to Oxbridge!'
'I want her to be free to discover herself.'
'I want him caned when he gets above himself.'
'The basics are the only important things you teach.'
'Why is there no A level Spanish on the timetable?'
'You are always picking on my son.'
'Why don't you do something about the litter?'
'I'll not have my child stay behind for detention.'
'There's no discipline at that school.'
'Why isn't she in the hockey team?'
'You can't teach Economics below undergraduate level.'
'Why aren't school leavers economically literate?'
'You are not going to teach my child sex.'

'Why don't you prepare children for the real world?'
'Teaching my boy needlework is a waste of time.'
'I'll report you to the Equal Opportunities Commission.'

There is no consensus among the clients. Any educationalist who looks for one will seek in vain. But that is only half the problem. There is also no consistency to the human material within the process. Boys and girls arrive at schools with a rich variety of backgrounds and having achieved a wide range of skills – the able, the retarded; the culturally rich, the environmentally deprived; the loved, the unwanted; the ill, the well; the introvert, the extrovert; the talented, the limited; the fully facultied, the partially handicapped. The simplistic view of education assumes a common starting point for all children who are then engaged in a broadly common experience which will fit them generally and equally for their future roles in society. Nothing could be further from the truth.

Denial of the simplistic, however, does not imply that secondary education is without fundamentals, which represent the highest common factors for all its clients. Analyse any lively secondary school and two objectives should emerge as relevant for all consumers.

That children should learn.
That they should grow into maturity.

Set in context, these objectives assume that no matter how diverse client demands may be, children at secondary stage should gain as much information and develop as many learning skills as possible, and secure an understanding of the world around them. At the same time, their human environment requires personal development as an equally legitimate priority. How well their network of relationships functions determines their social skills as wives, husbands, parents, co-workers, employers, neighbours and citizens. What they know and how they relate form two interwoven dimensions of their whole being. The resources of the school should be directed to achieving the highest standards on each front consistent with the ability and environmental background of each individual.

Such objectives may be framed as a model in which a child at the onset of secondary education sets out from a notional starting point in the middle and moves progressively outwards towards the furthest ring of the target at as many points as possible. In a comprehensive school some may not get very far; others will go a very long way indeed. From the standpoint of our clients, the target model will act as a reference point from which to compare and contrast perceptions (fig. 9.1).

Cognitive   Affective

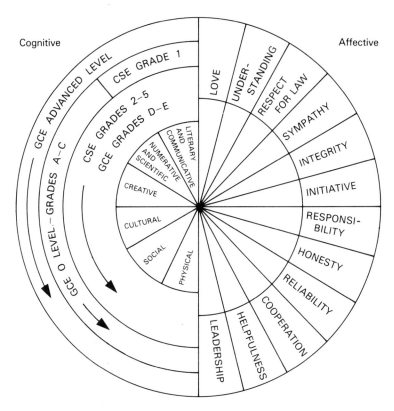

Fig. 9.1 Comprehensive objectives.

Parents

However clear the school's objectives may be, the ultimate responsibility for the upbringing of children remains with their parents. The status of the school *in loco parentis* reflects and enshrines this reality. In practical terms, therefore, the rôle of the school is to act as a logical extension of the learning and socializing function of the home; a function which can only be fulfilled if the two act in partnership. It is not difficult for a school to set out its position clearly as a basis on which such a partnership can grow.

Families are diverse; they span a broad spectrum of assumptions and expectations. Much has happened to the institution of the family over the past quarter of a century. Some changes have been beneficial: fewer children become seriously ill during their earlier years; fewer children are unplanned; more grandparents are alive and active during the whole of a young person's secondary education; family size has been reduced; greater material benefits surround its members. Viewed over the span of the century, housing has improved out of all recognition. Extreme poverty and debilitating material environments are problems which, by and large, schools in the 1980s are spared.

The physical problems of the early years of this century have been replaced by social and psychological ones in the later years. These problems are harder to combat and impinge more acutely on educational activity. In particular, they make universal consensus between school and home especially difficult. From the 1950s onwards there has been a significant growth in domestic tension and upheaval. The pursuit of self-centred ends has shifted values to a significant degree. The casualties have been and continue to be the children. The partnership between school and home referred to above can only flourish where values and expectations are held in common, but family unity is not a bedrock which can be assumed. The affective objectives on the right of the target model cannot be taken for granted as being synonymous with the expectations of all families. Increasingly, schools are called on to perform caring functions which more properly belong to the home. On the physical level, children are sent to matron with ailments which could and should have been dealt with by parents the night before. Does a head instruct her not to deal with them? Or is a disproportionate amount of time given over to solving situations with which the school is not resourced to deal? On the emotional level, family disputes can tear a child's psychological well-being apart. With the divorce rate standing at 1 marriage in 4, a significant proportion of secondary stage children will be affected by family conflict. Is it a head's right to intervene when divorced parents use their children to denigrate their ex-spouses' child-rearing policies? Is a school equipped and staffed to work in the field of marriage guidance counselling? How does it absorb the catastrophic effects on pupil behaviour and relationships when family tension is at its height?

Whatever shock waves inundate them, schools are expected to be a rock of stability. They are expected to understand, advise on and tolerate the behavioural repercussions. Moral values, based on a broad acceptance of the Christian ethic, which characterized the majority of homes in the mid-twentieth century, have been replaced in some cases by a philosophy which regards freedom more highly than responsibility. A curious paradox remains, however. The society which acquiesces in shoplifting and fare-dodging still expects its schools to be temples of purity in behaviour, speech and honesty. A coat taken by another pupil, in school, is seen as a crime more heinous than the same coat removed from a public disco. In the former the school is held in some way to blame. Two children have a row which gets out of hand during the day: the school is judged to be, to a degree, responsible. The dispute could just as easily have been sparked off at the weekend, in which case the school would have been deemed blameless.

COUNTY OF AVON EDUCATION COMMITTEE
Guidelines for Home and School

The Avon Local Education Authority has a duty to provide an education for children of school age in the County, but a child's education starts in the home and is continued as a partnership between home and school.

So that this partnership will give every child the best possible chance of success, the partners should be clear about what each can reasonably expect of the others. The Authority expects them to co-operate fully and to accept the responsibilities set out in these guidelines.

Responsibilities of the School

1 to develop each individual pupil's talents as fully as possible;
2 to teach effectively and to set the highest standards in work and behaviour;
3 to care for each child when at school as a good parent of a large family;
4 to help pupils to leave school able and anxious to make the best possible contribution to the community at large;
5 to encourage regular communication with parents as a basis for close co-operation between home and school.

Responsibilities of Parents

1 to show by their own example that they support the school in setting the highest standards in all it tries to do;
2 to make sure that their children come to school regularly, on time, refreshed, alert, correctly dressed and ready to work;
3 to take an active and supportive interest in their children's work and progress;
4 to support the authority and discipline of the school, helping their children to achieve maturity, self-discipline and self-control;
5 to control the development of their children's use of leisure time activities and entertainments.

Responsibilities of Pupils

1 to attend school regularly, on time, ready to learn and take part in school activities;
2 to aim at the highest standards in all aspects of school life;
3 to co-operate with the staff and to accept the authority and rules of conduct of the school;
4 to consider and respect the feelings and property of other people both in school and in the wider community;
5 to care for the grounds, buildings, furniture, equipment and books provided for the school.

Geoffrey Cummy

Director of Education

Fig. 9.2 Guidelines for home and school.

Two questions must be asked. First: how realistic is it to set and maintain high standards of social behaviour in schools irrespective of the standards demonstrated by society at large? And second, if the affective objectives of the target model (fig. 9.1) remain valid: how far can or should a school compensate for the ills of society and provide a social structure to which pupils can sensibly relate? There is no logical alternative to seeking the highest possible standards in the education of children and their relationship with others. To pretend they are of no account would be a travesty of principles. To quantify 'realistically', however, is an impossibility. There are only ways of working towards a goal.

The most practical approach lies in the concept of partnership between home and school. Where genuine cooperation exists, based on a relationship which is lasting, with partners who know each other, who exercise respect based on understanding, where good humour counterbalances prickles and complaint, a chance exists that school and home can work together – social and moral differences notwithstanding. The genesis of such a relationship is contained, for example, in the 'Guidelines for home and school' published by the County of Avon Education Committee and issued to all parents at all points of admission. If nothing else, they provide base lines from which to operate and to which to return when problems arise (fig. 9.2).

Guidelines are only a first move. Implementation is more time consuming. Take the entry of the new generation each September: an eight-step approach can be identified to put this partnership into action (fig. 9.3).

Not all can be guaranteed to proceed smoothly. Possible tensions can be identified at virtually every stage.

1 At step 1, parents who show insufficient interest to come to the open day but accept the 11+ transfer place, begin the partnership in a trailing position. Further strategies like home visiting may be pressed into service.
2 Also at step 1, the production of a prospectus analysing the exam results which appeared a matter of days earlier presents practical problems.
3 At step 2, parental prejudices cannot always be allayed by logical discussion. And if the parents of the most able decline to support the neighbourhood comprehensive, local confidence can be sapped to a devastating degree.
4 The open evening to display work makes considerable demands on staff who may not find shop window activity congenial.

	Date	Event	Purpose
1	September-a year prior to entry	Parents' open evening. Prospectus and Annual Report for previous year published and issued.	To build confidence and begin a relationship built on evidence and personal contact.
2	November prior to entry	Discussion groups with parents undecided about accepting a place in the area school.	To explore doubts and allay anxieties.
3	February/ March prior to entry	Visits to feeder primary schools by head of lower school. **OR** Individual family interviews.	To increase family interest and expectations.
4	May prior to entry	Visit of new intake to school for an afternoon of music-making.	To give the anticipation of the new school a more practical emphasis.
5	June prior to entry	Visits of new intake in small groups around the school.	
6	May/June prior to entry	Receipt of records from feeder primary schools summarizing progress and pointing out problems.	Transfer records provide an informed base on which to build.
7	July prior to entry	New parents' evenings (held on two successive evenings, to reduce numbers involved, thus making the occasion more personal). Talks from senior staff on expectations, procedures etc. Fashion parade of uniform. New parents shown around school. 'Notes for new parents' issued – a comprehensive statement of policy, rules, first year syllabus and advice.	To provide parents with practical information and begin a home/tutor relationship.
8	The day prior to the beginning of term	Each family invited to the school on a tutor group basis phased throughout the day to ensure only one group is present at any period of time. Child and parents meet tutor again, child taken to tutor base, allocated desk/locker. Free orange squash and biscuits provided.	Territorial and procedural anxieties allayed whilst older children are not present in school.

Fig. 9.3 Eight-step approach for new entrants.

5 The time required by the head of the lower school to visit or interview is expensively acquired – normal teaching timetables can be seriously disrupted.

6 May music demands the cooperation of a number of music teachers across the 11+ divide in a variety of schools. No one is in a position to command it.

7 New parents' evenings are most successful when the tutor is personally present to be introduced. If that tutor will be joining in September and is currently teaching 200 miles away, there are problems.

8 Records completed by primary teachers in many schools will lack consistency with each other. Parental choice can provide an 8 form entry with up to 30 feeder schools to contact.

9 The practicality of the pre-term activity depends entirely on the willing cooperation of tutors to relinquish a day's holiday for the purpose.

Through this welter of activity, none of which is set out in any teacher's contract of service, one message is being transmitted: that the secondary school welcomes and values the arrival of each new entry as an individual and that a firm, constructive parental relationship is the *sine qua non* of the five or more years to follow.

Children who are admitted during a school year require particular attention. The mobile society which a school serves can present over 60 families in an academic year requiring admission for their children. Not having experienced the induction process, such families need individual attention. This is a task which should not be delegated. There is a natural parental expectation to see the head – and conversely the head is in a strong position to interpret the appropriate stage of the school to the new entrant as well as effecting the compromises which ill-timed admissions can involve. It is a time consuming process, but immensely worthwhile.

One of the indicators of the quickening interest of parents is the degree of concern expressed over the curriculum. The secret garden has indeed become a public park. No longer can teachers expect total acquiescence over what is taught in the classroom. The reasons for this are not difficult to find. At a time of shrinking employment opportunities connections are being drawn between marketable subjects and career openings. The social gap between teachers and parents is narrowing. Parents rightly feel they can take an intelligent interest in curricular affairs. The open-door policy in the best of infant school sets up a pattern of expectation which can carry through the whole of the process. Partnership on these terms is healthier but the tensions can be sharper in the later years of schooling:

1 Teachers may view Latin and computer studies on equal terms. Parents may not.
2 There remains an obstinate connection between social class and academic success. The middle-class parent will demand seven years of homework, as per schedule, every night from the point of entry to 18. It was a working-class parent who wrote to a head: 'I understand she is given homework. This also has to stop as you are paid to teach her in school. If you cannot do this, you should not be in the job.' Satisfying both clients is not easy.
3 Parents argue the toss about examination entry, regarding GCE as the desirable qualification, to be preferred to CSE.
4 The demands placed on schools by the Sex Discrimination Act are not always appreciated by parents who object to their sons taking needlework but are more sanguine over daughters including technology.
5 The myth still persists that educational activity can only take place when teachers are in front of children. Closure for in-service education, a reformed school day or other devices designed to improve on planning on the hoof can be questioned by parents who see education as little different from a branch of automated industry.
6 Parents judge curricular activity by their own classroom experiences several decades previously. A school which seeks to change the thrust of its learning activity from content to process may find it hard to take its articulate parents with it.
7 The starting point for parental evaluation of a school includes a perception of eager but biddable children, taught by a competent, experienced teacher in a well resourced classroom which leads to excellent examination results. How can they come to terms with the real world which presents schools with a proportion of less amenable pupils in classrooms which show clear evidence of economic contraction? And how can they fully understand that a school faced with a vacancy on 31 May in a shortage subject has to accept an inexperienced teacher who could be less than ideal but is certainly not incompetent? And still the confidence level has to be maintained.

Nonetheless, the theme of partnership must persist and schools need to explore as many ways as possible to tap the goodwill and channel it constructively. Take an experiment to harness parental involvement in geography homework. The school wished parents to participate in critical evaluation of second year project work. Each family was issued with a comment sheet to be completed as the project progresses (fig. 9.4).

				Parent's
Week	Time spent	Work done	Parent's comments	signature
Week one	2 hours 16/11	Tasks 1–3	Kay found the instructions a little difficult to follow at first. They were not absolutely clear for Task 1. Tasks 2 and 3 presented no problems to her.	M.A.P.
Week two	2 hours	Tasks 4–8	Kay worked systematically through these tasks, finding it easier to concentrate for one longer spell rather than several short attempts.	M.A.P.
Week three	1 hour	Tasks 9–11	No problems. Gave Kay a definite sense of achievement on completion.	M.A.P.

Name of Pupil: KAY PXXXXXXXX Tutor Group T2Z
Project Title: The Population Explosion
Date of issue: 8th November
Completed Project to be handed in by: 12th December
Project to be brought to the Geography lesson on each day 4

Parents' general coment on the success of the project for daughter: Although Kay did not find the subject matter of this particular project very interesting, she quite enjoyed tackling this type of work. Further projects of a similar type would be very worthwhile. She welcomed the opportunity of having some scope for imagination, e.g. in lay-out and graphs/diagrams/etc. I would consider this project successful in its aim to give scope for varying abilities. As yet, Kay has not been 'stretched' unduly and we welcome this type of work. Kay took great care with the general presentation.

M.A.P.

Fig. 9.4 Parent's comment sheet.

Another parent commented : 'Once again this is an excellent project. This type of homework is welcome. It encourages Mark to think of others and we as parents can assist and become involved.'

A regular individual report, however, presents the most fruitful scope for continuing dialogue. Traditionally it is sent home, but there are alternatives. It can be handed over personally and its content discussed – an opportunity for a school both to listen and to explain to its principal clients the total process. The quality of care arising from such a practice is always enhanced. Danger exists for a head or head of house who takes precipitate action with a pupil without likely parental reaction being known – be it over work or behaviour. A false move made in ignorance can increase parental alienation. The consequent line up of forces which reads : *child + parents v school* provides the child with what he considers a pearl of very great price and the school with an unnecessarily intransigent problem. Conversely, cohesive cooperation, be it praise or punishment born of a spirit of trust and understanding, is the making of success. But how to achieve this dialogue with the vast majority of the clients? Certain practical considerations are important:

1 Parental visits to the school need to be crisp, businesslike and competently managed.
2 Long queues are anathema to the less than enthusiastic parent.
3 The task of report interpretation given over to the tutor provides an opportunity to give broad-based advice to a manageable clientèle. It also enhances the tutor's role out of all recognition.
4 If the school operates a 'continuous belt' tutor system, the parents attend the school to see a known person with whom, after the first contact, they have a developing relationship.
5 Heads of year/houses and the entire senior management team need to be present to pick up issues and problems as the needs arise.
6 Appointment times must be given to parents which are known to be convenient.

A report evening which takes cognisance of these considerations may be organised in the following way:

1 The tutor writes to each home informing parents of the date and asking for a return on which parents indicate all possible and convenient times on that evening.
2 An appointment schedule is drawn up based on this information and the tutor issues a second letter inviting attendance at a time which is known to be acceptable.
3 All the interviews are held in the hall where background noise ensures confidentiality but where the operation can be easily controlled and where referral to senior staff is readily managed.
4 The hall is arranged in a manner which promotes the smooth flow of parents (fig. 9.5).
   Such a scheme has regularly ensured an average response of over 90 per cent of parents on each evening. If follow-up interviews were added, the percentage involved would be recorded at an even higher level. There are potential disadvantages. If contact with subject teachers is required, this has to take place on a subsequent occasion. A head has to place great trust in tutors as they explain policy or make value judgements on behalf of the school as a whole. The tutor is acting as head for the evening – delegation par excellence. But

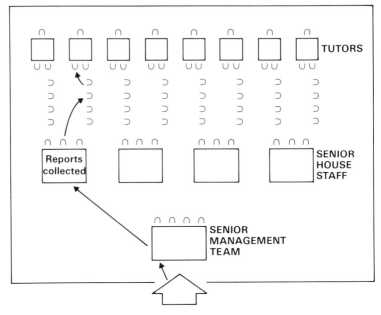

Fig. 9.5 Parents' report evening.

usually little goes wrong and, with experience, the kind of professional relationship which develops over the years is not dissimilar to that which obtains between a patient and the GP – dormant for periods of time but springing into action as the need arises based on mutual trust developed over the years.

Lest too rosy a picture is being painted, reference must be made to disagreements with which all heads have to deal, some of which stem from an increase in society's expectations of schools. In the 1930s the task was very simple – literacy and numeracy for all and for some, higher standards in the humanities, sciences, languages and perhaps the arts. The affective objectives of the target model (fig. 9.1) were seen as the responsibility of the home. Extend the school's remit to include the entire affective development of young people, set in a context of declining family skills in coping and conflict is inevitable. A fifth year boy is away from school. The head telephones his home to enquire his whereabouts. The mother informs the head that her son is still in bed at 10.00 am and won't get up; would the head get him out of bed? In such a situation, not only has expectation run away with itself but the head is in a quandary. If he agrees and intervenes, he puts himself in the centre of domestic strife; to back off is to let the parent down when help has been requested and appear to condone the truancy.

In an age which enjoys attacking authority most heads will at some time face the angry parent whose ire is roused, not so much by a proven injustice but because 'that school' is the nearest scapegoat when life becomes turbulent. A detention argued over, a complaint that 'my child is being picked on by your teachers', too much homework, not enough homework, lost property, squabbles between pupils – parental complaints which are the outward and visible signs of inward, invisible stress. A head serving the community in the latter years of the twentieth century requires infinite patience, the gift of logical thought, eloquence with which to express it and an inbuilt capacity to de-personalize the wrath. Occasionally the attacks are personal: usually they are not. Many caring heads are not always prepared to see the difference and pay heavily for their sensitivity.

Through the 1960s and early 1970s, the client relationship between schools and parents was able to develop in a relatively stable context. The last decade, however, has seen great changes. Two developments have come upon the scene which are having a profound effect on home/school relations. The first is increasing consumerism, represented by the freedom parents have been given to choose their school, enshrined in the 1980 Education Act. Superficially it is an attractive proposition. Choice of school should enhance family motivation and provide a headstart of support and enthusiasm. As a concept it has attracted the attention of politicians and pressure groups and has been specially welcomed by middle-class parents who tend to have more motivated youngsters. The criteria through which parents exercise that choice and the decisions which they make can cause serious problems of distortion for the secondary head. All schools' public examination results are now public property in the local library. It may only be a matter of time before the first 'Good learning guide' compiled by a parent pressure group along the lines of a 'Good eating guide' appears on the local newsagent's shelves. Value judgements are arrived at without taking account of staff movement, quality of entry, local authority policy or any of the other multifarious factors which skew results in a particular subject in a particular year.

The only way in which a head can set the record straight in sensible terms is to publish an annual report which allows all a school's constructive achievements to be set in context alongside examination results, and these make more sense when set out not by subjects but in a year profile with a national comparative (fig. 9.6). Results set out in this way are more meaningful than comparing small subject entries which are not statistically significant.

If pecking orders become a consuming passion within an area, there are dangers for the quality of secondary provision as a whole.

DES categories	National statistics	Loamshire County High School
1 Pupils leaving school without qualifications	11.38	3.3
2 Pupils achieving CSE grades 2–5	35.94	47.8
3 Pupils achieving 1–4 GCE grades A, B or C or CSE grade 1	26.61	26.7
4 Pupils achieving 5 or more GCE grades A, B or C (but no A levels)	9.61	10.4
5 Pupils achieving 1 GCE A level	3.00	2.7
6 Pupils achieving 2 GCE A levels	4.11	1.7
7 Pupils achieving 3 GCE A levels	9.35	7.4

Fig. 9.6 Academic achievements of leavers expressed as a percentage of the total number who left during the year.

Favoured schools, and that normally means those which serve more up-market housing, cream off the more able and biddable pupils from adjoining schools whose catchment area is less well endowed. The latter obtain poorer public examination results and have smaller, less viable sixth forms. So fewer parents choose them and the attrition continues in a vicious, downward spiral. If the balance is more even between competing schools, however, heads could find themselves pursuing a less innovatory curricular policy since parents who appreciate choice tend to opt for the familiar.

The effects of the onset of consumerism have been sharpened by contraction. From the school's point of view parental choice and falling rolls relate disastrously. If the schools are left part empty because other more popular establishments have room, full curriculum provision in the first sector is hard to maintain. Staff redeployment becomes inevitable and morale dips. Planned admission levels fixed by an LEA seek to sustain a policy of sharing the misery equally. They can still fail to provide a balanced entry. In the final battle of wills at an appeal hearing, the rights of particular parents may receive more attention than the educational welfare of the children as a whole who live in that area.

These are forces beyond the power of a head to control, though there are certain principles which stand immutable:

1 Parental enquiries must be given a high priority.
2 The law requires full information to be supplied.
3 LEA rules regarding planned admission levels must be strictly
  adhered to.
4 Good relations with neighbouring schools remain a top priority.
5 All heads will seek to do the best for their own schools.

On occasion these principles can be diametrically opposed. It is at
such times that management skills are at a premium.

With so much activity on the parental front, the question must be
asked: is there an ideal parent/teacher relationship? Chapter 8 ex-
plores some of the many ways in which parents can help a school
and enrich the quality of its life. It must nevertheless be recognized
that from time to time there is likely to be tension between the natural
over-riding concern of parents for the progress of their own child,
and the equally proper concern of the school for the welfare of the
pupils as a whole. Sometimes it may be impossible to reconcile the
two; constructive compromise will then be the only way of resolving
the issue.

Schools are not ends in themselves. They serve communities
beyond their walls, various though they be: the area in which the
school is situated, local firms, further education colleges, and institutions of higher education. In differing ways these too are clients
of the school since they will accept or reject its products and therefore
have a legitimate voice and one which must be listened to.

The local community

Take first the community – not one whit concerned with the cognitive
objectives of the target model (fig. 9.1) but liable to become
especially heated over certain facets of the affective objectives. Local
residents hold views about schools which are in direct proportion to
their proximity to the flight path. Children going to and from school
en masse and without supervision are not always at their best. The
blandishments of mobile sweet or fish-and-chip vans result in litter;
modern methods of merchandizing play into the hands of the shop
lifter; heavy urban traffic encourages cycling on pavements; and the
complexities of adolescent relationships are such that when schools
close, they do not remain frozen until 9.00 am the next day but erupt
on the streets after youth club sessions, at hours and in ways not
approved of by the community.

Here are another set of tensions which come the way of the head.
The question needs asking: how far can or should a head be

responsible for actions of pupils outside school? The law allows heads to take measures with pupils who misbehave travelling to or from school but it does not lay a requirement upon them. The community takes a different view. From a bus company: 'We have children presenting old tickets to conductors; will you please deal with them?' From a letter in a local paper: 'I have challenged youngsters who are the cause of most of the paper, cans and litter and I have written to the head since I noted that his (sic) pupils were the worst offenders. He said he was not responsible for what takes place outside the school but he did say he would draw pupils' attention to the matter. If he did, there's been no improvement.' In both instances, complaints were being registered because of the alleged offenders' membership of a school community, though in the first case their status was as passengers in a public service vehicle (for whom inspectors are at work to prevent fraud). In the second the alleged offences were committed in their capacity as community residents (for whom the police act as watchdogs) and their parents bear responsibility.

In both cases the head is called on to solve community ills. It is an unreasonable demand since the scale of operation is too great and the resources inadequate. The head is a head and not an omnicompetent local marshal. To ignore this dimension, though, is to court disaster and cause other problems. The public will say: 'The school is not interested, ∴ the school cannot care less about standards, ∴ that is not the school to which we will send our children' (especially if they are bright and there is a range of local choice). So the school loses out in reputation and pupils.

Again compromise is necessary. Limited, well-thought-out strategies can produce surprising results. The head who occasionally parks his car on the pupils' route home and merely observes can have a beneficial effect far beyond the size of the input. Cultivating the goodwill of the police can move mobile fish-and-chip vans with surprising alacrity. Giving positive assistance to a shopkeeper who has been the victim of theft but who wishes to use the school rather than the courts to recover her goods can improve local goodwill to the school enormously. Other preventative work is possible. Looking for openings for community service, especially to the young, old or handicapped builds up local community contacts which are invaluable sources of easement when problems arise. In compact areas where a number of social services make a contribution to a defined area, there are not infrequently monthly working lunches where the professionals of the caring services from a width of disciplines meet to discuss common problems and ideas. A community-minded head can give and receive valuable assistance.

The community at large will appreciate its school if it believes in it –

a trust which is rooted in justification by works. The head who is alert to the value of public prestige will make every endeavour to provide good foundations for that belief, or the school as a whole will suffer.

Employers

Among this community at large stand employers who are clients with quite specific requirements. Their future prosperity is determined by the quality of their workforce, progressively made up by school leavers who in return seek the economic freedom which employment brings. Such a mutually dependent situation argues for a close working partnership between school and industry. In reality it is often an uneasy relationship. The connections are not always securely founded. From the school side there lies a fundamental anxiety. While it is accepted that the economic well-being of the country will founder if industry is not well served by the products of the schools, heads and staff fear that if the learning process is totally subservient to the requirements of industry, liberal education will die. It is a key tension. It manifests itself in workaday decisions over curricular planning, fourth and fifth year option models, sixth form provision and careers counselling. How far should educational opportunity be open-ended and how far tailor-made to meet particular industrial needs? The kind of issues which arise may be instanced:

1 Industrialists have always taken a distorted view of the target model (fig. 9.1) above. The engineers put a premium on physics; the food industry sets chemistry on a pedestal; most employers demand mathematics at a pre-conceived level when what they mean is arithmetic. Some professional bodies will not even count certain GCE O-level 'passes' in some subjects they believe to be irrelevant – an arrogance which does not make for good relations. Does an employer exist who regards all areas of the curriculum as equally important?

2 Standards of judgement also differ. A pupil struggling with arithmetical computation in the fifth year gets a mark of 7/10 together with encouraging praise from his teacher. The same pupil, employed perhaps by a carpet-fitter, will soon find that he will lose his job unless his sums are invariably right – 7/10 will not do. The distinction needs to be recognized by teacher, pupil and employer alike.

3 'Close gap between school and jobs,' cries the Institute of Directors in a submission to the Secretary of State in April 1984. It is a plea to which many heads would subscribe until it is appreciatd that one

of the directors' propositions is that O level has proved its worth and should be retained. Are the potential advantages of a 16+ examination not known or just not appreciated? And whose fault if they are not?

4 An introduction to high technology is an obvious curricular need for future school leavers. The schools who have become involved with the range of equipment provided under the MSC-funded TVEI scheme have been impressed by its facilities and the way in which pupils of all abilities have profited from it. If this is a fundamental need for all, how can such curricular development be funded from normal resources?

5 A think-tank report submitted to government suggested that schools would serve industry more usefully if they were all privatized and were financed by direct company funding. If this ocurred, would art, drama, music, poetry and other related 'non-essentials' survive?

6 Difficulties arise in providing pre-vocational courses in sixth forms where there is an obvious demand, in opposition to government sponsored YTS schemes; and advising students appropriately.

7 Schools are not only preparing their pupils for employment but also for lack of it. Such a situation requires schools to re-think curricular priorities, with coping skills set as equal objectives to working skills.

These are only a few of the many tensions which a head and staff face as they consider their responsibility to industry. A middle road is called for, which could include the following suggestions:

1 Providing careers education to all pupils as part of the care curriculum to ensure a measure of economic literacy in all abilities.

2 Restructuring syllabuses, where the subject allows, to develop technological capability and encourage creativity.

3 Including information technology at a broad and basic level, sufficient to enable a student to embark on specialist training, which assumes the fundamentals, after leaving school.

4 Constructing a balanced curriculum which will close no career doors up to 16, yet provide satisfactory springboards for those who wish to move in specialist directions beyond that age.

5 Strengthening pre-vocational education in the upper levels of schools in terms of simulated company experience, work experience, residential opportunities and community service and in other ways which bring young people into contact with the world beyond the school gates.

6 Pursuing close local industrial links which bring each into active partnership without subservience.

Industrialists could contribute helpfully to most of these propositions. Whether they do in a given local situation is dependent on
many factors. One thing is certain: such partnership has to be worked
for. Directed cooperation is not within the head's gift: it has to be
striven for beyond the boundaries of the school. Considerable rewards, however, exist for the school whose head shares the same
entrepreneurial skills as the best of his local employers.

Higher education

Heads of 11 to 18 schools or post-16 colleges can add one further
member to their list of clients – the world of higher education in the
personalized form of admission tutor, course directors, heads of
departments and professors. One common theme which runs
through this chapter is the lack of unanimity among individual clients.
To expect it is to anticipate the impossible. Vice-chancellors talk
persuasively of curricular innovation while admission tutors are concerned that their future students have studied the right things in the
right way. No two academic institutions are likely to hold the same
views about sixth-form courses and what should be included. The
only common ground which can be identified is the current interest
in the cognitive and affective areas of the target model (fig. 9.1).

Traditionally heads have stereotyped the universities in the role of
ogres as a result of the pressure they inflict both in kind and extent on
sixth-form courses and examinations. It is not difficult to justify this
contention. Competition for places is fierce and conditional offers for
the more sought-after courses in the more popular places are so high
that A-level work can be an intense experience, with little
opportunity to move away from the strict confines of the scheme of
work – especially in the sciences, where the expanding frontiers of
knowledge are making syllabus-loading particularly onerous. The
national failure rate of undergraduate students is as high as 20 per
cent and heads are deeply concerned that their star pupils can
become a wastage statistic. There is too much evidence of unhappy
interactions between student and institution to allay school disquiet.
Higher education defines particular goals to be achieved within a
prescribed time limit, and provides what has been described by Dr A.
Ryle, Director of the University of Sussex Health Service, as a
'combination of pressure and supports and a fair degree of chaos'.
The study skills requisite for success and the personal qualities
necessary for survival must be of a high order. Both need time and
space in which to mature in the sixth form and heads generally are
concerned that the 1¾ years available is too brief a time to prepare

their students properly for all eventualities in higher education. Heads would also argue that the top 10–15 per cent of the country's intellects will only pass through the system once and since they are likely to make a major contribution to the economy of the country they are a precious resource and no stage of their development should be left to chance. Universities could use the same argument to press for greater control over the preparatory years. One easement would be lengthening the undergraduate course, but this is hardly likely at a time of financial retrenchment.

A head has other problems than those relating to pressure and grades. Contemporary sixth formers reflect a much broader academic profile in comprehensive schools than can be found in selectives. Not all A-level students could or should go on to higher education, for the sixth form provides a valuable learning experience for all abilities. Such a width of interest, however, makes a common purpose difficult to inspire. If a school regards the potential under-graduates as a first priority, the 'new' sixth formers could be short-sold. If the non-traditional members occupy the lion's share of staff time and resources, some who could have gone on to higher education may not. If this occurs to any significant degree, the school suffers a loss of confidence and individuals lose opportunities. The contraction of sixth form rolls represents a further pressure point. To offer a reasonable choice to all, there is an acceptable irreducible range of 12 A levels which should be on offer: shrinking numbers may curtail that curriculum. The prospect of broadening sixth-form studies with the introduction of A/S levels could be useful to many students but whether this is the most propitious time with regard to numbers and staff is debatable.

A look into the future also gives cause for disquiet. Two current issues relating to the world of higher education have serious im-plications for schools. The first relates to the projection for university places over the next decade. The government has calculated that because there will be fewer 18-year-olds in the 1990s, higher education places could be cut. This was begun in 1981. The statistics on which the calculations were based have come in for considerable criticism since they appear to have failed to take into sufficient account factors which will significantly affect demand – in particular the social class of prospective undergraduates. The fall in the birth rate has affected working-class families more than middle-class ones where demand for higher education is stronger. This situation will put more pressure on heads and schools and worsen the tensions mentioned above.

Not only is the number of undergraduates to change by the 1990s but so too will the balance of degree courses on offer if the

Swinnerton-Dyer document 'Development of a strategy for higher education into the 1990s' is accepted. The thrust of these proposals produced by the chairman of the University Grants Committee is that the country needs more good science graduates and fewer in arts and social sciences. If universities respond to a 'shift towards the technological, scientific and engineering courses and other vocationally relevant forms of study' what effect will that have on schools? The national advertisement placed by a head for a physicist to teach to O level, which received one application, is a salutary demonstration of the head's dilemma. There can be no effective channelling of students into technology if the teachers are not available to take them there – to say nothing of the moral issue of whether student undergraduate places should be the subject of coercion at all. Freedom to study what one wishes is a long and deeply cherished tradition which heads would not relinquish without a struggle.

In examining the tensions inherent in meeting the needs of a diversity of clients, one factor remains constant: the rôle of the head is crucial to their satisfaction. Rarely is this a simple demand-and-response operation. More often it is a matter of setting out fundamentals, perceiving what is going on in the world and deciding priorities. Since instability created by changing circumstances is the only permanent feature of the scene, the result will always be compromise – each successive issue, it is hoped, obtaining an inspired solution but not a perfect one. Perfection is not on the agenda.

10 Changing the curriculum in a school

George Gyte

The issues and their backcloth

The challenge of changing the curriculum is one to which every head seeks to respond at some time during a headship. How that response is shaped and textured will vary enormously depending on the individual, the circumstances, the needs, the resources available, the 'climate' prevailing in the school and the support – or lack of it – from the LEA. I shall seek to describe my own perceptions concerning change, the curriculum and the school. It will be, inevitably, subjective and descriptive rather than objective and universally valid. (I am not in fact sure that this area of work can be objective and universal since it appears to me that the factual knowledge isn't yet available or systematized.) Certain assumptions will be made about the process of innovation in school and while they may be stated assertively, nevertheless their validy is a question of belief rather than knowledge.

While I shall be discussing the nature of changing the curriculum in a general way, I shall draw, inevitably, on my seven years experience of headship at the Springfield/Keldholme School and relate to facets of change there. In particular, the introduction of a social education programme with substantial community and industrial involvement will be an important experience I shall draw upon, as will be the planning for amalgamation during the year 1982–83. While several aspects of school life altered and changed during those seven years, these two key experiences will illuminate some important considerations thought to be necessary as reflections on the process and practice of changing the curriculum in a school.

When I arrived at Springfield in 1977 the school had been marked by a long period of stable leadership given by the headmaster who had opened the school in 1959. It was organized on traditional, streamed lines, certain key academic departments having a very influential 'say' in the management and organization of the school. Decision-making rested very much with the head, with some delegation to the deputy head. The school served a markedly deprived catchment area: it was one of the three schools in the county of Cleveland defined as a social priority area school and given the appropriate allowances. There was no parent-school association, hence parental involvement was minimal and turn-out at consultation evenings very low. However, its top-stream children did very well in examinations, and the school had a good reputation locally in this respect.

In many ways it was a school ready for change with several staff who were anxious for a different approach to the organization and management of the school as well as to curricular considerations and questions concerning teaching styles and relationships. The important headship task was to give that group a focus of interest and energy while providing enough safeguarding processes to ensure initiatives would not founder on reactionary rocks, nor be carried away by a bubbling enthusiasm which fizzled out when faced with the logistical problems of implementation.

An important coincidence of needs emerged during the autumn term of 1977. The Schools Council Industry Project was sifting through LEAs for prospective project areas. It settled on Cleveland as one of the five, and the LEA, in turn, settled on the Middlebeck base as the location within the county: Springfield was one of the four schools on that base. SCIP was a project jointly sponsored by the CBI and the TUC and was concerned to encourage liaison and links between schools and industry. Thus we had a school ripe for change (though not likely to acknowledge that!), a staff with certain members at an important stage in their professional development and looking for a way forward, an untapped community anxious for a way in, a national project aimed at fostering and encouraging local initiatives, and a new head looking for starting points for change. The big question was *how* to do it.

Before I proceed to tackle that question there is a further element which must be outlined. Cleveland was a county that boomed in the sixties. By the late 1970s it was clear that the industrial base of the county would need to shed manpower on a massive scale in order to survive in the eighties. Because Cleveland had a higher-than-average child population it was inevitable that the resulting unemployment would have an enormous impact on school leavers. Thus, the way in which the school responded to the curricular reach-back of youth unemployment and prototype YTS schemes was bound to have a bearing on the morale and motivation of its young people. To that backcloth must be added the critical issue of falling rolls (30 per cent in Cleveland) with its attendant anxieties over curriculum planning, staffing, re-deployment, morale and professional development of staff. Altogether this is a pretty bleak picture which contrasts sharply with the 'growth and change' era of the sixties when I cut my early teaching teeth. This was a contrast which presented a rather daunting prospect in 1977–78, but in point of fact the gloomy scenario was vividly and widely off the mark, as events were to prove.

Literature concerning the process of innovation in the comprehensive school is rather scarce. Thus there were no handy 'ready references' to which we could turn for guidance or advice. Incidentally, I make no apologies for referring to the *process* of innovation. It is all too easy for schools to be obsessed with the change *product* – its packaged outcomes and cosmetic issues – rather than with the difficult, painful, daunting, exciting and demanding process which has to be gone through in order to find the methodologies and strategies which work for you and the rhythms for teaching and learning in the new situation which will secure the developments into the wider practice of the whole school.

Rogers states what he considers to be five important stages that the innovation process must go through: awareness, interest, trial, evaluation, adaptation.[26] His work has run into criticism in that several have argued that his model cannot easily be applied to the school situation since the individual teacher (let alone pupil!) does not have the freedom which one of his basic assumptions implies: that at any point in the process he or she can decide whether to try it or not.

Gross, Giacquinta and Bernstein argue that the organizational structure prevailing in schools suggests that the change process in a school works differently to that in other institutions or organizations.[27] They suggest that the process moves through three critical phases.

1 The period of the initiation of an organizational innovation.
2 The period of its attempted implementation.
3 The period during which an innovation is incorporated into the organization.

Furthermore, Gross et al would argue that the most under-studied and under-valued phase has been that concerned with understanding the 'implementation period' of the innovation process. Interestingly, they went on to isolate five conditions which they felt had to be fulfilled before a change in a school could be said to be successful:

1 Participants in the project concerned must have understood the new method of working *on their own terms* [my italics].
2 Participants must have, or be able to obtain, skills in working in the new ways.
3 Participants must have access to materials and resources which enable them to work in the new way.
4 The school organization must be open enough to accept the change in parts other than the one in which the change project is being undertaken, in order that the change is not blocked.
5 Those who participate in the proposed change must not feel they have been compelled to participate.[28]

While I am not sure that all of these five conditions were understood (let alone met!) in the Springfield situation of 1978, nevertheless the five key figures provide a useful evaluation check list for readers, and indeed a planning guide for would-be innovators.

The practice of changing the curriculum at the Springfield/ Keldhome school had as much to do with altering the nature of relationships – between teacher and young people, teacher and teacher, teacher and adult-other-than-teacher – as it did with working methods, materials and resources. Thus a research project which I found came closest to my own view of the innovation process undertaken by schools was that produced by Ekholm, Sandström, Svanberg and Tjellander.[29] In their work they analyzed four phases: preparation, accommodation, application and circulation. While the phraseology might strike English ears as rather quaint on translation, nevertheless those stages did strike me as very pertinent to our operation in Cleveland. I felt that our attempts to change the curriculum and hence organization at the school moved through four similar cycles of activity: (i) preparing for change; (ii) implementing the change; (iii) incorporating the change into the school structures; and (iv) disseminating the change in the wider school and community context. I shall proceed then to describe our work under those four adapted headings.

Preparing for the change

When I reflect on the attempt to introduce a social education programme into a tightly packed academic offering for years four and five at Springfield School, it does appear to me that several preparatory ingredients were responsible for its later success. Three key ingredients were: a fairly bold (in hindsight!) marking out of timetable time, the multi-disciplinary teaching team and the creation of a working party composed of teachers from the school, employers, industrialists, small businessmen and women, trade unionists, parents, an industrial chaplain, a careers officer and a school psychologist. Perhaps, though, the cornerstone of this phase was a shared recognition of the problem: the need for a programme of activities and experiences which prepared our young people for life after school. This was accompanied by an equally recognized and shared awareness that in 1978 in Cleveland, no one group of people – teachers, employers, parents or pupils – had a monopoly of wisdom as far as that programme was concerned.

Discussion about this curricular innovation took place within school in a changed decision-making framework. We had evolved a system of forum groupings – a mix of staff with different curricular backgrounds and levels of experience in each group, which numbered no more than twelve and which had a chairman who was no higher than scale 2 in the scales hierarchy – reporting to senior staff meetings, the senior decision-making body in the school. Thus there was ample opportunity for a wider discussion concerning the social education programme by those staff who were not directly involved – a participative audience whose strategic importance we did not recognize until later!

The new course had certain objectives and approaches that broke with the tradition of the school:

1 It had a full half-day block of time with a full year group operating in mixed ability groups: a flexible structure.
2 It brought together a multi-disciplinary team of teachers drawn from different academic backgrounds and with a range of expertise which we hoped would make for experimentation of approach and variety of initiatives in the work. (This feature was to prove crucial in gaining acceptance by heads of departments for the necessary time allocation for the course.)
3 It had a view of the community as provider, influence and user. This view enabled us to establish links with industry, the trade unions, commerce, the worlds of work and unemployment, and other facets of community life; and this in turn stretched our imagination and widened the scope of what we were able to offer.
4 The methodology chosen for teaching was a group work approach with outsiders (adults other than teachers) closely involved in building up relationships with youngsters.
5 The working party saw its work as being concerned as much with

the process of learning as with the product. It was for this reason that right from the outset we began to create frameworks for enabling adults other than teachers to be involved in planning curricular activities and in the actual teaching situations.

The kinds of teaching units and modules which have emerged have been well documented elsewhere and to describe them is not the purpose of this chapter.[30] Rather, I have chosen to illustrate how the aims and nature of that work were such a change of direction for the school – in terms of the relationships between teachers and pupils they were almost a scene change.

Several crucial elements need to be borne in mind:

1 Sharing a defined view of the problem and hence the need for change.
2 Using outsiders from the wider community so that their experience and expertise is a significant resource, not to replace the teacher but to enhance his work.
3 Having an 'open agenda' approach to the initial discussions and meetings before moving to concrete and practical applications and to lesson planning, jointly carried out by teachers and AOTs.
4 Taking a considerable amount of time over discussion and de-liberations at meetings both of the working party and of the teaching team, and taking time over – at this stage – short-term evaluation.

The first point is very important and it is imperative that prime attention is given to gaining a shared view among the people con-cerned, whether that be via meetings during or after school, at a local teachers centre or at a school-based residential in-service course. We found the second point concerning outsiders most fruitful in that they performed a variety of rôles: as teaching resource, consultant, critical evaluator, alternative viewpoint, champion of pupils' rights and res-ponsibilities, trainer, motivator and encourager. Indeed, several be-came true critical friends.

The third issue is of even more vital importance since the great danger involved in curriculum innovation occurs at two levels. There is the danger of the teachers concerned becoming isolated from their colleagues. Rumours and myths abound and can quickly lead to unnecessary resistance, as the social education teaching team at Springfield found when it began the relationships module involving various kinds of games and rôle-play exercises. Furthermore such attempts at breaking new ground can easily be construed as a damning criticism of existing teaching approaches. Thus, the need for an *open* approach to discussions where staff not directly involved can sit in, will go some way to avoiding unnecessary friction. Equally, of course, it is carrying the debate about innovation into a wider sphere: clarity of purpose, direction and application on the part of innovators will always help scotch unnecessary and damaging speculation.

The final concept has very considerable relevance to a successful undertaking. It became a paramount concern at Springfield/ Keldholme that in those areas where we were taking new curriculum initiatives there was a need to talk the issues through, to share individual and mutual apprehensions as well as provide opportunities and structures for mutual support. Teaching team meetings took place monthly during the evenings in different team members' homes. They alternated between structured and open agenda meetings and enabled clarification of policy and practice, and sharing and support to take place, as well as continuing evaluation. These meetings were open to the members of the working party and many took advantage of the opportunity to build and strengthen their links with the school and staff.

Implementing the change

Once the heady level of discussion involved in planning and pre-paring a major curricular initiative has been undertaken, the crunch arrives when implementation takes place. This period in the in-novation process occurs when ideas, tactics and strategies are tested out. In our case two needs quickly became apparent: the adults (teachers and AOTs) needed to share responses, feelings and reactions in order to change tack on emphasis, while we needed to find out how the pupils were reacting and responding to the new approaches.

In the case of the Springfield social education programme the structures were available for the teachers and other adults to discuss and consider their progress so far at the monthly working party meetings, at the weekly lunchtime team meetings which occurred after the morning's programme of activities, and at the ad hoc meetings of the small sub-groups of teachers and other adults who had planned the teaching units. Finding out how the youngsters responded to the new teaching units and the different teaching methodology was a different and, at first, difficult proposition.

Most of our past normal teaching strategy had been based on 'sensing' a class's response to the work, and using a kind of dipstick approach when talking with individuals about particular lessons. The working party members, though, were anxious to gain information about how, for example, the programme about trade unions had been viewed by the youngsters. They weren't deflected by such generalized teacher statements as 'Well I think my group enjoyed it'. They wanted to know what the kids themselves thought! This really began an important process of devising appropriate methods for pupil evaluation for the whole course. We developed a strategy of using questionnaires, pair work or quartet work and whole group de-briefing and evaluation. The information received proved to be, at different times, encouraging, satisfying, daunting, shattering or demanding. By way of example: a sub-group of teachers and five trade unionists spent several days planning the unit of lessons con- cerned with this aspect of the course. They gathered together useful video material, worksheets, booklets and specialist inputs from known and sound sources. It was a very thorough and well-planned scheme of work. After the three weeks' work was completed we evaluated the work with the groups and they tore it to shreds! We quickly gathered the view that it had been too 'expert orientated', too much like a bad set piece history lesson, too passive, and too 'boring'. The planning group sat down to consider the feedback and pick up the pieces: the outcome was a highly successful simulation experience with the emphasis on an active, experiential learning process with youngsters, teachers, trade unionists, managers and parents rôle-playing different personae on a construction toy car assembly line. The preparation, experience and subsequent evaluation proved to be one of the most significant turning points in our course.

Thus, this second phase of implementing a change in the curriculum is important for the testing out of ideas, ways of working and methods of relating to each other. It is a stage at which strategy needs to be capable of being altered without any accompanying sense of insecurity, uncertainty or failure. There is a vital need then for structures to exist which enable reflection and short-term analysis to take place. Really it is a justification for the kind of catalytic and process-aiding function of the agent of change as defined by Havelock whereby there is a recognition that for successful school curricular innovation to take place there is an important need to be aware that the rôle of the teacher and the rôle of the pupil are inextricably bound up together. A change in the rôle of one in- evitably leads to a demand for changes in the other.[31]

One other key facet of this second phase of implementation was the growing recognition that whilst the course was *working* there was an overwhelming demand for an in-service course for the teachers and other adults. With LEA and central project help we mounted a first two-day venture at a North Yorkshire country hotel in

Goathland. It consisted of the teaching team of twelve, a similar number of adults other than teachers, together with (significantly and strategically) six staff who, while they did not want to teach on the course nevertheless were interested in what was happening. They came to call themselves 'touchliners': while they did not want to play in the game, they were interested spectators. What is more, they proved useful allies in terms of allaying fears, anxieties and mis-understandings which might have arisen between the team and the other departmental areas.

Incorporating the change

The third decisive phase in a curricular development process is when the change is bedded down into the rhythm of the school. It is at this stage that acceptance can be safely assumed. New patterns of work-ing and ways of relating become a normal feature of the life of the school and clearly indicate that the philosophy on which they are based has now been internalized and fundamental rôle changes made.

Our third stage at Springfield was characterized by such features as more shared responsibilities for the different teaching units; a clear pattern for introducing and supporting new teaching team members; short in-service courses (half-day) prior to each new term's work led by existing team members to introduce new members to the activities and approaches as well as to refresh and replenish older and more experienced colleagues; and a markedly more confident and more determined in-service input from the AOTs.

This third phase appears to be a safe one: in fact it hides some profound dangers for would-be curriculum developers! There is a real risk that the converts to the change may make the mental leap of assuming that the new ways of working have a universal application for the whole school – indeed for all schools! Some American research has suggested that the longer an individual has been in-volved in an attempted change, the greater the need he or she has to maintain that the basic idea on which the change rests is worthwhile and useful, that it has an almost extra truthfulness and validity. However this tendency must be guarded against since it often pro-vides ammunition for the cynics. More importantly though, it works against a pluralist view of the teaching experience and it can lead to the feeling that the 'right approach' has been found, when the search is on for an open school which embraces a variety of teaching approaches. Certainly there were problems that arose from this novel experience – not least in staffroom dynamics.

Another anxiety concerned the youngsters themselves. With the early cohorts the new patterns of working and ways of relating in the groups had an excitement and momentum that was different and unique. Later groups were more familiar, had experienced similar approaches in other areas of the lower school curriculum taught by team members or those interested in the methodologies (for example, drama), and therefore their levels of expectation were that much more demanding. The openness of the group situation meant that the teacher/leader had to learn to use the group itself as the disciplining process with would-be saboteurs, and perhaps recognize that the initial level of conflict might be higher than exists in a traditional classroom situation.

The way through the incorporation phase of changing the curriculum for us was a rather different strategy. In order to clarify the stage which had been reached and to allow for a total evaluation of the course, plans were laid for an evaluation day course involving pupils, parents, teachers and adults other than teachers. The local college of education was borrowed for a Saturday and some seventy individuals met reflecting those different interest groups. There were small group and plenary sessions which enabled thoughtful and shared reflection on the two-year programme together with suggestions for alterations, deletions and additions for the next two-year course. This particular event proved to be yet another turning point in the course, and in the personal and professional development of all involved. Equally, it was a crucial part in the renewal process so necessary to maintain the programme's momentum.

Disseminating the change

One clear measure of the extent to which a change in the curriculum has penetrated is the way in which participants have entered into the business of spreading their ideas, tactics, methods and approaches with other groups they work with and with other colleagues. This is an important and necessary clarifying phase since it serves several useful purposes. The hesitant change agent has become a successful initiator and is vested with an important task of dissemination which does wonders for doubting self-confidence. Additionally the process of explaining to others has a way of refining concepts and practice in our own minds and serves a useful focusing purpose. A questioning audience of whatever size is a fine sounding board for the intellectual and practical justification for our purpose and practice in changing the curriculum. I argue then, that this phase of dissemination within and outside the school is a very important part of the innovation process; that it would be foolish to underestimate its importance, since it marks the completion of the change circle for the individual teacher and the point of renewal for others who need to be encouraged. The Springfield-Keldholme staff have been involved in several INSET programmes with other schools which would fall into the dissemination category. Those experiences were powerful growth and development stages for the team members concerned and having grown, several of them have now moved on: promoted to more senior posts in other schools to initiate similar developmental approaches elsewhere.

It is interesting to note the pace and direction of curricular change at Springfield/Keldholme school against the kind of turbulent social and economic backcloth in the area which I outlined earlier in this chapter. I am sure that the nature of the managerial and decision-making structures which were evolving at the time had a great deal to do with enabling energy and dynamism to be released. In their study of traditional firms adjusting to the new situation of continuously changing technology and markets, Burns and Stalker (1961) were led to describe two ideal types of organizational structures which are the extreme points of a continuum along which most organizations can be placed. In stable conditions with a stable technology one will find a *mechanistic* type of organization where individuals will carry out their assigned, precisely defined tasks: there is a clear hierarchy of control with responsibility for overall knowledge and coordination resting exclusively at the top of the hierarchy; vertical communications and interactions (superior to subordinate) are stressed with an insistence on loyalty and obedience to superiors.[32]

However, in an unstable and turbulent environment where new ground is reached continually and unfamiliar problems arise which cannot be broken down and distributed among existing specialist roles, then our *organic* type of organization emerges. This is characterized by a continual adjustment and re-definition of individual tasks, 'less attention is paid to formal rules, more decisions reached at lower levels and communication is more common among lateral positions than vertical ones'.[33] More importantly, a much higher degree of commitment to the aims of the organization as a whole is generated. It does seem to me that where a school seeks to bring about a major curricular change, then some serious thinking has to take place about the nature of the climate within the school and the decision-making structures which best encourage innovation, adaptation and flexibility. At Springfield/Keldholme, the working party was an ad hoc arrangement charged with real responsibility for a major block of timetable time; the teaching team was a democratic and open gathering with no recognized head of department or acknowledged leader; and the work of these two groups took place against a changing backcloth towards a more open, consultative and participative school. I am sure that this context was responsible in great measure for the successful change which took place.

I am equally sure that successful innovation needs to move through the four phases I have attempted to describe if the changes are to reach a point of stability. It would be foolish not to recognize that a school's capacity for stability is in many ways a powerful resource, and one that is often neglected by the inexperienced cavaliers of the curriculum development world, who possibly see it as dogged resistance to change. Stability enables us to save those features we cherish and value for reasons other than habit. I suppose I am arguing that it is a good thing that changing the curriculum of a school is a difficult and long process: it means, as Sir Lincoln Ralphs once suggested, that the changes we perceive to be needed and work so hard for will be just as complex and demanding to disentangle. They need the application of a disciplined intelligence as much as of an enthusiastic heart.

11 Independent schools

Pamela Stringer

One of the features of the independent schools least-comprehended by colleagues in the maintained schools is probably their sheer variety. There is certainly no prototype 'independent school', and their very variety affords parents who elect to send their children to an independent school an extremely wide choice. Nor is there a typical pupil (or parent); many of the young people at present being educated in independent schools are first-generation pupils.

Analysis of variety

1 Provision   (a) fully boarding (b) fully day (c) day with some boarding (d) boarding with some day (e) weekly boarding. Length and timing of the school day (and indeed of school terms) are conditioned by the nature of such provision.

2 Educational tendency   (a) full ability range (b) upper ability range (c) highly academic (d) special abilities e.g. music, ballet, art, drama (e) special educational disabilities e.g. dyslexia.

3 Size   (a) very large e.g. Eton, Cheltenham Ladies' College (b) moderate (350–700) (c) relatively small.

4 Clientèle   (a) by *sex of pupils* (i) single-sex boys (ii) single-sex girls (iii) fully co-educational (iv) boys' schools with a small pro-portion of girls (often only in Sixth Form) (b) by *source of fees* (i) parents in 'socio-economic groups I and II (ii) grandparents (iii) emoluments for executives (largely contributions paid towards fees by firms employing parents overseas) (iv) long pre-planning by par-ents for school fees via various insurance-linked schemes (v) services and diplomatic etc. contributions (vi) scholarships offered by schools themselves from their own resources (vii) endowments and benefactions (viii) special charitable links e.g. freemasons, the army, the navy (ix) government assisted places.

5 Affiliations   (a) nil, except to national organizations (b) religious affiliations e.g. (i) Roman Catholic, run by either religious or lay personnel, or by a mixture of the two; (ii) Church of England, run by either religious or lay personnel, or by a mixture of the two – these include 24 boys' schools in the High Anglican tradition administered under the Woodard Corporation, and 8 girls' schools administered by the Church Schools Company. (iii) Methodist; (iv) Quaker, commonly, but not always, co-educational; (v) Girls' Public Day School Trust (GPDST): founded in 1872, it now comprises 24 schools. The Trust was a pioneer of day schools for girls characterized by both high academic standards and a broad general education.

That this wide variety appeals to parents is beyond doubt; it can even produce an *embarras de richesses*, but organizations such as the Independent Schools Information Service (ISIS) can do much to help prospective parents to make a systematic and realistic choice.

Responsibilities of the head

One of the immediately obvious effects of the fact of wide choice for parents is the consequent accountability of the head: one must provide what is appropriate for the pupils and attractive to parents, and also try to promote the merits of what is on offer without meretriciousness.

Both head and parents can, and should, learn a great deal of reciprocal benefit from an initial visit to the school and interview with the head. Prospective parents, when choosing their child's school, are contemplating an investment often nearly as costly and certainly no less important than the purchase of a house. Some parents may seem only too content to make over all responsibility, at least during term-time, for their childrens' education, moral and social welfare, recreation, health and emotional development to the school, particularly (but not exclusively) if it be a boarding school. In some parents this is a conscious and a positive virtue; in most it is born of a mixture of inertia, ineptitude and an attitude of 'after all, what am I paying for?' One of the really significant and salutary features of parental choice is that the parents do always have the choice of removing their child from a school – as heads, too, have the ultimate recourse of asking them to do so.

In assessing the needs and the actual requirements of prospective parents, the head needs insight mingled with entrepreneurial skills –

and needs to assess both what the pupil and parents will derive from the school and what they have to offer to the school. This latter idea often appeals to parents, who can sometimes help with, for example, arranging special access for school expeditions or educational visits, or sharing an interest or enthusiasm. Practical help of this kind further strengthens the bond between parents and school.

As the head is going to be *in loco parentis* to the child (and, in the case of a boarding pupil, to be so for 24 hours a day for 8 months of the year) the more the head can understand what that *locus* is, the better. Quite apart from meeting prospective parents (individually, as far as possible) a head's task vis-a-vis parents commonly and properly includes talking with them and counselling them where appropriate on any matter (i.e. almost everything) that could affect the child's life in school and his future. This communication is enhanced if it includes the head's seeking advice and responses from parents of present or recently-past pupils.

The rather 'contrived' atmosphere of open days, commemoration weekends, parents' association meetings, etc. is not and never should be considered as the only suitable ambience in which to meet parents: those parents who come to see you occasionally for no 'better' reason than that you have their child in your care are welcome but few. One important meeting point between parent and school is the written report. The content of such reports is of crucial importance in establishing good public relations. What a teacher writes should always be something which she would be prepared to say and to substantiate in a face to face meeting. Sometimes a report can turn out to contain nine or ten derogatory comments about a pupil's work and/or behaviour, so that parents are startled into the supposition that they have bred a stupid, idle or evil child. Not one of the writers may have had any intention to convey that message, imagining perhaps that the incidents which they had recalled at report-time would be referred to by nobody else. And such misdemeanours may have been trivial and easily contained at the time. Parents deserve to be told the truth, but a constructive and proportioned truth, and in words which will foster the good as well as discouraging the bad.

The governing body

The head has a prime and clear responsibility to the governing body of the school – and the head of an independent school is in many ways fortunate in serving (usually) but one master – and that a group containing few, if any, statutory representatives of external bodies, not vulnerable to political change. The freedoms enjoyed by independent governing bodies and their heads are many but depend on mutual confidence. The head is normally responsible for the overall conduct of the school, for the direction of the teaching curriculum and for the maintenance of discipline; as an important corollary, the head is usually solely responsible for the appointment of all teaching staff. The wide autonomy afforded to the head means that the head must be able to inspire in the governing body full confidence that they will be kept continually well-informed about the state of the school so that they can discharge their responsibilities properly.

A prudent but democratically-inclined head must quite often these days, amid clamours for pupil-power, for parent-representation on governing bodies, and for ever greater consultation with all one's staff, be like someone trying to drive a double-decker bus along a corniche through thick fog with the help of sixty or so back-seat drivers. A head must aim for constructive reconciliation of conflicting claims and interests, while avoiding feeble compromise. It is essential in this difficult situation that the relationship between the head and the governing body be one of the fullest possible frankness and trust.

Staff and curriculum

The head's control over the appointment of staff gives an invaluable freedom (loaded with commensurate responsibility). Occasionally, heads of independent schools may find it useful or politic to seek specialist advice from one or more of the governing body with regard to a key appointment. But they do not commonly suffer the frustrations and delays of waiting for an appointments board to convene (meanwhile almost certainly losing one's most favoured applicants to another school); and all heads would as a matter of course consult the relevant heads of department already on their staff. Independent heads normally enjoy control over the actual deployment of staff, within the constraints of the budget; this clearly makes both innovation (e.g. craft, design and technology) and con-servation (e.g. Classical Greek) in the curriculum much easier for heads in the independent system.

The head's responsibility for the curriculum, in consultation with the staff, is a heavy one, but again carries concomitant power. The allocation of time between subjects, the bias (or lack of it) demon-strated by the range of subject-options at, for instance, 14+ and 16+, the importance attached to minority and general subjects, particularly in the sixth form, the time devoted to physical education and organized sport, all reflect and inform the ethos of the school. Some heads extend their control of the curriculum to the actual making of the timetable themselves. Where this task is delegated, the head rightly shoulders any burden of odium and would probably accept the bouquets (if there ever were any).

Selection of pupils

The selection and the mode or modes of selection of pupils is a further prime responsibility. 'Selection' does not always or necessarily spell academic selection. Some independent schools quite deliberately engineer an ability-mix in their schools; some choose to cater for the all-rounder as well as for academic high-fliers; some show marked artistic, musical, athletic preferences, but a degree of selection is virtually inevitable as most independent schools are heavily over-subscribed.

Many, but by no means all, independent schools make use of the Common Entrance examination as an instrument of selection; for boys this is usually taken at age 13, for girls at 11, 12 or 13. Entry is normally at 11+ to those independent schools which were previously direct-grant grammar schools. Independent secondary schools using Common Entrance mark the papers themselves and can be as flexible or inflexible about pass marks as seems appropriate; there is certainly room for a head to take into account candidates' talents and qualities which do not readily lend themselves to formal testing. Those schools which do not use Common Entrance normally have their own entrance examination, and entry is almost always competitive rather than by qualification. Some heads prefer the convenience (to parents even more, perhaps, than to the schools) of the readily-comprehensible and clearly-formulated Common Entrance system; others painstakingly guard their autonomy and the presumed superior predictive powers of their own entrance tests. With any mode of selection for entry to independent schools, importance is attached to an interview with the prospective pupil, and most heads give weight to a confidential report from the candidate's previous school. Those schools which cater for a wide-ability range commonly teach some subjects over the whole range but other subjects (e.g. mathematics, French) in smaller sets of matched ability, so that the specially gifted as well as the strugglers can all have individual attention. Some schools make special provision for pupils with learning problems such as dyslexia, and help them to master the basic skills at their own speed in special groups.

Selection, then, for independent schools, is not in general according to any closely pre-structured scheme – and most heads will give special consideration to a candidate who already has a sibling in the school; to filial or sentimental connections with old pupils; and, most importantly, to marked parental preference.

Finance

While Heads and Bursars of Independent Schools are expected to operate in close liaison, it is usual for the Bursar to be primarily responsible to the Governing Body for the care and control of the finances of the School, for the administration and upkeep of the buildings and grounds and for the supervision of domestic and catering arrangements. It is to be expected that Head and Bursar will often consult each other and it is desirable that each appreciates the distinctive and complementary role of the other.

Ethos of the school

The head of any school conditions the ethos of that school, and the greater the freedoms of the head the heavier the responsibilities and the more immediate the blame. The sanctions available to the independent school head can be quickly implemented, and, if they be just, can be of instant assistance to the head and the staff in the maintenance of good order. The penalty of explusion can be, and in very serious cases is, invoked; it can be veiled as a 'request for the withdrawal' of a pupil. Even in an independent school which has not yet used this sanction, it is salutary for both pupils and their parents to know that it could be. Rustication and suspension are normally reserved for serious but not 'terminally serious' offences – and to back up these sanctions there is normally a battery of relatively minor punishments – for example, detentions, returned work, putting a pupil 'on report', withdrawal of privileges, and demotion.

Most heads find that the less codification and rule-listing there is, the better; the personal influence of staff and senior pupils is the strongest single factor likely to make for good discipline. Discipline is most efficiently maintained by force of personality, and the general sense of a well-ordered community getting on with things: the positive side of discipline, as enabling a young person within a community to 'do his/her own thing' in a variety of important ways, rather than the negative and disabling aspect of discipline, needs to be kept before our pupils.

Boarding

Those independent schools which are predominantly for boarders make demands on management and staffing extending well beyond the administrative demands of a purely day school. They draw their pupils from a very wide catchment area, and their clientèle includes expatriates and foreign pupils as well as young people from the

United Kingdom. It is very important that schoolchildren whose parents are resident abroad should have guardians in this country, to whom the Head can look, for example, for detailed arrangements for half-term holidays and occasional exeats; for confirming or disputing recommendations about course-choice, examination entry etc. when distance makes the quick implementation of parental decisions difficult. There could also be occasions such as the necessity for consenting to an emergency operation in the absence of a parent. The head does, of course, stand *in loco parentis* for all the boarders on a full-time, whole-term basis, so it is a safeguard and a reassurance to head and parents alike if there is the possibility of communicating quickly with a representative of the parents in this country.

Most independent boarding schools operate a house-system. The social structure of the houses varies, as might be expected, from school to school. Often, each house contains pupils from the whole age-range for which the school provides, for example 11+ – 18+, 13+ – 18+. Some schools have vertical grouping for the majority of their pupils but separate out, for example, the under-12s and/or the second-year sixth, into houses of their own. Whichever system operates, a usual boarding-house size is 50–60 pupils. The number and, much more importantly, the quality of the house staff in each house is a crucial factor in the happiness and success of any boardng-school.

Boarding-school life certainly can make young people more reliant and perhaps less self-centred: they have a chance to stand on their own feet; they also have to learn to live with people whose company they have not personally chosen and whose idiosyncrasies they have to accept. Remember Peanuts? – 'going to our school is an education in itself, which is not to be confused with actually getting an education'. This, whether we like it or not, is probably what boarding education is all about. There are, however, obvious dangers and difficulties arising from prolonged and continuous exposure to the society chiefly of one's own peer group. It is highly desirable, then, that in each boarding-house there should be enough responsible resident adults for their presence to be felt by the young and for the adults themselves not to become isolated or starved of adult society. If house supervisory staff do their job properly, it is an extremely exhausting one; if they are ineffective, the house suffers. Many heads have, we can be sure, had the experience of employing a succession of likely and likeable people who have simply not been able to stand for more than a few terms the inevitable wear and tear of living at close quarters with a crowd of energetic adolescents. Perhaps the stage has been reached at which boarding-school life is so enjoyable and eventful for the pupils that it is almost unendurable for the supervising adult.

Significant differences exist between the expectations of parents for their daughters in boarding care and their expectations for their sons – and these expectations are usually reflected in the regimes of every type of single-sex (male and female) as well as co-educational school.

The 24-hour commitment of top-line management in boarding-schools is clear where the health of boarders is concerned. Apart from general maintenance care (teeth, eyesight, skin problems, puberty, postural defects etc.) there is the responsibility for ensuring nursing care in cases of sickness, accident or infectious diseases; for the provision of skilled and competent first aid; for psychiatric and sometimes for sexual counselling. The provision of a full-scale sanatorium is less common than it used to be; it is more usual these days for each boarding house to have a small sick wing, with (probably) an isolation room, a small ward (2–6 beds), and a general 'surgery'. If there is a widespread epidemic in a boarding-house, it is fairly easy to annex adjacent dormitories as additional ward-space. It is clearly uneconomical to have a large sanatorium with most rooms lying idle. Barring accidents, a relatively empty sick bay is a far surer sign of the presence of a good matron who believes in positive health care than is a sanatorium packed with patients held in duress to give nursing-staff a *raison d'être*.

The curriculum of boarding-schools naturally spills outside the confines of a day-school teaching-day. This allows remarkable leeway for extra-curricular activities both educational and re-creational – it also inevitably poses heavy administrative and strategic problems for heads and house staff of boarding-schools. The chief potential problem is adolescent ennui; this, of course, is not peculiar to boarding schools or to single-sex schools. Most young adolescents seem to feel bored: one bored and restless 13–14 year-old in a household can be wearing; multiply this by 100 or so, and you have a real problem. Young people are, too, very apt to use 'I'm bored' as a get-out. It is occasionally salutary to tell them that they are boring – this is quite a new idea to many. Young people think they are happy if they are not organized – but are they? Parents judge a boarding-school partly by the quality and diversity of the provisions for the children's free time; it is as well for them, sometimes, that they are not judged by the occasional revealing remarks made by their children on their preferred activities outside the school term when the responsibility falls back on their parents.

Special problems and challenges facing heads of independent schools.

1 The task of reconciling the needs of the pupils with the expectations of their parents, with the standards demanded by the staff, with the strengths and the limitations of the staff, with the financial viability of the school; and with the need to keep up with (and/or pioneer) educational change.

2 The financial need to know the school's market well – and not to be forced by external (particularly financial) pressures into expedient tampering with the 'product'.

3 Pastoral care – at all hours, quite frequently.

4 The need to link the school with the local community. This can be achieved in many ways, not least by sharing the use of the school's facilities, for example swimming pool, sports centre, theatre. Also by opening the entire campus with all its resources, for example for holiday courses. Practical social service, for example helping the mentally handicapped or elderly, is another valuable link.

5 The need to discourage staff as well as pupils from becoming insular.

6 The need to know when to allow the governing body to know better than you do, even when you know you are omniscient in school matters!

7 The realization of the rôle ambiguity of the head – one of the most important causes of stress. The head has to be parent and mentor to the children and love them even if he or she doesn't, on occasion, actually like them; must be both colleague and leader to staff; is often called upon to act as marriage guidance counsellor, confessor, specialized careers adviser, psychologist, psychiatrist to parents; and is expected to be 'respectable' as well as 'human'.

8 The over-riding need to maintain a sense of proportion – the commonest of all casualties in the life of any school.

Associations and their abbreviations

GBA Association of Governing Bodies of Public Schools

GBGSA Association of Governing Bodies of Girls' Public Schools. GBA and GBGSA together act as the coordinating organizations for independent secondary schools. They act as advisory bodies for the governors of such schools on educational and administrative matters.

GSA Girls Schools Association. Membership around 200. Heads in membership are also members of SHA. The stated objects of GSA are (i) to discuss matters concerning the policy and administration of such schools, (ii) to consider their relation to the general educational interest of the community, and (iii) to express the views of heads on such matters and to take such action as may be appropriate.

HMC Headmasters' Conference. Traditionally, this is an association of individuals not of schools. It has a limited membership of just over 200. It was founded in 1896 when twelve headmasters met and conferred at Uppingham. Heads in membership are also members of the Secondary Heads Association (SHA).

IAPS Incorporated Association of Preparatory Schools

ISAI Independent Schools Association Incorporated. This includes both preparatory and secondary schools.

ISBA Independent Schools Bursars' Association

ISJC Independent Schools Joint Committee, which represents independent education at national level. This committee is the main financial sponsor for the Independent Schools Information Service (ISIS). ISJC consists of GBA, GBGSA, GSA, IAPS, HMC, SHMIS, ISBA, ISIS and ISAI. It speaks collectively on behalf of its members and considers matters of policy and administration common to its members.

SHMIS Society of Heads of Independent Schools. This consists mainly of Heads of smaller Independent boarding schools not in membership of HMC.

12 Community schools

Veronica Kerr

What is a community school?

The first point which must be established is that community schools are not a variation on the traditional theme – they are not ordinary schools which indulge in an additional, esoteric activity. Community schools are based on a radically different concept of education to that underlying the mainstream structure of formal education.

Extending Bernard Shaw's famous dictum that 'education is wasted on the young', why should education be exclusively the prerogative and duty of the young? The community school philosophy rejects both of these conditions. Andrew Fairburn (CEO Leicestershire from 1971 to 1984) wrote in 1978: '. . . the college can be regarded as a base where all members of the community can be involved in their own education'.[34] This approach encompasses a dual thrust: on the one hand it means making the enormously rich resources of schools freely available to the whole community; on the other hand it implies a fundamental change in the institutionalized process to which our young are statutorily submitted. The economic logic of opening up schools to a wider public is surely self-evident. In most communities, the school is the largest single public investment of buildings, material and expertise. Whether primary or secondary, the riches of modern carpeted rooms, catering facilities, gymnasia, swimming pools, pottery kilns, design work shops, computers etc. cannot justifiably be closed at 4 pm every day and closed entirely for 175 days each year. The school is not of course merely a physical resource. Again, in most communities it combines the greatest concentration of professional skill and knowledge with an extensive natural network of connections with most sections of the community. The impact of the community school on the education of the school-age child will be dealt with more fully towards the end of this chapter;

at this stage I will simply reflect on the following statement taken from the DES report *Curriculum 11–16. Towards a statement of entitlement.*

General social, political and moral considerations have posed curricular questions for schools. How do we help children to understand sexual relationships and their implications? Do we prepare children well enough for more leisure and less work as unemployment becomes more structural and less cyclical? How do we prepare them to understand the social and political impact of unemployment? To what extent do we enable pupils to understand and use computers? Do we try to help them understand the ethical problems raised by new technologies which can, for example, create nuclear weapons and make possible surgical transplants? Do we give pupils an understanding that they are living through a third industrial revolution which may lead to social and personal disturbance, to population shifts and a consequent restructuring of society as its predecessors did? (The first industrial revolution was concerned with coal, steam, iron and steel and early forms of mass production; the second with electricity, oil, the internal combustion engine and extended forms of mass production; the third with nuclear power, microtechnology and robot production methods.) When pupils can legally marry at 16, and vote at 18, what should the curriculum do to help pupils with these matters of fundamental importance to adult life?

It is in this context that the conviction has grown that all pupils are entitled to a broad compulsory common curriculum to the age of 16 which introduces them to a range of experiences, makes them aware of the kind of society in which they are going to live and gives them the skills necessary to live in it.[35]

It is difficult to reconcile such aims with an institutionalized system which not only isolates young people from the adult world but effectively even attempts to cut off one year group from the next. This latter criticism is one which many of the more traditional public schools can reject with greater ease than most state schools.

The product of this sort of thinking is an organization which is quite different from that of schools – an organization which by its very nature is de-institutionalized and which re-defines authority. Geoffrey Holroyde, writing as the head-master of Sidney Stringer Community College, uses the following description.

A community College is created by the coming together of people in the Community. They meet for education and recreation and to work together for their mutual benefit.

A college building is not essential, but helps greatly, and it belongs to the people in the Community.

It may be that we can pick out groups of people in that Community, for example

- *Young people of compulsory school age*
- *The parents of those young people*
- *Adults and young people over the school leaving age*
- *Members of recognized and established groups*
- *Professional teachers, community workers, social workers, health visitors, politicians and other agents.*

Such groups may have little in common, and the College does not attempt to force them into artificial associations with each other. There is no 'one' Community, but an amalgam of many formal and informal groups working and playing alongside each other.

It is sensible to base the School in the Community College so that school and non-school activities support each other, and extra resources can be put in by combining those normally available to a school with those provided for Further Education, Youth and Community.

A Community college is not an extension of the School; the School is part of the Community College.[36]

Management structures

The system of government for a true community school must provide two vital elements which may seem paradoxical: there must be unified control but there cannot be concentration of power. Stewart Mason who worked with Henry Morris in Cambridgeshire before moving to Leicestershire as CEO, established the principle of unified control in his 'Memorandum on community education' presented to the Leicestershire Education Committee in March 1949:

It is, I believe, essential for the successful implementation of the community college idea that there should be no diarchy of authority over the school use and the community use of the buildings. If school and centre are two uneasy bedfellows in rivalry with each other, and frequently at cross-purposes, the result will be failure. If the institution is to teach community living, it must in itself illustrate that harmony and integration which it is the job of education to give to each individual. This in practice will only be achieved if one man is ultimately responsible to the Committee not merely for the proper use of the whole set of college buildings, but for the success of the community centre as much as for the success of the school. It will therefore be necessary to appoint a warden of the college who will combine in one office the duties of headmaster and warden of the community centre.[37]

Experience in Leicestershire has completely vindicated these views (although 'one man' is now replaced by 'one person'!)

This sort of position could of course – seen in isolation and in the wrong hands – lead to the very concentration of power and authority which is the antithesis of community education. The solution to the paradox lies in the democratic structures which are essential expressions of the ideal. In the same Memorandum advocating unified control, Stewart Mason says:

A positive attitude of enthusiasm, pride and affection towards a community centre can be achieved only when the day-to-day government of the institution is in the hands of the people who use it. If real success is to be achieved, it must be the Committee's policy to encourage true democracy in these adult institutions by leaving the daily management to the people themselves, and by throttling down officialdom to the minimum. Ultimate responsibility for the proper care and use of the buildings will always remain with the Committee, but it is hoped that, like a wise friend, it will stand unobtrusively in the background and grant the utmost delegation to the people on the spot. Nothing worth having is attained without an element of risk.[38]

Inevitably, the management structures form a complex web with lines of public accountability criss-crossing lines of professional responsibility. A typical model is shown in fig. 12.1.

In practice the community council is usually a rather large and unwieldy body which devolves its executive function to a series of committees – finance and management, bar and catering, youth club management, class programme etc. The relationship between the various elements is somewhat analogous to that of parliamentary government. The committees represent the executive branch and are serviced by the professional staff who assume a civil servant role. The community council fills the function of the parliament. The whole must of course be held ultimately responsible to the statutory political system via the governors. At its best, this sort of arrangement can produce genuine democracy enabling a community to direct its own affairs with vitality and purpose.

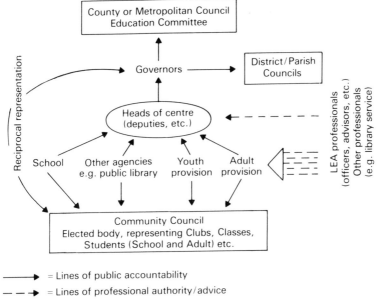

Fig. 12.1 Structure of a community college.

Financial structures

Separation of funding provided for school functions from those designated for community functions contradicts the basic concept – most people involved in community education are ardent advocates of virement and the block grant. Control of money is usually the most obvious and direct expression of power; the democracy inherent in the community school concept will always be largely sham unless it involves a real say in the distribution of resources. Few LEAs have found the courage and administrative simplicity needed to hand over a given sum annually for the entire operation and then rely on audit to ensure honesty. Some authorities do provide for community use by a block grant but still provide school resources in the traditional way (staffing establishment, per capital allowances etc.) It must be said, however, that a well-run community school will gradually find it quite impossible to maintain this artificial distinction between two functions. The boundaries between education and other services also become blurred. A new piece of equipment for a gymnasium may well be bought from school funds or youth service funds and be of obvious benefit to both. The provision of a special toilet for the handicapped may well be funded by social services and immediately enable the school to respond more fully to the Warnock Report. The over-riding concern is always to simplify the bureaucracy, to stop the labelling of little bits of finance and above all to stop the transferring backwards and forwards of bits of finance at great administrative cost. One LEA has recently set up a new set of procedures which will involve the community school remitting all monies generated by catering etc. to the LEA only to be given it back at the end of the year! Simplicity and flexibility are vital – provided always that proper accounting procedures are used and that audit is sure and strict.

Obviously the community activities based on a school will cost money and will require funding. Unfortunately the cost cannot be accurately predicted. Unlike the statutory sector, community activities tend to operate as a market economy and need similar financial structures. Financially, running a community school is much more like running a small business than running a school. The most satisfactory way of organizing the system is for the local authority to budget for certain costs, for example caretakers, wages, heating and lighting etc. and then make a block grant at the beginning of each year which the community council will then augment in various ways – membership, booking fees, class tuition fees etc. From the combined income, the community council must then reimburse the LEA for certain costs which have to be administered through the LEA.

Thus a community council will be balancing a set of accounts with the following sort of headings:

Income

1 **Block grant (LEA)**
(to include monies for youth service, adult education etc.)

2 **Booking fees**
(e.g. letting of gym to badminton clubs etc.)

3 **Class fees**
(i.e. income from adult classes)

4 **Membership fees**
(individual and club)

5 **Grants from public bodies**
(e.g. sports council/district council grants for new swimming pool)

6 **Bar/catering profits**
(can be very large)

7 **Fund-raising activities**
(raffles etc.)

8 **Quasi-commercial activities**
(e.g. printing, book shops, etc.)

Expenditure

1 Claw back to LEA

(a) Salaries for staff employed directly by LEA, mainly tutors for adult classes.

  (b) Caretaking and cleaning costs above that budgeted for by LEA, e.g. caretaking after 10 pm.

  (c) Realistically estimated heating and lighting costs above that budgeted for by LEA.

  (d) Notionally estimated costs of wear and tear on equipment and fabric.

2 Staff wages
(for staff employed directly by the community council e.g. bar/catering staff)

3 Administrative costs
(paper, phone bills etc.)

4 Subsidies to groups/ activities
(e.g. grants to adult literacy)

5 Goods and services
(e.g. equipment)

The books do of course need to balance annually. The element of risk is obvious. In Fairbairn's words:

> The advantages of this system are described later. At this point, it suffices to say that colleges, released from the need to recruit specific numbers to establish classes, are now able to cater for minority groups with very much smaller numbers in them if they so desire. The devolution of responsibility is real: one management committee evinced a healthy caution when it asked 'What happens if we get in the red?' recognizing after more discussion that, in that event, they would be on their own and would have to get into credit again by their own efforts.[39]

Accommodation

The community schools in Leicestershire which have been built as such and not produced by adaptations of existing buildings are designed so 'that the buildings should not resemble the common conception of a school'. This is vital for the community side of the operation – perhaps it should be vital for the school population as well. As said earlier, community activities are subject to market forces. People will only come into a community school if they want to, if they feel welcomed and that there is something of value to be gained. Many of our schools seem designed to prevent children from unauthorized departure rather than to make their arrival pleasant! No matter what the buildings are to start with, they must be made open and welcoming.

The first essential is that there must be an artistic visual policy and that aesthetic qualities be seen as central and not as unnecessary frills. This need not cost a great deal of money. Often it can be achieved by the removal of walls and railings, and the application of some paint, jobs which lend themselves to a self-help approach. This sort of possible transformation is on view in all our major cities, where old schools have been closed down and then re-opened as community centres, wall murals and all. If only the transformation had been done before the school died. Every community has local artists who are only too grateful for an opportunity to display their work.

Another vital ingredient is the sign-posting which is needed. Few schools have anything in the way of sign-posting for and within their buildings, and often what there is is negative. The community cannot and will not wander helplessly about looking for 'N12' which may or may not be the room they want; they will simply go away and not come again.

Specialized accommodation needs

These are really very few and are often already present in a reason-ably well-endowed school. The first requirement is for an attractive and obvious reception area at the front of the building. Ideally the reception area should be close to the administration centre with immediate access to information and telephone communication. There should be a pleasant waiting area, for notices, leaflets, news sheets etc. and provided with easy chairs. The reception area should serve both school and community activities. Any separation of function at this stage undermines the unity underlying the concept of a community school.

There is a real need for a pleasant social area – a room provided with easy chairs, coffee tables, etc. Such an area, which should be as attractive as funds will allow, provides an excellent base for the display of arts and crafts, produced by both adults in the community and children within the school. There is no reason why such an area cannot also be the social area provided for sixth form or other school students – indeed there are positive advantages if the area is shared.

Catering facilities are essential. Ideally there should be a snack bar type of service provided during most of the time the school is open. There are obvious advantages if the catering facilities are adjacent to the social area. The change in character of the school meals service, which is taking place in many LEAs, now enables this sort of function to be taken on relatively easily. The trend towards a commercial approach, cafeteria service and the use of modern fast foods puts the running of a snack or coffee bar comfortably within the abilities of school meals personnel. Should this prove difficult, an independent unit can be created; the initial capital costs need not be prohibitive. Either approach does, of course, give the possibility of job creation – a move which is much appreciated by the local community in the present economic climate. Both approaches are, however, subject to the same cold economic reality: one cannot afford to run such an operation at too great a loss. A certain amount of subsidy may be acceptable but ideally the aim should be to break even or make a profit. Profit is possible, but it will only be achieved by the skilled application of commercial principles. There is an inherent advantage over 'straight' commercial catering concerns in that there will be no outlay on rates and a reduced outlay on heating, lighting, cleaning and security – these latter being already in part provided. Another prime feature of catering is that being open for long hours to serve occasional trade almost certainly produces a loss. But catering for special occasions, e.g. wine and cheese parties for social clubs, can always be made to produce a profit.

A licensed bar can be a tremendous asset. Again there are obvious advantages if a small bar can be incorporated into the social area, with the facility to close it if and when appropriate. The capital outlay in setting up a reasonably equipped bar is large. However, most major brewing companies are only too delighted to provide capital or equipment in return for the franchise on sales. As with catering, occasional trade tends to produce less profit; however, this can be easily offset by the opportunities to provide for special occasions. There is a very large market for weddings, parties, club socials etc.

Central to the philosophical theme is that the community facilities must not be separated from the school. A community or adult wing in some distant part of the school site will simply encourage the development of a community centre which might as well have been put in another part of the town. As the Newsome Report 'Half our future' put it: 'The less his school . . . is an island to itself the better. If it is to serve this generation, it needs to be joined to the mainland of life by a causeway well trodden in both directions.'

Dual use

Many of our schools which are used in the evenings for further education by a disconnected organization are living proof of the worst consequences of dual use. Cupboards locked, equipment hidden away, the constant flow of complaints about misuse, the caretaker assuming Machiavellian powers to cause trouble etc. Indeed the folk-lore of horror stories which circulate in the teaching profession has put more than one head off any sort of community involvement. Experience shows that the biggest single cause of these problems is likely to be the separation of school and community functions. Tribal loyalties to one group or another can build up and are quickly compounded by bloody-mindedness. Once the rot has set in it is almost impossible to cure: the PE teacher will *never* lend the footballs to the youth club; the home economics teacher will believe that every mark on the cookers is directly attributable to the Indian cookery class; and so on.

Where there is unified control and different sections of one organization share facilities, dual use can not only run smoothly but can even have its advantages. If the different sections of the community are involved with each other and recognize their common membership of the same body, they will care about each other's needs. This effect is particularly marked in the school population. Community schools typically suffer far less vandalism from their captive population than do many ordinary schools. It is a brave child who will adorn a lavatory with his name if his father/grandfather/ elder brother is likely to use the same toilet later that evening!

Unified control also, of course, enables sensible channels of organization and information to be established right from the beginning. Often a simple but quick and sure method of reporting problems is all that is needed to prevent friction between different users. The same lines of communication can be used to effect improvements which will be of mutual benefit to all concerned. One complaint about court markings in a sports hall from the tennis club resulted in the discovery that the badminton club (who met on a different night) had a member who was a painter, and the sports hall was re-marked within a fortnight!

Incorporation of non-school public buildings

Many of the public institutions (and indeed private ones) can easily be incorporated into the community school building or campus. The material advantages, especially where the buildings are all newly constructed, are often great. The cost of land for each section is often less than that of a plot bought independently. The cost of actual building can also be significantly less, especially if there is shared accommodation.

Savings on cost of care and maintenance are almost guaranteed. Cleaning, repairs and caretaking can all be proportionately cheaper.

The non-material gains are enormous. A significant proportion of our adult population found little in the schools which they attended which captured their interest or enlisted their personal commitment. They do not therefore expect that anything which contains the word 'school' in its title will be likely to be on their wave-length. Many adults simply lack the self-confidence to join organizations or even come into large and imposing buildings. If they can be helped to break the ice by coming in for some non-school, non-educational reason, for some service which they really need, then there is at least a chance that they will stay long enough to get interested in other activities. A lonely old person who lacks the courage to join a 'drop in', may well cope with a visit to the public library, have a cup of tea in the adjacent lounge and make the connection with the community college.

Relationships with other agencies

An ordinary school is usually involved with a limited number of outside agencies or groups. Regular interchange is often confined to the LEA, governors, parents, sporting organizations, other educational institutions and academic bodies. There will of course be occasional contacts with the police, social services, the probation service, local charities, local government etc. However, these contacts tend to be either concerned with individuals or with particular events. A community school will soon find itself involved in regular dialogue with an almost unlimited number of other bodies. This is a natural consequence of the widening of purpose of the organization. A community school is trying to cater for a much wider range of people than is a traditional school. The following is a list of some of the external agencies with which one such community school is involved. In each case there is a brief note as to the possible project or joint concern under consideration.

One of the main factors operating in these dealings with other bodies is the fact that the wider set of objectives enables legitimate application to be made for funding. There is a great deal of overlap between education and recreation, and between education and community service. The grey areas are not, however, reflected in the political and bureaucratic structures which our society uses to provide for their needs. The LEA will provide a table-tennis bat for educational purposes but not for adult recreation. The social services will provide a modified mini-bus to transport the handicapped but not to enable a school to gain educationally through work with the handicapped. In order to obtain concrete support from the outside

External agency	Project/mutual concern
1 Sports council District council Parish council	Provision of swimming pool sited at the school. Jointly financed and jointly managed.
2 Arts Council	Subsidies for programme of art exhibitions, music concerts and the publication of work of local writers.
3 Social services	Provision for groups of elderly house-bound, physically and mentally handicapped.
4 Age Concern	Work with housebound.
5 Local hospital/day centre	Reciprocal visits – volunteers to hospital, patients to school.
6 Royal Society for the Blind	Provision of a garden for the blind plus a course in gardening at the school.
7 Local chamber of commerce	Provision of courses for pre-retirement.
8 Local ethnic groups	Provision of facilities for cultural activities e.g. weddings.
9 Probation service	Formation of local intermediate treatment group.
10 Adult literacy	School acting as administrative base and providing additional funding.
11 Local Anglican and Methodist churches	Links between school and YTS scheme and local needs through community service.
12 Public library service	Public library sited within the school.
13 Local jobcentre	Reception area of school used as advertising outlet.

agencies one must be fulfilling their primary aims. A community school is in a position to do exactly this and, at the same time, fulfil its own additional aims of enriching the educational experience of its students.

Consequences for staffing and staff

A community school needs skills, abilities and attitudes from its workforce which are in many ways different from those needed to run schools. The first source of these differing needs is the organization's genuine commitment to objectives which are not normally expected of schools; the second is, as mentioned earlier, the operation of the community activities in the market place. Until the 1980 Education Act came into operation, giving parental choice of schools, teachers have rarely had to sell their product. A community school must do exactly this and the classical techniques of business soon come into play: market research, product design, product packaging, advertising and, lastly but by no means least, the maintenance of financial solvency. A school knows at the beginning of a year pretty accurately what functions and events are going to occur during that year. Furthermore it knows what its income is going to be and how it will be spent. A community school has far less certainty. The analogy with a commercial enterprise is an illuminating one, but it cannot be pressed too far. For one thing, a community school has no need to declare a profit for its own sake. For another, it will carry out its market research against a background of its own broad educational philosophy and what it sees as its own legitimate function. A closer analogy in this sense might be with the BBC.

Specialized staff

There are, therefore, several key personnel needed in a community school who are not necessarily part of the staff of a traditional school. These are listed below with a brief indication of their role:
If these people are to be part of a community school rather than a community centre, it is vital that each and every one also has a clear role within the school. Where appropriate they should form part of the school teaching staff and have curricular commitments – these can range from a straightforward teaching load to responsibility for an aspect of student life, for example active tutorial work, work experience. Where curricular responsibility is not appropriate, the integration can be achieved directly: clerical, catering, sporting personnel can all contribute a part of their time to the school student population – the bar staff may well have to confine their attentions to the adult community!

The main teaching force

In the best community schools all the teachers have a commitment to the wider concept. The most exciting translation of this commitment into a working reality is the creation of the Leicestershire Phase III Colleges in which all the teachers are recruited on the understanding that a percentage of their time will be devoted to work outside the school. Contracts known locally as '90–10s' or '80–20s' are agreed whereby teachers spend 90 or 80 per cent of their work load with school pupils and the remaining 10 or 20 per cent with adult groups or classes. This sort of arrangement does of course mean funding the cost of staff from both the education budget and from the further education and youth budgets.
Such a post is very different from that of an ordinary classroom teacher. It often attracts a particular sort of teacher and teachers are changed by the experience of such a post. Most people with direct experience of such community schools will claim that the quality of teaching is raised by the experience of working in different ways at least some of the time. Adult and voluntary youth groups simply

Head of centre	Who must encompass the headship of the school and the leadership of the community-based functions. Essential requirements are: the stamina to work well beyond normal school hours and terms; a high level of political awareness and competence; courage to take large financial and social risks.
Head of community activities (Ideally of deputy head status)	Liaison with the community; working with and through identifiable groups and individuals; liaison with outside agencies; entrepreneur who translates ideas into action; mobilizer of diverse groups, people, resources to attain ends.
Assistant heads of community activities. In a large community school there can be natural subdivisions:- youth, adult, sport and recreation, disadvantaged etc. Each area has an assistant community head in charge.	As for the head of community activities, and under his guidance and supervision; e.g. organization and management of youth club, planning and execution of adult class programme.
Secretarial and accounting staff	Additional to normal school requirements. Fairly standard job descriptions modified by the need for work of a very varied kind, often during anti-social hours.
Catering (and bar) management staff. One manager unless the operation is large enough to justify separating catering from bars. Supplemented by the requisite number of junior staff.	These must be experienced and trained personnel. Ideally recruited from industry, but must be committed to the community school ethos and temper commercial sharpness with sensitivity. Function: to run a small business within the organization.
Other management rôles As required, e.g. swimming pool manager, sports hall manager etc.	Again requires trained professionals

cannot be reached by some of the attitudes and methods which have been commonplace in schools. An hour of 'shut up and do exercise 8 because I say you should' is guaranteed to close down an adult class after a week! In coming to terms with the problems of adult education, teachers can improve their performance with children, sometimes to a remarkable degree.

Consequences for school students

The hidden curriculum

The recognition of the 'hidden curriculum' is perhaps one of the most significant things which has recently affected our perceptions of schools. One of the best illustrations of the phenomenon of the hidden curriculum known to the author was the published statement of the following education aim: 'To encourage pupils to appreciate the virtues of co-operation, to foster habits of responsibility and self-discipline, and to promote initiative, endeavour and the exercise of individual judgement' – combined with the practice of confining the junior pupils on an enclosed tennis court during breaks and lunch-time with staff on duty to ensure captivity and insisting that a pupil must request permission to remove his or her blazer in warm weather.

Essentially the hidden curriculum is a matter of recognizing that actions speak louder than words and that all too often the actions of the institution are conveying a hidden set of value judgements which are the opposite of those theoretically espoused. Because a community school is subject to far more involvement with people from outside the teacher-pupil axis, it is far more difficult for both teachers and pupils to ignore paradoxes of this sort. The presence of one adult in a class is enough to question most of the rituals which teachers and pupils have mutually conspired to create – most of which are of course designed to ensure behavioural submission of the pupil but which may often extend to intellectual and personal submission. Indeed much of the artificial and ritualized rôle-play in which both teachers and pupils take part can be embarrassing when performed in the presence of 'outsiders'. It is a regular experience in community schools that teachers become less authoritarian and that pupils become better behaved.

Parents

Many parents find the traditional school a daunting prospect. Their own memories of the experience are often negative and their current dealings often confined to an annual 'parents evening' which may seem to focus on inadequacies (their children's and sometimes by implication their own) rather than on achievement. Any teacher who is tempted towards complacency about the 'parents evening' would be well advised to read the report on research into such interviews by the Nottingham University School of Education.[40]

The community school offers two immediate advantages when it comes to dealing with parents. The first is that the physical environs are by definition more welcoming and more like 'home territory' for the parent. The second is that there is at least a possibility that parents will be involved with the community school in their own right and will, therefore, have a familiarity with and confidence in the organization which can help them when dealing with the emotional and critical business of their children's development.

Timetables: school and adult students

Unified control reflecting wider but unified aims for the institution allows a range of curricular possibilities which is difficult to envisage in a traditional school.

The simplest and easiest arrangement is the admission of adults to school classes. Again economic advantage is combined with psychological gain. The presence in a fourth or fifth year class of one or two adults who have 'chosen' to be there and furthermore may well be paying to attend does wonders for the school student's evaluation of the experience. Furthermore the adults can bring a contribution to discussions, which adds an extra and rich resource to the classroom. Imagine the effect of the presence of a retired miner in a literature class studying D. H. Lawrence!

Many of our community schools have, however, gone much further, and now interchange school and adult provision in complex and adventurous ways. The school day and week have always produced timetable constraints which have thwarted curricular ambitions. The possibility of one or two 'extra' sessions at tea-time or in the evening can give a wonderful flexibility to the timetable. Bretton Woods now offers both adults and older school students an array of courses and combinations which can only be matched by the larger and more adventurous public schools (who achieve the range in the same way – by extension of the school day). An essential element of their approach is, of course, that activities out of normal school hours have to be voluntary; and experience shows that many pupils will attend voluntary sessions with greater enthusiasm than they show for the statutory ones. It is a common experience to find pupils who would normally be described as 'less-motivated' doing more rather than less.

Politics of community education

Ever since Henry Morris, starting the Village Colleges in Cambridgeshire, talked about the development of a 'rural democracy', the community education movement has been political in the best sense of that word. At the heart of the concept is the determination to stop seeing education as a didactic imposition on people between the ages of 5 and 16. Large institutions and formal organizations are necessary – twentieth-century society is too complex and technological even to pretend that Huxley's first solution, proferred in *Brave New World*, is viable:

> Over population and over organization have produced the modern metropolis, in which a fully human life of multiple personal relationships has become impossible. Therefore if you wish to avoid the spiritual impoverishment of individuals and whole societies, leave the metropolis and revive the small country communities or alternatively humanize the metropolis by creating within its network of mechanical organizations the urban equivalents of small country communities, in which individuals can meet and co-operate as complete persons, not as the mere embodiments of specialized functions. . . .

But the alternative which he here proposes has at least offered the hope of success and can be interpreted through the concept of the community school approach. Fairbairn uses the following words.

> Every society needs common institutions that are capable of bringing together people of diverse interests and positions to share experiences ranging beyond and above the immediate claims of self-interest. This role has always been claimed by the churches, but in the temper of the present age, they tend to have an ever-diminishing importance at least numerically. The rapid increase of smaller houses, motorcars and televison means that the family unit, now rarely exceeding father, mother and two children, can be virtually self-sufficient for its entertainment. More and more men and women indeed live only in pairs or alone. Although people tend to be herded together during working hours in bigger and bigger complexes of industry and commerce, this does little to satisfy more than material needs. The decline of the cinema has deprived many of a gathering ground which was at least warm and comfortable at little cost and small compensation is to be found in the dwindling camaraderie of the football stands.[41]

The community school is a participatory organization in which members of the community attempt to fulfil their own aims and ambitions within a framework of expertise and professional support. The 'community' includes the students who are of statutory school age. As Bob Aitken (CEO Coventry) states, 'Democracy is a learning process, a changing process, one becomes accustomed to it, you mature in the experience, and the very nature of the process changes thereby.'

Appendix

Leicestershire Education Committee revised scheme of management for a community college

1. **Aims and Objectives**
   The   Community College has been established to provide for the social, cultural and recreational activities of the community of   and the surrounding area.

2. **Constitution**
   Subject to the general supervision of the Governors of the Community College and the direction of the Local Education Authority, the policy and general management of the affairs of the Community College shall be directed by a Council.

3. The Council shall consist of representatives to be appointed annually as follows:

   (i)   One elected from the individual College membership for each fifty members of the College.
   (ii) Two from each of the affiliated bodies.
   (iii) The Chairman of the Council.
   (iv) The Honorary Treasurer.
   (v)   The Principal of the College, and his full-time professional staff.
   (vi) Six representatives of the teaching staff, and part-time professional staff of the College and its extra-mural classes.
   (vii) Six representatives appointed by the Governors.
   (viii) Not more than eight members to be co-opted by the Council under such conditions as it may determine from time to time.

   All members of the Council shall retire annually at the Annual General Meeting, but shall be eligible for re-appointment.

4. The Council shall appoint a Committee of Management and may appoint such other committees as it may from time to time decide including, if desired, members of the College who are not members of the Council, and shall determine their powers and terms of reference.

5. The Committee of Management shall consist of not less than twelve nor more than sixteen members of the Council, together with the officers of the Council. The Council shall delegate to it the management of the College subject to the general policy of the Council, together with such other duties as the Council may, from time to time to determine. The Committee of Management shall contain at least one member from each of the groups (other than co-opted members) enumerated in paragraph 3: not less than three representatives shall be under the age of twenty-one.

6. The Chairman of the Council, the Principal or his representative and other officers of the Council shall be ex-officio members of all committees. Each committee shall elect its own Chairman.

7. **Annual General Meeting**
   As early as possible in each Autumn term the Council shall convene an Annual General Meeting of the College which all members shall be entitled to attend for the purpose of:-

   (i)   Receiving the annual report of the Council and the annual audited statement of accounts.
   (ii) Appointing Honorary Officers of the College.
   (iii) Electing representatives of the individual membership to serve on the Council.
   (iv) Appointing auditors.
   (v)   Making recommendations to the Council upon any matter affecting the College.

   The Annual General Meeting shall elect:-

   (a)   The Chairman of the Council.
   (b)   An Honorary Treasurer.
   (c)   Such officers as it may determine from time to time.

   The Principal or a member of his staff nominated by him shall be Secretary of the Council and of the Committee of Management.

8. **Procedure**
   All decisions taken, whether at a general meeting or a meeting of the Council or a Committee shall be determined by a majority of

those present, and voting and the decision shall be binding and conclusive, providing that the Principal, if he considers any decision to be contrary to regulations or intentions of the Local Education Authority, may defer taking action on any such decision and refer the matter for consideration by the Governors at their next meeting. If the Principal exercises his powers under this provision, he shall send a full account of the reason for his action to the Director of Education.

9. The Chairman of the Council may, at any time at his discretion, and within twenty-one days of receiving a written request so to do signed by not less than twenty members having the power to vote, and giving reasons for the request, arrange through the Principal to call a Special General Meeting of the College.

10. For the purpose of securing uniformity of administrative practice, the Governors, the Council and the Committee of Management in the exercise of the functions delegated to them, shall comply with any regulations that may be made by the Local Education Authority.

11. In the event of any disagreement between the Governors and the Council of the Community College connected with the Scheme of Management the matter shall be referred to the Local Education Authority for decision.

12. Minutes shall be kept of the proceedings of all General Meetings and meetings of the Council and its Committees. The Principal shall send to the Governors copies of all minutes of the Council and the Committee of Management which have taken place since the previous meeting of the Governors. The minutes of all other Committees of the Council shall be open to inspection by the Governors.

13. The Council shall have the power to make rules and regulations for the management of the College, subject to any direction of the Local Education Authority and subject to review by the Governors acting on behalf of the Local Education Authority.

14. Subject to such limitations as are contained in this Scheme of Management, the Council shall draw up rules of procedure and shall determine constitutional matters, including voting powers, quorum and the size and composition of Committees. These matters shall be determined in consonance with the wishes of

the Annual General Meeting and shall be subject to the approval
of the Governors.

15. **Finance**
    The Council shall receive all monies by or on behalf of the
    College. It is also authorised to approve expenditure within the
    limits of the budget for the College as agreed annually with the
    Local Education Authority. Unless specifically authorised by the
    Education Authority, the Council shall have no power and shall
    not purport to authorise any expenditure from public funds or to
    represent the Council as acting on behalf of the Local Education
    Authority in any matter. The Council, or if the Council so
    delegates, the Committee of Management, shall fix rates of
    subscriptions for the various classes of membership and shall
    have the power to make membership of the College compulsory
    for all who enrol for classes, or join the Youth Centre provided
    always that the Local Education Authority may, at any time,
    require the Council to make use of this power of compulsory
    membership.

16. The Council shall be responsible for ensuring that proper
    accounts of the finances of the College are kept and audited at
    least once a year by auditors appointed at the Annual General
    Meeting. Audited statement of accounts for each financial year,
    1st April to 31st March shall be submitted to the Governors and
    shall be presented to the Annual General Meeting.

17. **General**
    The Committee of Management shall have the right for good
    and sufficient reason to terminate the membership of an indi-
    vidual member or an affiliated body, provided that the indi-
    vidual member or a person representing the body shall have the
    right to appeal to the Council.

18. The Council (or the Committee of Management acting on its
    behalf) shall decide the annual programme of the College and
    shall inform the Governors of the requirements of the College
    for the use of the school premises for community purposes. The
    Governors shall arrange for the accommodation required to be
    made available and the Principal shall be empowered to make
    such adjustments in the arrangements for the use of the pre-
    mises as may become necessary as a result of changes in the
    programme of the College. In accordance with the Articles of
    Government of the School, the Governors shall determine the

use to which the school premises, or any part thereof, shall be put, out of school hours when not required by the College.

19. The Council and Committee of Management acting on its behalf, shall be responsible to the Governors for the conduct of the College and the care of the premises when in use for community purposes.

Note: The above scheme of management is currently under review.

February 1985.

References

2 Finance, plant and administration

Note that *Government grants: a guide for voluntary organizations*, The National Council for Voluntary organizations, Bedford Square Press, is an invaluable guide.

3 Staff Management I

1 Everard K B June 1982 *Management in Comprehensive schools – what can be learnt from industry*. Report commissioned by the Centre for the Study of Comprehensive Schools p 9.
2 See current recommendations to the Secretary of State from the Advisory Committee on the Supply and Education of Teachers, 1984.
3 Lawton D 1981 *Curriculum studies and educational planning*. Hodder and Stoughton
4 August 1983 Criteria and mechanisms for the approval of initial training courses. DES, See also Circular No. 3/84 DES
5 Hilsum S Strong C 1978 *The secondary teacher's day* NFER National Foundation for Educational Research.

7 The Curriculum

6 See 22 December 1983 Industry and Schools: a memorandum by the CBI to the National Economic Development Council.
7 March 1981 The School Curriculum. HMSO, p 3
8 1981 The Practical Curriculum. Schools Council WP 70, Methuen, p 15
9 1978 Curriculum 11–16: working papers by HM Inspectorate. HMSO.
10 December 1983 *SHA Review* **243**
11 1981 The Practical Curriculum. op. cit. p 21
12 1979 The curricular needs of slow learners, Schools Council WP 63.

13 1978 Special educational needs. HMSO.
14 Wilcox B, Eustace P J 1980 *Tooling up for curriculum review.* NFER.
15 1983 Science education 11–16. *Secondary Science Curriculum review.*
16 1983 Foreign Languages in the School Curriculum. DES.
17 January 1984 Co-operation over pre-vocational education. CGL/BTEC joint press release.
18 March 1984 Improving secondary schools. Report by the Committee on Curriculum and Organisation of Secondary Schools, ILEA.
19 1982 The arts in schools – principles, practice and provision. Gulbenkian Trust.
20 December 1983 Life and social skills – an unfinished tale. *SHA Review* **243**
21 Duffy M N 1982 Options for the fourth: different perspectives. Schools Council.
22 Hargreaves (1984) op. cit. pp 74–6
23 For foreign languages, for example, the courses of the Institute of Linguists; and the 'Foreign languages at work' project of the London Chambers of Commerce.
24 1979 A basis for choice. DES; and 1981 ABC in action. DES.
25 1975 *16–19: Growth and response.* Schools Council WP 53, Evans/Methuen.

10 Changing the curriculum in a school

26 Rogers E M 1962 *Diffusion of innovations.* The Free Press of Glencoe, New York.
27 Gross N, Giacquinta J B, Bernstein M 1971 *Implementing organisational innovations: sociological analysis of planned educational change.* Harper and Row, New York.
28 ibid.
29 Ekholm M, Sanström, Svanberg G, Tjellander B 1983 Studies of the process of innovation in the comprehensive school. The Innova Project, Institute of Education, University of Linköping, Sweden.
30 Jamieson I, Lightfoot M 1982 *Schools and industry.* Derivations from the Schools Council Industry Project, Methuen Educational.
Holmes S, Lightfoot M 1981 The world in the classroom. Times Educational Supplement, 30 Jan 1981.
Gyte G 1982 Some links – YOP and others – at Springfield

School. In Watts A G (ed) *Schools, YOP and the new training initiative*. CRAC Publications.

Gyte G 1982 Case study: Springfield School. Youth in need: a call to action. SHA Topics.

BBC Television series (1980) Is there life after school: Programme 2. Produced by Ian Woolf, accompanying discussion notes by John Storey.

BBC Radio 4 (1981) File on 4 education special. Produced by David Rogers.

31 Havelock R G 1973 *Planning for innovation through dissemination and utilization of knowledge*. University of Michigan.
32 Burns T, Stalker G M 1961 *The management of innovation*. Tavistock Publications.
33 Schein E 1970 *Organisational psychology*. Prentice-Hall Inc.

12 Community schools

34 Fairbairn A N 1978. *The Leicestershire Community Colleges and Centres 1978.*
35 1983 *Curriculum 11–16: Towards a statement of entitlement.* DES.
36 A case study in management: Sidney Stringer School and Community College. 1976. The Open University Press.
37 Fairbairn A N, op. cit.
38 ibid.
39 ibid.
40 Teacher parent interviews. 1983. Nottingham University School of Education.
41 Fairbairn A N, op. cit.

Index